FORMAL SPOKEN ARABIC
FAST COURSE WITH MP3 FILES

Georgetown Classics in Arabic Language and Linguistics
Karin C. Ryding and Margaret Nydell, series editors

For some time, Georgetown University Press has been interested in making available seminal publications in Arabic language and linguistics that have gone out of print. Some of the most meticulous and creative scholarship of the last century was devoted to the analysis of Arabic language, to producing detailed reference works and textbooks of the highest quality. Although some of the material is dated in terms of theoretical approaches, the content and methodology of the books considered for the reprint series is still valid and in some cases, unsurpassed.

With global awareness now refocused on the Arab world, and with renewed interest in Arab culture, society, and political life, it is essential to provide easy access to classic reference materials such as dictionaries and reference grammars, and language teaching materials. The key components of this series of classic reprints have been chosen for quality of research and scholarship, and have been updated with new bibliographies and introductions to provide readers with resources for further study. Where possible, the original authors have been involved in the reproduction and republication process.

Georgetown University Press hopes hereby to serve the growing national and international need for reference works on Arabic language and culture, as well as provide access to quality textbooks and audiovisual resources for teaching Arabic language in its written and spoken forms.

Books in the series:

Arabic Language Handbook
    Mary Catherine Bateson

Audio CD for A Reference Grammar of Syrian Arabic
    Mark W. Cowell

A Basic Course in Iraqi Arabic with MP3 Audio Files
    Wallace M. Erwin

A Basic Course in Moroccan Arabic
    Richard S. Harrell with Mohammed Abu-Talib and William S. Carroll

A Basic Course in Moroccan Arabic MP3 Files: Audio Exercises
    Richard S. Harrell

A Dictionary of Iraqi Arabic: English–Arabic, Arabic–English
    B. E. Clarity, Karl Stowasser, and Ronald G. Wolfe, editors; D. R. Woodhead and Wayne Beene, editors

A Dictionary of Moroccan Arabic: Moroccan–English/English–Moroccan
    Richard S. Harrell and Harvey Sobelman, editors

A Dictionary of Syrian Arabic: English–Arabic
    Karl Stowasser and Moukhtar Ani

FORMAL SPOKEN ARABIC
FAST COURSE WITH MP3 FILES

Karin C. Ryding and Abdelnour Zaiback

GEORGETOWN UNIVERSITY PRESS / WASHINGTON, D.C.

Copyright Statement for Formal Spoken Arabic *FAST* Course

This book is largely based on the Formal Spoken Arabic Familiarization and Short Term (FAST) course developed at the Foreign Service Institute from 1981 to 1986. Since leaving the U.S. Department of State, Dr. Ryding has, among other things, revised the transcription system, revised and expanded the exercises, grammar explanations, preface, and introduction, and reformatted the text. The authors claim no right to U.S. Government work or other material in the public domain.

The original audiotapes for the spoken dialogues on the seven cassettes that accompany this text were engineered at the Foreign Service Institute Language Laboratory.

Georgetown University Press, Washington, D.C.
© 2004 by Georgetown University Press. All rights reserved.
Printed in the United States of America

10   9   8   7   6   5   4   3   2   2006

This book is printed on acid-free paper meeting
the requirements of the American National Standard
for Permanence in Paper for Printed Library Materials.

First published in 1993.

Library of Congress Cataloging-in-Publication Data

Ryding, Karin C.
   Formal spoken Arabic FAST course : with MP3 files / Karin C. Ryding and Abdelnour Zaiback.
        p.   cm.   (Georgetown classics in Arabic language and linguistics)
     ISBN 1-58901-106-6 (alk. paper)
        1. Arabic language—Dialects—Grammar.   I. Zaiback, Abdelnour.   II. Title.
III. Series.
PJ6713.R935 2004
492.7'7—dc22

2004040881

CONTENTS

MP3 FILES FOR THE SAMPLE DIALOGUES

Track	Page	Lesson	Unit	Time
1	1	Lesson 1	Sample Dialogue	1:17
2	1	Lesson 1	Sample Dialogue Read Slowly	2:28
3	2	Lesson 1	Vocabulary	6:43
4	3	Lesson 1	Supplementary Vocabulary	2:55
5	3	Lesson 1.II.A.	Matching Arabic with English	1:13
6	11	Lesson 1.IV.B.	Comprehension of Spoken Arabic	1:04
7	13	Lesson 2	Sample Dialogue A	0:57
8	13	Lesson 2	Sample Dialogue A read slowly	1:41
9	15	Lesson 2	Sample Dialogue B	0:54
10	15	Lesson 2	Sample Dialogue B read slowly	1:59
11	16	Lesson 2	Vocabulary	6:32
12	17	Lesson 2	Supplementary Vocabulary	3:19
13	17	Lesson 1.II.A.	Matching Arabic with English	1:22
14	21	Lesson 2.III.A.	bidd — "to want"	0:58
15	24	Lesson 2.III.E.	Subject Pronouns: Summary	0:46
16	25	Lesson 2.IV.B.	Comprehension of Spoken Arabic	0:54
17	27	Lesson 3	Sample Dialogue	1:27
18	27	Lesson 3	Sample Dialogue read slowly	3:08
19	28	Lesson 3	Vocabulary	5:39
20	29	Lesson 3	Supplementary Vocabulary	2:23
21	31	Lesson 3.II.A.	Matching Arabic with English	1:26
22	36	Lesson 3.D.	"on the phone"	1:01
23	36	Lesson 3.III.E.	Object Pronouns	1:04
24	39	Lesson IV.B.	Comprehension	1:07
25	41	Lesson 4	Sample Dialogue	1:35
26	41	Lesson 4	Sample Dialogue read slowly	3:14
27	42	Lesson 4	Vocabulary	5:15
28	42	Lesson 4	Supplementary Vocabulary	1:11
29	44	Lesson 4.II.A.	Matching Arabic with English	1:54
30	49	Lesson IV.B.	Comprehension of Spoken Arabic	1:13
31	51	Lesson 5	Sample Dialogue	1:27
32	51	Lesson 5	Sample Dialogue read slowly	2:17
33	52	Lesson 5	Vocabulary	8:03
34	54	Lesson 5.II.A.	Matching Arabic to English	1:33
35	59	Lesson 5.IV.B.	Comprehension of Spoken Arabic	1:23
36	61	Lesson 6	Sample Dialogue	1:25
37	61	Lesson 6	Sample Dialogue read slowly	2:53
38	62	Lesson 6	Vocabulary	3:03
39	62	Lesson 6	Supplementary Vocabulary	8:36
40	65	Lesson 6.II.A.	Matching Arabic to English	1:25
41	69	Lesson 6.IV.B.	Comprehension of Spoken Arabic	1:19
42	71	Lesson 7	Sample Dialogue	1:29
43	71	Lesson 7	Sample Dialogue read slowly	3:07
44	72	Lesson 7	Vocabulary	5:20
45	73	Lesson 7	Supplementary Vocabulary	3:52
46	75	Lesson 7.II.A.	Matching Arabic with English	1:46
47	77	Lesson 7.III.A.	kaan: Conjugation in Past Tense	1:08

TOTAL: 4:35:55

ARABIC RESEARCH AT GEORGETOWN UNIVERSITY

In the past forty years, the world of research in Arabic theoretical linguistics has expanded but the production of professional quality textbooks in colloquial Arabic has remained limited. Despite the passage of years, the Richard Slade Harrell Arabic series has consistently been in demand from Georgetown University Press because of the quality of research that went into its composition, the solid theoretical foundations for its methodology, and the comprehensive coverage of regional Arabic speech communities.

The Department of Arabic Language, Literature and Linguistics at Georgetown University (formerly Arabic Department) recognizes the need to sustain the tradition of research and publication in Arabic dialects and has continued dialectology field research and textbook production, most notably with Margaret (Omar) Nydell's *Syrian Arabic Video Course,* a three-year research project funded by Center for the Advancement of Language Learning from 1991 to 1994. Currently we are engaged in a four-year dialectology research project aimed at producing "conversion" courses to assist learners of Modern Standard Arabic in converting their knowledge and skills of written Arabic to proficiency in selected Arabic dialects. This project is part of a grant administered by the National Capital Language Resource Center under the directorship of Dr. James E. Alatis and Dr. Anna Chamot.

We pay tribute to the tradition initiated and led by Richard Harrell, the founder of this series, and of the original Arabic Research Program at Georgetown University. His scholarship and creative energy set a standard in the field and yielded an unprecedented and as-yet unsurpassed series of, as he put it, "practical tools for the increasing number of Americans whose lives bring them into contact with the Arab world." We hope that this series of reprints, and our continuing efforts in applied Arabic dialectology research, will yield a new crop of linguistic resources for Arabic language study.

Karin C. Ryding
Sultan Qaboos bin Said Professor of Arabic

FOREWORD TO THE GEORGETOWN CLASSICS EDITION

Formal Spoken Arabic FAST Course with MP3 Files is being reprinted for several reasons. First, it is important to provide the learner with updated formats of the listening materials; instead of audiocassettes, Georgetown University Press now provides these same listening materials in MP3 file format on a CD. Second, and most important, at a time when the acquisition of spoken Arabic has suddenly been thrust to the forefront of U.S. national security as a result of the tragedy of September 11, *Formal Spoken Arabic FAST Course with MP3 Files* provides the learner with a model of Arabic used in everyday situations by educated Levantine speakers of Arabic.

For far too long, government and university educators have consistently striven to teach Arabic learners the literary standard of Arabic for use in routine, everyday spoken interaction, though the literary standard is rarely, if ever, used this way. Consequently, when this book was originally published in 1993, it was groundbreaking. Its authors targeted the needs of U.S. diplomatic and government cadre in the field and those of the Arabic learner population at large for a functional, proficiency-based course that takes the learner from a Foreign Service Institute proficiency rating of 0 to at least 1+, a limited working proficiency in the language. The authors achieve this by developing linguistic creativity and building communicative competence in spoken Arabic through realistic role-play, listening comprehension, expansion drills, and the like. Those goals are still valid and make the *Formal Spoken Arabic FAST Course with MP3 Files* a viable option for Arabic language learners today. The authors' use of a consistent, learner-friendly transliteration system as a tool to accelerate the learners' speaking ability—which is usually the first thing they want to do—is another important reason why Arabic learners stand to benefit greatly from this course. An additional enduring quality is the book's use of cultural notes on topics such as bartering and price haggling with taxi drivers or confronting a hostile authority, which are still vital for survival in Arab society. Learners who want to experience spoken Arabic in conversation will find this course indispensable.

David Mehall
Georgetown University

PREFACE

This text is based on materials developed for use by the U.S. Department of State in the Arabic training section of the Foreign Service Institute (FSI) during the years 1981–86. The original version was developed to serve as the core of a six-week intensive *FAST* (Familiarization and Short-Term) course tailored to provide maximum linguistic and cultural exposure in a short period of time for U.S. Government employees heading for posts in the Arab world. It is designed to cushion culture shock and bolster student confidence in handling day-to-day situations.

The lessons deal with typical situations Americans are likely to encounter. Each dialogue is between an American and an Arab, so that students always play realistic parts in rehearsing situations. Transcription is used instead of Arabic script in order to accelerate spoken performance. However, students interested in seeing the dialogues in Arabic may review the script at the beginning of each lesson.

Students and teachers should both keep in mind the six principles on which this course is based:

1. It is designed to make life more manageable in the host country. It is not strictly a language course.

2. It is organized around selected situations, not around bits of language; it is not grammar-based.

3. The text is a resource; it is not the entire course. The course is what the teacher arranges for the students to do and experience.

4. Grammar explanations and drills are included to clarify and facilitate practical use of the language. Grammar and other explanations in English by the teacher are best used sparingly.

5. A substantial amount of time is devoted to role-playing and to creative, realistic use of the language.

6. The main criterion for measuring students' performance is their demonstration of ability to manage situations as they talk with and to people.

The Linguistic Situation in the Arab World

The Arab world is characterized by a linguistic phenomenon known as "diglossia," meaning that the spoken and written languages are divergent and substantially different. Whereas the literary language (Modern Standard Arabic or MSA) has essentially retained the lexical and grammatical features of Classical Arabic (CA), and is the same from one Arab country to another, spoken Arabic has been much less codified and more pliant, adapting swiftly to the everyday needs of colloquial speech, incorporating foreign words, reducing grammatical categories and evolving into regional variants characteristic of specific geographical areas. Many of these regional variants are mutually intelligible to native speakers, but some widely separated ones diverge considerably from each other. The issue of which form of spoken Arabic to teach to foreigners has therefore traditionally been a thorny one, with little choice between teaching a spoken form of literary Arabic (MSA) or one specific dialect (e.g., Syrian, Moroccan, Egyptian, Saudi).

Formal Spoken Arabic

The type of spoken Arabic taught in the United States to most of the students at the Foreign Service Institute (FSI) has traditionally been called Formal Spoken Arabic (FSA).[*] Because FSI trains students who are going to all parts of the Arab world, it

---

[*] Other English terms for this type of spoken Arabic include "Educated Spoken Arabic," "Inter-Arabic," and "Middle Arabic."

has settled upon teaching a form of Arabic *lingua franca* to people posted to the Arab East. The reasons for this are both logistical and practical: logistical because resource limitations do not allow FSI to teach every possible form of spoken Arabic, and practical because feedback from officers in the field indicates that FSA is the most efficient, flexible, and useful brand of Arabic for Foreign Service personnel who need Arabic language skills to serve them in a variety of posts.

It has long been recognized that there are shared language features that characterize most urban colloquial forms of Arabic[*] and that these common features are regularly used by Arabs from different regions when they need to communicate with each other. These features are part of the language variant that is called Formal Spoken Arabic.

Although pronunciation and internal vowelization of FSA generally reflect the conventions of literary Arabic, shared dialect features constitute its core (lexical items such as *raaH* for the verb "to go," *jaab*, "to bring," *mish* for negation of phrases and non-verbal expressions, and *laazim* to express necessity; morphological features include elimination of case and mood inflections, dual and feminine person plural verb forms). Where spoken Arabic diverges by dialect and choices had to be made (such as the terms for "what" and "now"), Levantine items (i.e., terms common to Lebanon, Syria, and Jordan) were selected for this text. Of course, the teacher may modify these items or offer other options, depending on both experience and judgment and the needs of various students.

THE AUTHORS

---

[*] See Ferguson, Charles. 1959. "The Arabic Koine," in *Language*, 35:616–30.

ACKNOWLEDGMENTS

The text of *FAST* was developed under the supervision of Karin C. Ryding who planned it and made arrangements for its publication. Abdelnour Zaiback was responsible for developing the Arabic language dialogues and exercises as well as the notes for the instructor, whereas Dr. Ryding supervised and prepared the work, wrote the grammatical explanations, compiled the glossaries, and revised the final version. Mr. Zaiback was further responsible for field-testing the text and for word-processing the original version.

Sincere thanks go to all the Formal Spoken Arabic instructors at FSI who contributed suggestions and taught the course in its various stages. Special acknowledgment goes to Naim Owais, who, as senior Arabic instructor, proofread the text many times and made valuable recommendations regarding linguistic usage.

Finally, our thanks are extended to all the FSI students who survived various versions of this course, and who provided important feedback as to its appropriateness and effectiveness.

NOTES FOR THE INSTRUCTOR

In addition to a sample dialogue and vocabulary list in each lesson, there are five basic segments in each of the fourteen lessons you will be using:

I. **Working with Words and Phrases**
II. **Working with Sentences**
III. **Working with the Language**
IV. **Working with Variants**
V. **Working with the Situation**

Segments I and II focus on the retention of new words and basic functional lines, while Segment III deals with the language itself: the mechanics of spoken Arabic—how it works. Segments IV and V deal with learning expansion: enrichment of the basic lines and building communicative competence. Lessons are typically developed in two logical stages: first, by presenting language structure (Segments I to III), and then by expanding learning (Segments IV and V).

STRUCTURED STAGE

A. PREVIEWING EACH LESSON (Listening to the Sample Dialogue)

Initial Exposure
As the first step in each lesson plan, you will have the class listen together to the dialogue. This provides students with an opportunity to make subjective assessments based on actual perception of Arabic. What does it sound like? Is it very different from what they as students are used to? Does it sound easy to imitate? What about the people using the language? What mood are they in?

You, the instructor, should ask such questions to stimulate discussion. The nature of these questions should change from subjective to more objective with later lessons, e.g., What is the situation about? Who said what?

Setting the Scene
By providing a vivid context for the lesson situation, you will enable your students to associate new vocabulary with powerful imagery. As their instructor, you will describe when, where, and with whom students can typically use the language of the lesson. Because many students at FSI have previous experience overseas, they can often be first-hand informants on the anticipated needs of a situation.

B. LAYING THE FOUNDATION (Working with Words and Phrases)

Vocabulary learning is an essential process in the Arabic *FAST* course. Students do not have to internalize completely the vocabulary of a lesson before moving on to the next step, but the more familiar the vocabulary, the more meaningful the activities that follow.

To ensure sufficient familiarity, you, the instructor, should go through the following steps—first with the Sounds and then with the Meaning:

Familiarity with Sounds—the First Emphasis
1. Teacher reads vocabulary words aloud (each three times) to the listening students.

2. Students listen to each sample dialogue on the cassettes and attempt to recognize familiar sounds or sound sequences.

3. Students repeat vocabulary words chorally after the teacher. This is also done three times, and should be done briskly.

4. Students repeat Step 2.

5. Students repeat each vocabulary item after the teacher chorally, then individually.

6. Students alternate reading vocabulary aloud as many times as the number of students in class (thus each has a chance to read all the words aloud). This assumes that the number of students in the class ordinarily does not exceed five or six.

Familiarity with Meaning—the Next Emphasis

1. Students read aloud the Arabic words and their English equivalents (preferably as many times as there are students in the class—but at least three times if there are only one or two in the class).

2. Teacher reads the Arabic words aloud; students give the English meaning (*books closed*).

3. Students read aloud the English meanings and the equivalent Arabic words.

4. Teacher quizzes students by randomly giving them the Arabic words and students give the appropriate English equivalents.

5. Teacher quizzes students by randomly giving them the English meanings and students give the equivalent Arabic words.

If retention remains weak after these successive steps, more drilling is essential before moving on. In any case, vocabulary drills do not end at this point. Do selected vocabulary drills *repeatedly* at different points during the lesson, both to reinforce retention and to break the monotony of other activities.

C. FEELING OUT THE MEANING (Working with Sentences)

Once a foundation has been established with the vocabulary items, students are ready to shift focus from individual words to the sentences as a whole. Thus student attention is focused not on retention, but on meaningful and creative use of words in context. Successful work in this section often stimulates interesting questions and observations, not only on sentence meaning, but also on language structure and on its cultural implications.

Familiarity with the dialogue should be given early priority at this stage. The first task is to establish good comprehension, then to work on producing the American's lines. Students are not expected to recite the Arabic speaker's lines in the dialogue, but careful listening is an obvious essential.

Working on Audio Comprehension (Using the Taped Dialogue)

1. Students listen to the dialogue twice without looking at the text.

2. Students listen to the dialogue again while looking at the text.

3. Students take turns reading the Arabic lines aloud and translating them into English.

4. Students all listen to the taped dialogue and then say the English equivalent line-by-line, as directed by the instructor.

Working on Speech Production (Using both the American's and the Arab's lines)

1. Teacher reads the American's lines, students repeat them two times chorally.

2. Teacher reads the American's lines and the students repeat, first chorally, then individually.

3. Teacher and students role-play the dialogue one-on-one (students play the American role and the teacher plays the Arab role).

4. Students listen to the taped dialogue to compare and self-critique their performance.

5. Teacher says the Arab's lines out of sequence and students take turns responding with an appropriate American line.

6. Teacher again role-plays the situation with individual students. Teacher may at this point introduce some variation in the Arab's lines, as long as the essential meaning is not changed.

EXPANSION STAGE

After moving carefully through Steps A, B, and C of the initial structured stage of each lesson and working up to sentence-level production and comprehension, the next step is out of the structured stage and into the expansion stage of the lesson. It is called the expansion stage because: first, it aims at helping the student attain as much flexibility as possible within his or her limited knowledge of vocabulary. This enables the student to develop communication strategies by exploiting what he or she already knows. Second, the teacher is now in a position and is expected to expand, vary, and intensify learning activities.

A. TAKING IT APART (Working with the Language)

This consists of Section III, Working with the Language, plus systematic review of the material covered in the previous stage. It is a transitional section designed to bridge the gap between memorized sentence-level "chunks" of language and conversation-level flexibility. In order to achieve flexibility of expression or comprehension, the rules of word combination and inflection need to be grasped and applied. Thus, this section consists of what is traditionally called 'grammar.' It is not grammar for grammar's sake, but grammar as a tool to expand and fortify student performance in real-life situations.

An important pedagogical point is to avoid overdosing students with grammar. That means you will break up the presentation of Section III by using other learning activities, such as vocabulary review and dialogue rehearsal. A typical Section III presentation would be as follows:

1. Introduce a grammar point.
2. Go over related drills.
3. Engage in rehearsal or review activity.
4. Introduce another point of grammar and related drills.
5. Engage in rehearsal or review activity.
6. Continue the above process with the remaining grammar points.

Although the section **Working with the Language** is important, it should not dominate and take too much of the students' time or energy. If students do not quite get the idea after a grammatical point is made and the drills that follow, go on with the lesson. Come back to the point later. Students can often manage a situation without complete mastery of grammar, so the rehearsal of a situation should have priority over any other activity. There is a danger here: students may become frustrated if they are unable to grasp a grammatical point (and some of them may not be sure what the grammatical terms mean, even in English). As the teacher, you may consider attempting to dispel that anxiety by going over the point with an extended explanation, but this is generally not the best course.

As the teacher, emphasize that it is not absolutely essential for students to master every grammatical point, and reflect this in your teaching.

A useful rule in *dealing with grammar* and drills is not to spend more than fifteen minutes at a time on any one point of grammar. One way to do it, as mentioned above, is to switch back to the *rehearsal of a situation* with special emphasis on a single point of grammar. Another way is to review vocabulary. For example, vocabulary can be reviewed in quiz form, on flash cards, or in translation of short sentences.

Grammar drills should be done and reviewed in class, whether they are assigned for homework or not.

B. CREATING NEW LINES (Working with Variants)

This is a transitional step in which you aim at helping students develop their skills in managing and generating language to adapt to new situations. Build on the students' growing reservoir of vocabulary items and their ability to manipulate and recombine these items into meaningful phrases that will help them manage simple conversation.

Variation on the basic dialogue lines has already been introduced by you, the teacher, in rehearsal activities. In this section, there is a special effort on the part of students to create new lines that are functional and practical in given situations. This activity is extremely valuable to talented and experienced language learners. Slower students may not appreciate too much variation, as it burdens their resources.

A basic principle when dealing with new elements is to work on comprehension first, then on production. Thus, a recommended sequence:

1. Students translate simple new sentences (written and taped).

2. Students create lines applicable to the situation.

3. Teacher engages students in mini-conversations, using language generated in earlier activities.

4. Teacher and students engage in restricted role-playing to practice variation.

When they are creating new lines, students may initially use the text to look up words. However, maximum benefit from this exercise occurs when students create the new lines by using words they already know.

This illustrates how important it is for students to master vocabulary and for the teacher to conduct review exercises systematically and regularly.

Students are ready to move on to the next activity when they can demonstrate their ability to generate new lines in an acceptable form.

C. EXPERIENCING LANGUAGE IN CONVERSATION
(Working with the Situation)

This is a simulation of the ultimate goal: to use the target language confidently to manage, cope, and survive in a given situation. The preceding activities have been steps preparatory to this experience, and should help students to develop appropriate conversation management strategies to tackle this "experience" task step by step:

1. Teacher and students rehearse the situation, incorporating variations on the theme.

2. Teacher and students rehearse similar situations, and other possible situations, including those covered in earlier lessons (*these interactions are to be taped*).

3. Teacher critiques each student's performance, with specific advice for improvement.

4. Students listen to their own tapes to monitor and analyze their performance.

5. Teacher and students role-play the simulated situation.

NOTES & INTRODUCTION FOR STUDENTS

THE SOUNDS OF ARABIC

Vowels

Arabic has long vowels and short vowels. This difference in length is not a difference in sound quality, but rather in the length of time that the vowel is held. Listen intently to your teacher as you go over these sounds.

The long aa sound is pronounced most often like the a in English "dad," but in some words it sounds more like the a in "father." Its sound quality depends on the surrounding consonants. The *ii* sound is like the i in English "machine." The *uu* sound is like the u in "rude." The long *ee* is like the ei in English "freight," and the *oo* is like the o in "hope."

Long vowels	**Examples**	*Diphthongs*	**Examples**
aa	shaaf, aaxudh, naas, maaDi, raaH	aw	mawjuud, mawDuuʕ, Hawl
ii	miin, kabiir, saniin	ay	mayy, ghayyar, sayyaara
uu	fuluus, ruTuuba, kuusa		
ee	beet, masheena, eesh		
oo	mooz, hadhool, yoom		

Short vowels	**Examples**
a	raH, maTbax, ana, abda'
i	ibn, biddik, mumkin
u	kull, ghurfa, uktub, umm

Consonants

Most of the consonant sounds in Arabic are similar to English sounds. Some, however, are sounds with which English speakers are not familiar. The unfamiliar sounds are described briefly, but the best way to grasp them is to listen carefully to the tapes and to your teacher.

Consonants	**Examples**	*Consonants*	**Examples**
b	biddi, qabl, jaab	q	qaliil, baqar, daqaa'iq
d	dafaʕ, qadar, bariid	r	rashiid, baarid, qamar
D	Daruuri, HaaDir, riyaaD	s	salaam, nasi, dars
dh	dhaalik, haadha, nabiidh	S	Sabi, baSal, xalaS
DH	DHuhur, naDHiif, alfaaDH	sh	shii, sharshaf, mish
f	feen, Hafla, ashraf	t	tamriin, atakallam, beet
gh	gharb, baghdaad, mablagh	T	Tayyib, aʕTiini, fuwaT
h	huna, sahl, fahd, allaah	th	thaani, kathiir, athaath
H	Hilu, suHuun, sabaaH	w	walad, aswad, aw
j	jiddan, shajar, dajaaj	x	xalaS, daxal, wasix
k	kiif, akil, hunaak	y	yoom, thiyaab, swayy
l	lamma, balad, fuul	z	zeet, nazal, ruzz
m	muslim, samak, salaam	'	su'aal, abnaa'
n	naʕnaʕ, diinaar, furn	ʕ	ʕarab, naʕam, usbuuʕ

Unfamiliar Consonants

There are sounds in the preceding list that do not occur in English. These include the following:

D	a "heavy" d sound, pronounced with a raised, stiff tongue
dh	the voiced th sound in English "than," "though," or "them"
DH	a "heavy" th sound, pronounced with a raised, stiff tongue. Many Arabic speakers pronounce it as a heavy z sound. If this is easier for you, pronounce it that way.
gh	a "gargled" sound similar to French r; a voiced velar fricative
H	a "whispered" h, pronounced much deeper in the throat than regular h; a voiceless pharyngeal fricative
q	a "clicking" sound made by touching the back of your tongue to your uvula; a voiceless uvular stop
r	a "flapped" or "rolled" sound like the r in Spanish or Italian
S	a "heavy" s sound pronounced with a stiff, raised tongue
T	a "heavy" t sound, pronounced with a stiff, raised tongue
x	sometimes written "kh," in English transcription; a sound like German ch as in "ach" or Scottish "loch"; a voiceless velar fricative
'	a glottal stop, i.e., like the catch in the voice between the parts of "oh-oh"
ʕ	a sort of "strangled" sound made deep in the throat; a voiced pharyngeal fricative.

The best way to acquire accurate pronunciation of these sounds is to listen very intently and attentively to your teacher, to the tapes, and to any native Arabic speakers you encounter. Also, do a great deal of oral drilling yourself in order to train your articulatory muscles to these new positions. Practice using these sounds in single syllables at first, then in short, common words (such as naʕam for "yes"), and then build up to phrases and longer words.

Doubled consonants

Sometimes consonants are "doubled" in Arabic. This means that they are pronounced with more emphasis and held for a longer period of time. Listen to your teacher pronounce the following words:

Hatta	xabbar	mukaddas	naDHDHaf
xallaS	mufakkir	nashshaf	marra
awwal	Haarr	taʕʕab	ta'axxar
kull	lamma	tafaDDal	muwaffaq

THE ARABIC ALPHABET

As a Final Letter	As a Medial Letter	As an Initial Letter	In Arabic (alone)	Transliteration of Letter	Name of the Letter
			ا	aa	'alif
ـب	ـبـ	بـ	ب	b	baa'
ـت	ـتـ	تـ	ت	t	taa'
ـث	ـثـ	ثـ	ث	th	thaa'
ـج	ـجـ	جـ	ج	j	jiim
ـح	ـحـ	حـ	ح	H	Haa'
ـخ	ـخـ	خـ	خ	x	xaa'
ـد			د	d	daal
ـذ			ذ	dh	dhaal
ـر			ر	r	raa'
ـز			ز	z	zaay
ـس	ـسـ	سـ	س	s	siin
ـش	ـشـ	شـ	ش	sh	shiin
ـص	ـصـ	صـ	ص	S	Saad
ـض	ـضـ	ضـ	ض	D	Daad
ـط	ـطـ	طـ	ط	T	Taa'
ـظ	ـظـ	ظـ	ظ	DH	DHaa'
ـع	ـعـ	عـ	ع	ʕ	ʕayn
ـغ	ـغـ	غـ	غ	gh	ghayn
ـف	ـفـ	فـ	ف	f	faa'
ـق	ـقـ	قـ	ق	q	qaaf
ـك	ـكـ	كـ	ك	k	kaaf
ـل	ـلـ	لـ	ل	l	laam
ـم	ـمـ	مـ	م	m	miim
ـن	ـنـ	نـ	ن	n	nuun
ـه	ـهـ	هـ	ه	h	haa'
ـو			و	w, uu	waaw
ـى	ـيـ	يـ	ي	y, ii	yaa'
			ء	,	hamza

الدرس الاول

مين حضرتك

١. العربــــي : صباح الخير .

٢. الاميركي : صباح النور ، كيف الحال ؟

٣. العربــــي : الحمد لله كويس ، وكيف حالك انت ؟

٤. الاميركي : كويس الحمد لله .

٥. العربــــي : حضرتك ساكن في العمارة ؟

٦. الاميركي : نعم ، انا ساكن هنا . وحضرتك ؟

٧. العربــــي : انا كمان ساكن هنا ، في الطابق الثالث ، من فين حضرتك ؟

٨. الاميركي : انا من أميركا .

٩. العربــــي : حضرتك اميركي ؟ شو اسمك ؟

١٠. الاميركي : اسمي "ستيف بلاك" واسمك ؟

١١. العربــــي : اسمي "ماهر النّشاشيبي " . انا موظف في وزارة الداخلية .
وحضرتك فين تشتغل ؟

١٢. الاميركي : اشتغل في السفارة الأميركية .

١٣. العربــــي : اهلا وسهلا في بلدنا . تشرفنا .

١٤. الاميركي : اهلا بك . الشرف لنا .

LESSON ONE: Who are You?

id-dars il-awwal: miin HaDirtak?

Sample Dialogue:

ARAB says:

1: *SabaaH il-xeer.*
Good morning.

3: *il-Hamdu li-llaah kwayyis, wa kiif Haalak int?*
Thanks be to God, fine. And how are you?

5: *HaDirtak saakin fi l-Samaara?*

Do you live in the building?

7: *ana kamaan saakin huna, fi T-Taabiq ith-thaalith. min feen HaDirtak?*
I live here too, on the third floor. Where are you from?

9: *HaDirtak ameerki? shu ismak?*
You're American? What's your name?

11: *ismi maahir in-nashaashiibi. ana muwaDHDHaf fi wazaarat id-daaxiliyya. wa HaDirtak feen tashtaghil?*
My name is Maahir An-Nashashiby. I'm an employee at the Ministry of the Interior. And you, where do you work?

13: *ahlan wa sahlan fi baladna. tasharrafna.*
Welcome to our country. Pleased to meet you.

AMERICAN says:

2: *SabaaH in-nuur, kiif il-Haal?*
Good morning, how are you?

4: *kwayyis, il-Hamdu li-llaah.*
Fine, thanks be to God.

6: *naSam, ana saakin huna. wa HaDirtak?*
Yes, I live here. And you?

8: *ana min ameerka.*
I'm from America.

10: *ismi 'Steve Black.' wa ismak?*
My name is Steve Black. And yours?

12: *ashtaghil fi s-safaara l-ameerkiyya.*
I work at the American Embassy.

14: *ahlan biik. ish-sharaf la-na.*
Thank you. The pleasure is mine.

VOCABULARY

dars
lesson

awwal
first

SabaaH il-xeer
good morning

SabaaH in-nuur
(*as response*)
good morning

kiif
how

Haal
condition

kiif il-Haal?
how are you?

il-Hamdu li-llaah
thanks be to God

kwayyis
good, fine

wa
and

Haalak
your condition

kiif Haalak?
how are you? (*m*)

int/inta
you (*m*)

HaDirtak
polite form of 'you'

saakin
living, dwelling

fi
in, at

ʕamaara
building

naʕam
yes

ana
I

huna
here

kamaan
also, too

Taabiq
floor, storey

thaalith
third

iT-Taabiq ith-thaalith
the third floor

min
from

feen
where

ameerka
America

ameerki
American (*m*)

shu
what

ism
name

ismak
your (*m*) name

ismi
my name

muwaDHDHaf
employee (*m*)

wazaara
ministry

wazaarat id-daaxiliyya
Ministry of the Interior

tashtaghil
you (*m*) work

ashtaghil
I work

safaara
embassy

ameerkiyya
American (*f*)

ahlan wa sahlan
welcome

baladna
our country

tasharrafna
pleased to meet you
("we are honored")

SUPPLEMENTARY VOCABULARY

inti
  you (f)

HaDirtik
  polite form of "you" (f)

Haalik
  your (f) condition

kiif Haalik?
  How are you (f)?

kwayyisa
  good, fine (f)

saakina
  dwelling, living(f)

muwaDHDHafa
  employee (f)

tashtaghili
  you (f) work

ʕarabi
  Arab (m)

ʕarabiyya
  Arab (f)

saʕuudi
  Saudi (m)

saʕuudiyya
  Saudi (f)

lubnaani
  Lebanese (m)

lubnaaniyya
  Lebanese (f)

kabiir
  big (m)

kabiira
  big (f)

Saghiir
  small (m)

Saghiira
  small (f)

miin
  who

I. WORKING WITH WORDS AND PHRASES

A. Matching English with Arabic
Match the English expressions with their Arabic equivalents by writing the appropriate numbers to the right of the letters.

1.	Good morning.	a. _____	*kwayyis*
2.	How are you?	b. _____	*safaara*
3.	fine, good	c. _____	*ʕamaara*
4.	living	d. _____	*ish-sharaf la-na.*
5.	What's your name?	e. _____	*SabaaH il-xeer.*
6.	building	f. _____	*ahlan wa sahlan.*
7.	embassy	g. _____	*kiif Haalak?*
8.	Welcome.	h. _____	*shu ismak?*
9.	The pleasure is mine.	i. _____	*ashtaghil*
10.	I work	j. _____	*saakin*

3

B. Completion of Arabic Dialogue

In the following Arabic version of the dialogue certain words have been left out. Complete each of the fourteen sentences by writing in the missing words.

ARAB says:

1: SabaaH _____.

3: il-Hamdu li-llaah _____, wa kiif Haalak _____?

5: HaDirtak _____ fi l-ʕamaara?

7: ana _____ saakin huna, fi T-Taabiq ith-thaalith. min _____ HaDirtak?

9: HaDirtak ameerki?_____ ismak?

11: ismi maahir in-nashaashiibi. ana _____ fi wazaarat id-daaxiliyya. wa HaDirtak feen _____?

13: ahlan wa sahlan fi _____. tasharrafna.

AMERICAN says:

2: SabaaH in-nuur, kiif _____.

4: kwayyis, _____ li-llaah.

6: naʕam, ana saakin huna. wa _____?

8: ana min _____.

10: ismi 'Steve Black.' wa _____?

12: ashtaghil fi _____ l-ameerkiyya.

14: ahlan biik. ish-sharaf _____.

II. WORKING WITH SENTENCES

A. Matching Spoken Arabic with Written English

Listen either to Cassette 1 (side 1) or to your teacher, and match what is said in Arabic with the eight English sentences below. Write the number of each Arabic sentence in the blanks to the left of the English.

_____ Good morning.
_____ Good morning. How are you?
_____ Fine (praise be to God).
_____ Yes, I live here.
_____ I am from America.
_____ What's your name?
_____ I work at the American Embassy.
_____ Welcome to our country.

B. Scrambled Arabic Dialogue

Reconstruct the sample dialogue by numbering the fifteen sentences below so they are in a meaningful sequence.

_____ il-Hamdu li-llaah kwayyis, wa kiif Haalak int?
_____ SabaaH in-nuur, kiif il-Haal?
_____ ashtaghil fi s-safaara l-ameerkiyya.
_____ kwayyis, il-Hamdu li-llaah.
_____ ismi 'Steve Black.' wa ismak?
_____ ahlan biik. ish-sharaf la-na.
_____ ana kamaan saakin huna, fi T-Taabiq ith-thaalith.
_____ min feen HaDirtak?
_____ ahlan wa sahlan fi baladna. tasharrafna.
_____ HaDirtak ameerki? shu ismak?
_____ naʕam, ana saakin huna. wa HaDirtak?
_____ ismi maahir in-nashaashiibi. ana muwaDHDHaf fi wazaarat id-daaxiliyya, wa HaDirtak feen tashtaghil?
_____ SabaaH il-xeer.
_____ ana min ameerka.
_____ HaDirtak saakin fi l-ʕamaara?

C. Matching English with Arabic

Match the English sentences with their Arabic counterparts. Either draw a line to connect the two or write the number (English) next to the letter (Arabic). You can also respond orally by saying the English first and then the Arabic equivalent.

1. Good morning.		*a.* kwayyis, il-Hamdu li-Ilaah.
2. I'm from America.		*b.* SabaaH in-nuur, kiif Haalak?
3. Welcome to our country.		*c.* shu ismak?
4. What is your name?		*d.* SabaaH il-xeer.
5. Fine (Praise be to God).		*e.* ana min ameerka.
6. Yes, I live here.		*f.* ahlan wa sahlan fi baladna.
7. Good morning, how are you?		*g.* ashtaghil fi s-safaara l-ameerkiyya.
8. I work at the American Embassy.		*h.* naʕam, ana saakin huna.

D. Matching Arabic Remarks to Appropriate Responses

Match the eight Arabic sentences on the left with the appropriate response among the seven on the right.

1. SabaaH il-xeer.		*a.* naʕam, ana saakin huna.
2. kiif il-Haal?		*b.* ahlan biik.
3. HaDirtak saakin fi-l-ʕamaara?		*c.* ashtaghil fi s-safaara l-ameerkiyya.
4. min feen HaDirtak?		*d.* SabaaH in-nuur.
5. wa kiif Haalak int?		*e.* ish-sharaf la-na.
6. ahlan wa sahlan.		*f.* ana min ameerka.
7. feen tashtaghil?		*g.* kwayyis, il-Hamdu li-Ilaah.
8. tasharrafna.		

E. Translation into Arabic

Go back to Exercise **A** and convert those eight sentences into Arabic.

III. WORKING WITH THE LANGUAGE

A. Pronunciation of the Definite Article

The word for 'the' in Arabic is *al-*. It is most often pronounced *el-* or *il-* in everyday speech. In this text, it is spelled *il-*:

> *SabaaH il-xeer.*
> Good morning.

If it is preceded by a word that ends in a vowel, it becomes just *-l-*:

> *fi-l-ʃamaara*
> in the building

The '*l*' of the definite article often assimilates to the initial sound of the following word:

is-safaara the embassy	*ith-thaalith* the third
iT-Taabiq the floor	*iS-SabaaH* the morning

The sounds that cause '*l*' of the definite article to assimilate are: *t - th - d - dh - r - z - s - sh - S - D - T - DH - l - n.*

Drill 1: TRANSFORMATION OF NOUNS

Make the following twelve indefinite nouns definite:

1.	*xeer*	*5.*	*ameerki*	*9.*	*balad*
2.	*nuur*	*6.*	*daaxiliyya*	*10.*	*safaara*
3.	*ʃamaara*	*7.*	*muwaDHDHaf*	*11.*	*dars*
4.	*Taabiq*	*8.*	*sharaf*	*12.*	*ism*

B. Gender in Nouns

All Arabic nouns have gender. They are either masculine or feminine. Generally, feminine nouns end with an '*a*' sound:

balad country	*ʃamaara* building
ism name	*safaara* embassy
muwaDHDHaf employee (*m*)	*muwaDHDHafa* employee (*f*)

7

Drill 2: IDENTIFICATION OF NOUNS BY GENDER
Go over the vocabulary list for this lesson and identify the nouns by gender. Verify your identification with your teacher.

C. Adjectives: Gender and Definiteness
Adjectives agree with nouns in gender, and they usually follow the noun:

balad kabiir
a big country

ʕamaara kabiira
a big building

ism ʕarabi
an Arab name

safaara ʕarabiyya
an Arab embassy

Adjectives also agree with nouns in definiteness, i.e., if the noun has the definite article (*il-*), the adjective has one, too:

il-balad il-kabiir
the big country

il-ʕamaara l-kabiira
the big building

il-ism il-ʕarabi
the Arab name

is-safaara s-saʕuudiyya
the Saudi Embassy

Drill 3: COMPLETION
Complete Sentence *a* below with each of the noun-adjective phrases. Then do the same with Sentence *b*, using the same seven phrases appropriately.

a. ashtaghil fi _____.

1. s-safaara l-ameerkiyya
2. s-safaara s-saʕuudiyya
3. balad ʕarabi
4. s-safaara l-kuweetiyya
5. l-ʕamaara l-kabiira
6. s-safaara l-lubnaaniyya
7. balad Saghiir

b. ana muwaDHDHaf/muwaDHDHafa fi _____.

D. Equational Sentences
Arabic does not generally use an overt form of the verb "to be" in present tense sentences. Instead, they are phrased as below:

ana min ameerka.
I (am) from America.

shu ismak?
What (is) your name?

ismi maahir.
My name (is) Maahir.

ana ameerkiyya.
I (am) American.

Sentences that lack an overt verb are termed "equational" sentences.

8

Drill 4: IDENTIFICATION

Go over the Sample Dialogue at the beginning of this lesson and identify the equational sentences. Then verify your work with your teacher.

E. Verbs

Present tense verbs in Arabic consist of a **prefix** and a **stem**. Sometimes there is also a **suffix**. In this lesson the verb 'to work' (*ishtaghal*) occurs in the present tense. The forms that occur in this lesson are:

ashtaghil
  I work

tashtaghil
  you (*m*) work

tashtaghili
  you (*f*) work

Drill 5: CONJUGATION

Transform the following verbal sentences from the first person singular (I) to the second person singular (you) *masculine*, and then to the second person *feminine*.

Examples:
(ana) ashtaghil fi s-safaara l-ameerkiyya.--->

(inta) tashtaghil fi s-safaara l-ameerkiyya.--->

(inti) tashtaghili fi s-safaara l-ameerkiyya.

1. *ashtaghil fi balad ʕarabi.*
2. *ashtaghil fi l-ʕamaara l-kabiira.*
3. *ashtaghil fi s-safaara l-lubnaaniyya.*
4. *ashtaghil fi ameerka.*
5. *ashtaghil fi balad Saghiir.*
6. *ashtaghil huna.*

F. Pronoun Types: Independent and Suffixed

Arabic has two types of pronouns: independent and suffixed. The independent ones are separate words, and are subject pronouns, e.g.,

ana ameerki.
  I (am) (an) American.

inti muwaDHDHafa.
  You (*f*) (are) an employee.

inta min ameerka?
  Are you (m) from America?

9

Suffix pronouns are not independent words; they are attached to the ends of nouns to show possession. In this lesson we have used the suffix pronouns for "my," "your" (*m* and *f*), and "our." In Arabic these are: *-i, -ak, -ik,* and *-na*.

> *ism-i maahir.*
>> My name is Mahir.
>
> *fi balad-na*
>> in our country
>
> *shu ism-ak?*
>> What is your (*m*) name?
>
> *shu ism-ik?*
>> What is your (*f*) name?

When a possessive pronoun is suffixed to a feminine noun (ending in *a*), ordinarily insert a *-t* is before the pronoun:

> *ʕamaara*
>> (a) building
>
> *ʕamaarat-i*
>> my building
>
> *safaara*
>> (an) embassy
>
> *safaarat-na*
>> our embassy

Drill 6: PRONOUN USAGE IN CONVERSATION

a. Students use subject pronouns (*ana, inta, inti*) to ask each other where they are from.

b. Students practice attaching suffix pronouns (*-i, -ak, -ik, -na*) to the following ten words:

1. ism	*4. Haal*	*6. wazaara*	*8. ʕamaara*
2. balad	*5. muwaDHDHaf*	*7. safaara*	*9. muwaDHDHafa*
3. dars			*10. sharaf*

IV. WORKING WITH VARIANTS

A. Translation from English into Arabic
Convert the following eight sentences into Arabic.

1. Are you (*m*) American?
2. Are you Mahir?
3. Do you work at the Ministry of the Interior?
4. Do you live on the third floor?
5. I work here, too.
6. Where do you (*m*) live?
7. Are you Fatima?
8. Do you (*f*) work in this building?

B. Comprehension of Spoken Arabic
Listen to the Arabic sentences on the cassette and determine which of the following English sentences corresponds in meaning to one of the recorded Arabic sentences. Write the identification for the Arabic to the left of the English equilavent below.

1. _____ I am living on the third floor.
   _____ You are living on the third floor.
   _____ You work on the third floor.

2. _____ You work at the American Embassy.
   _____ You are an employee at the American Embassy.
   _____ I work at the American Embassy.

3. _____ Do you know Steve Black?
   _____ My name is Steve Black.
   _____ I your name Steve Black?

4. _____ I work in the American building.
   _____ You live at the American Embassy.
   _____ I live in the building.

5. _____ Welcome to our embassy.
   _____ Welcome to our building.
   _____ Welcome to our country.

V. WORKING WITH THE SITUATION

Any situation in the Arab East where you meet someone for the first time involves several linguistic and societal functions: offering a greeting, responding to a greeting, getting some basic information, giving some basic information, and concluding with a suitable courtesy expression. All of these are in the Sample Dialogue.

In a real-life situation, the Arab's part in such a conversation may vary, even though the content is essentially the same. Your teacher will role-play this situation with you, but he or she will not adhere to exactly the same lines as the Arab does in this lesson's dialogue.

Before you begin, discuss with your teacher what you think you want to say so that you have a set of "key lines" to use in this type of situation. These lines can be the same as the ones in the Sample Dialogue or you can add some new ones. For the time being, however, keep your lines simple, and rehearse this type of dialogue until it comes automatically.

The point of this exercise is to accustom you to functioning in this kind of situation even though you do not understand every word the Arab says. You are aiming at basic communicative competence, not total linguistic comprehension.

11

الدرس الثاني (أ)

التاكسي

١. الاميركي : تاكسي !
٢. العربـــي : تفضل بالسيارة .
٣. الاميركي : بدى اروح الى هذا العنوان .
٤. العربـــي : طيَب ، تفضّل .
٥. الاميركي : قديش لازم ادفع ؟
٦. العربي : الأجرة على العداد ، تفضل .
٧. الاميركي : طيب .
(بعد عشر دقائق)
٨. العربـــي : تعرف وين العمارة تماما ؟
٩. الاميركي : مش بعيدة من هنا ، افتكر قدام شوي .
١٠. العربـــي : هذي هي العمارة ؟
١١. الاميركي : ايوه ، قديش الأجرة من فضلك ؟
١٢. العربـــي : تسع ريالات .
١٣. الاميركي : تفضل ، هذي عشرة ريالات ، وخلَي الباقي .
١٤. العربـــي : شكراً ، مع السلامة .
١٥. الاميركي : عفواً ، الله يسلّمك .

LESSON TWO: Taxi

id-dars ith-thaani: it-taksi

Two dialogues are provided in this lesson in order to give alternative scenarios and to offer examples of interaction for both men and women. Listen carefully to Cassette 1 (side 2) and to your teacher.

Sample Dialogue A:

AMERICAN says:	ARAB says:
1: *taksi!* Taxi!	**2:** *tafaDDal bi-s-sayyaara.* Please, get in the car.
3: *biddi aruuH ila haadha l-Sinwaan.* I want to go to this address.	**4:** *Tayyib, tafaDDal.* Okay, get in.
5: *qaddeesh laazim adfaS?* How much do I have to pay?	**6:** *il-ujra Sala l-Saddaad, tafaDDal.* The fare is on the meter. Go ahead, get in.
7: *Tayyib.* All right.	

[AFTER ABOUT 10 MINUTES IN THE TAXI]

	8: *taSrif ween il-Samaara tamaaman?* Do you know exactly where the building is?
9: *mish baSiida min huna, aftakir quddaam shwayy.* Not far from here, I think a little ahead.	**10:** *haadhi hiya l-Samaara?* Is this the building?
11: *aywa, qaddeesh il-ujra min faDlak* Yes. How much is the fare, plea₂	**12:** *tisaS riyaalaat.* Nine riyals.
13: *tafaDDal, haadhi Sashar riyaalaat, ₁ xalli l-baaqi.* Here. This is ten riyals. Keep the change.	**14:** *shukran, maS is-salaama.* Thank you. Good-bye.
15: *allaah yusallimak.* Good-bye.	

الدرس الثاني (ب)

١.   الاميركية : تاكسي !

٢.   العربـــي : تفضلي بالسيارة .

٣.   الاميركية : بدى اروح الى هذا العنوان .

٤.   العربـــي : طيّب ، تفضّلي .

٥.   الاميركية : قديش لازم ادفع ؟

٦.   العربي : قدر ما بدك ، تفضلي .

٧.   الاميركية : اولا بدي اعرف قديش لازم ادفع .

٨.   العربي : خمسة عشر ريال .

٩.   الاميركية : لا ، هذا كثير ، سبع ريالات كفاية .

١٠. العربي : سبع ريالات قليل جدا ، معليش بعشر ريالات .

١١. الاميركية : طيب . هذا معقول .

(بعد عشر دقائق)

١٢. العربـــي : تعرفي وين العمارة تماما ؟

١٣. الاميركية : مش بعيدة من هنا ، افتكر قدام شوي .

١٤. العربـــي : هذي هي العمارة ؟

١٥. الاميركية : ايوه ، تفضل هذي عشر ريالات .

١٦. العربـــي : شكرا ، مع السلامة .

١٧. الاميركية : الله يسلّمك .

Sample Dialogue B:

AMERICAN says:

1: taksi!
   Taxi!

3: biddi aruuH ila haadha l-ʕinwaan.
   I want to go to this address.

5: qaddeesh laazim adfaʕ?
   How much do I have to pay?

*7: awwalan biddi aʕrif qaddeesh
   laazim adfaʕ.*
   First I need to know how much
   I must pay.

*9: laa, haadha kathiir, sabaʕ riyaalaat
   kifaaya.*
   No, that's too much. Seven
   riyals is enough.

11: Tayyib. haadha maʕquul.
   Okay, that's reasonable.

ARAB says:

2: tafaDDali bi-s-sayyaara.
   Please, get in the car.

4: Tayyib, tafaDDali.
   Okay, get in.

6: qadarma biddik, tafaDDali.
   As you want, please get in.

8: xamstaʕshar riyaal.
   Fifteen riyals.

*10: sabaʕ riyaalaat qaliil jiddan,
   maʕaleesh bi-ʕashar riyaalaat.
   tafaDDali.*
   Seven riyals is very little.
   Let's say ten. Please get in.

[AFTER ABOUT 10 MINUTES IN THE TAXI]

12: taʕrifi ween il-ʕamaara tamaaman?
   Do you know exactly where the
   building is?

*13: mish baʕiida min huna, aftakir
   quddaam shwayy.*
   Not far from here. A little
   ahead, I think.

14: haadhi hiya l-ʕamaara?
   Is this the building?

*15: aywa. tafaDDal, haadhi ʕashar
   riyaalaat.*
   Yes, here. This is ten riyals.

16: shukran, maʕ is-salaama.
   Thanks. Good-bye.

17: allaah yusallimak.
   Good-bye.

15

VOCABULARY

thaani
second

taksi
taxi

tafaDDal
please (m), go ahead

bi-
in, at

sayyaara
car

biddi
I want

aruuH
I go

biddi aruuH
I want to go

ila
to, towards

haadha
this (m)

ʕinwaan
address

haadha l-ʕinwaan
this address

Tayyib
all right, okay

qaddeesh
how much

laazim
it is necessary,
must, have to

adfaʕ
I pay

laazim adfaʕ
I have to pay

ujra
fare

ʕala
on, upon

ʕaddaad
meter

ʕala l-ʕaddaad
on / by the meter

min faDlak
please (m)

taʕrif
you (m) know

ween
where

tamaaman
exactly

mish
not

baʕiid (min)
far (from)

aftakir
I think

quddaam
ahead, in front of

shwayy
little, a little (bit)

haadhi
this (f)

hiya
she

aywa
yes (informal)

tisaʕ
nine

ʕashar
ten

riyaal (-aat)
riyal

xalli l-baaqi
"keep the change"

shukran
thanks, thank you

maʕ is-salaama
good-bye

allaah yusallimak
good-bye (as response)

tafaDDali
please (f) go ahead

qadarma
as much as

biddik
you (f) want

awwalan
first of all

aʕrif
I know

xamstaʕshar
fifteen

la
no

kathiir
much, too much,
many

sabaʕ
seven

kifaaya
enough

qaliil
little, few

jiddan
very

maʕaleesh
never mind; it's okay

maʕquul
reasonable

taʕrifi
you (f) know

SUPPLEMENTARY VOCABULARY

huwa
  he
	thalaatha
	  three
		thalaathataʕsh(ar)
		  thirteen

hum
  they
	arbaʕa
	  four
		arbaʕtaʕash(ar)
		  fourteen

intu
  you (pl)
	xamsa
	  five
		xamstaʕash(ar)
		  fifteen

naHna
  we
	sitta
	  six
		sittaʕash(ar)
		  sixteen

tadfaʕ
  you (m) pay
	sabʕa
	  seven
		sabaʕtaʕash(ar)
		  seventeen

taftakir
  you (m) think
	thamaaniya
	  eight
		thamantaʕash(ar)
		  eighteen

taftakiri
  you (f) think
	tisʕa
	  nine
		tisaʕtaʕash(ar)
		  nineteen

qariib (min)
  near, close (to)
	ʕashara
	  ten
		ʕishriin
		  twenty

waaHid
  one
	iHdaʕsh(ar)
	  eleven
		ameerkaan
		  Americans

ithneen
  two
	ithnaʕsh(ar)
	  twelve
		ʕarab
		  Arabs

I. WORKING WITH WORDS AND PHRASES

A. Matching English with Arabic Equivalents

Match each of the twelve English expressions with its Arabic equivalent by writing the appropriate numbers in the blanks after the letters.

1.	car	a. _____	baʕiid
2.	address	b. _____	quddaam shwayy
3.	I want to go	c. _____	qadarma biddik
4.	where	d. _____	kifaaya
5.	far away	e. _____	sayyaara
6.	how much	f. _____	laazim adfaʕ.
7.	enough	g. _____	aftakir
8.	ahead a little	h. _____	ʕinwaan
9.	I think	i. _____	xalli l-baaqi.
10.	as you wish	j. _____	qaddeesh
11.	I must pay.	k. _____	biddi aruuH
12.	Keep the change.	l. _____	ween

B. Completion of Arabic Conversation

In both Dialogues *A* and *B*, certain words have been left out. Complete the sentences in each version by writing in the missing words.

Dialogue A

AMERICAN says:

1: taksi!

3: biddi aruuH ila haadha _____

5: qaddeesh laazim _____ *?*

7: Tayyib.

9: mish baSiida min huna, _____ *quddaam shwayy.*

11: aywa, _____ *il-ujra min faDlak?*

13: tafaDDal, _____ *Sashar riyaalaat wa* _____ *l-baaqi.*

15: allaah _____ *.*

ARAB says:

2: _____
bi-s-sayyaara.

4: _____ *, tafaDDal.*

6: _____ *Sala l-Saddaad, tafaDDal.*

8: taSrif ween il-Samaara _____ *?*

10: haadhi hiya _____ *?*

12: _____ *riyaalaat.*

14: _____ *, maS is-salaama.*

Dialogue B

AMERICAN says:

1: taksi!

3: biddi _____ *ila haadha l-Sinwaan.*

5: qaddesh _____ *adfaS?*

7: awwalan _____ *aSrif* _____ *laazim adfaS.*

9: la, haadha _____ *; sabaS riyaalaat* _____ *.*

11: Tayyib. haadha _____ *.*

13: mish _____ *min huna, aftakir* _____ *shwayy.*

15: _____ *, tafaDDal haadhi* _____ *riyaalaat.*

17: _____ *yusallimak.*

ARAB says:

2: tafaDDali bi- _____ *.*

4: Tayyib, _____ *.*

6: qadarma _____ *, tafaDDali.*

8: xamstaSshar _____ *.*

10: _____ *riyaalaat* _____ *jiddan, maSaleesh bi-Sashar riyaalaat. tafaDDali.*

12: taSrifi ween _____ *tamaaman?*

14: haadhi _____ *l-Samaara?*

16: shukran, maS _____ *.*

II. WORKING WITH SENTENCES

A. Matching Spoken Arabic with Written English Equivalents (listening)
Listen to the cassette again or to your teacher, and match what is said in Arabic with the following eight sentences by writing the identification for each Arabic sentence in the blank preceding the English.

_____ How much must I pay?

_____ I want to go to this address.

_____ Do you know where the building is?

_____ How much is the fare, please?

_____ Not too far from here. I think it's a little ahead.

_____ That's too much. Seven riyals is enough.

_____ First of all, I need to know how much I must pay.

_____ Here's ten riyals. Keep the change.

B. Scrambled Arabic Dialogue
Reconstruct this Sample Dialogue by numbering the seventeen sentences below so they are in a meaningful sequence.

_____ la, haadha kathiir, sabaʕ riyaalaat kifaaya.

_____ shukran, maʕ is-salaama.

_____ Tayyib, tafaDDali.

_____ mish baʕiida min huna, aftakir quddaam shwayy.

_____ Tayyib. haadha maʕquul.

_____ aywa, tafaDDal. haadhi ʕashar riyaalaat.

_____ awwalan biddi aʕrif qaddeesh laazim adfaʕ.

_____ qadarma biddik, tafaDDali.

_____ taksi!

_____ sabaʕ riyaalaat qaliil jiddan, maʕaleesh bi-ʕashar
riyaalaat. tafaDDali.

_____ biddi aruuH ila haadha l-ʕinwaan.

_____ taʕrifi ween il-ʕamaara tamaaman?

_____ xamstaʕshar riyaal.

_____ haadhi hiya l-ʕamaara?

_____ qaddesh laazim adfaʕ?

_____ tafaDDali bi-s-sayyaara.

_____ allaah yusallimak.

19

C. Matching English with Arabic Equivalents

Match the English sentences with their Arabic counterparts. As before, you may either draw a line to connect the two or you can write the appropriate number next to the letters. You may also respond orally.

1. Get in the car, please.

a. shukran, maʕ is-salaama.

2. How much is the fare, please?

b. sabaʕ riyaalaat qaliil jiddan.

3. I want to go to this address.

c. qaddeesh laazim adfaʕ?

4. I want to know how much I must pay.

d. tafaDDal bi-s-sayyaara.

5. How much must I pay?

e. sabaʕ riyaalaat kifaaya.

6. Seven riyals is enough.

f. qaddeesh il-ujra, min faDlak?

7. Thank you. Good-bye.

g. biddi aruuH ila haadha l-ʕinwaan.

8. Seven riyals is (too) little.

h. biddi aʕrif qaddeesh laazim adfaʕ.

D. Matching Arabic Remarks and Responses

Match each of the eight Arabic sentences on the left with an appropriate response on the right. Write the remark number next to the letter of the response.

1. biddi aruuH ila haadha l-ʕinwaan.

a. tisaʕ riyaalaat.

2. qaddeesh laazim adfaʕ?

b. sabaʕ riyaalaat qaliil.

3. qaddeesh il-ujra min faDlak?

c. aywa.

4. maʕ is-salaama.

d. tafaDDal bi-s-sayyaara.

5. taʕrif ween il-ʕamaara tamaaman?

e. Tayyib. tafaDDal.

6. sabaʕ riyaalaat kifaaya.

f. il-ujra ʕala l-ʕaddaad.

7. haadhi hiya l-ʕamaara?

g. allaah yusallimak.

8. taksi!

h. mish baʕiida min huna, aftakir quddaam shwayy.

E. Translation into Arabic

Convert the English sentences in Exercise **A** of this Section (p. 19) into Arabic.

20

III. WORKING WITH THE LANGUAGE

A. bidd- "to want"
There are several ways to express the concept of wanting in Arabic. One of the ways most common in colloquial Levantine speech is to use the expression *bidd-*. But *bidd-* is not really a verb. It is a noun that takes pronoun suffixes. It is somewhat like saying: "[my] wish (is) . . .".

> *bidd-i taksi.*   *shu bidd-ak?*   *bidd-u xamstaʕshar riyaal.*
> I want a taxi.   What do you want?   He wants 15 riyals.

The complete forms of *bidd-* are:

> *bidd-u*   *bidd-ha*   *bidd-hum*
>   he wants   she wants   they want

> *bidd-ak*   *bidd-ik*   *bidd-kum*
>   you want   you (*f*) want   you (*pl*) want

> *bidd-i*   *bidd-na*
>   I want   we want

Note: For paradigms (examples of inflectional forms) in Arabic all persons are listed in the following traditional order:

> singular (*m*), singular (*f*), and plural.

Drill 1: CONJUGATION OF bidd- FORMS
a. Teacher says forms of *bidd-* on chart. Students listen.
b. Teacher says forms of *bidd-* and students repeat.
c. Students take turns reciting *bidd-* forms, referring to chart, if necessary.
d. Students practice changing the *bidd-* forms with the following sentences:

> **1.** *biddi sayyaara.*
> **2.** *biddi taksi.*
> **3.** *biddi xamstaʕshar riyaal.*

B. Demonstrative Pronoun Forms: Masculine, Feminine, & Plural
The words for "this" in Arabic are *haadha* and *haadhi*. *haadha* is masculine and *haadhi* is feminine. The word for "these" is *hadhool*, the plural.

1. Demonstrative phrases: "This" and "These" Usage
To say "this address," (for example) in Arabic, one says, literally, "this the-address," as shown in the three examples below:

> *haadha l-ʕinwaan*   *haadhi l-ʕamaara*   *hadhool il-ameerkaan*
>   this address   this building   these Americans

21

2. Demonstrative sentences: "This" and "These" Usage
To say something like "this is an address," the definite article is dropped from the noun:

haadha ʕinwaan.	haadhi ʕamaara.	hadhool ameerkaan.
This is an address.	This is a building.	These are Americans.

To say "this is **the** address," the subject pronoun plus the definite article is used:

haadha huwa l-ʕinwaan.	haadhi hiya l-ʕamaara.	hadhool hum il-ameerkaan.
This is the address.	This is the building.	These are the Americans.

Drill 2: DEMONSTRATIVES

a. Use the appropriate demonstrative in the six phrases below:

1. _____ s-safaara   4. _____ l-ujra
2. _____ l-ʕinwaan   5. _____ t-taksi
3. _____ s-sayyaara   6. _____ il-ʕarab

b. Form demonstrative sentences from the phrases, as in the three examples below:

1. haadhi l-ʕamaara ("this building") ---->
2. haadhi ʕamaara. ("This is a building.") --->
3. haadhi hiya l-ʕamaara. ("This is the building.")

C. Numbers: Counting and enumerating

There are some basic rules to remember when counting in Arabic:

1. Numbers 3 through 10 are followed by plural nouns.

2. When reciting the numbers 3 through 10 (without counted nouns), the feminine form is used. With most counted nouns, the masculine form is used.

3. Numbers 11 and above are for the most part followed by singular nouns.

4. Plural nouns that refer to anything other than humans take feminine singular agreement.

Examples:

a. 3 through 10 plus a noun when counting:

xams riyaalaat	arbaʕ sayyaaraat
5 riyals	4 cars

b. 3 through 10 when without a noun:

arbaʕa	xamsa	sitta
4	5	6

c. 11 and above:

xamastaʕshar riyaal	*sabaʕtashar sayyaara*	*ʕishriin muwaDHDHaf*
15 riyals	17 cars	20 employees

d. Non-human nouns:

haadhi ʕashar riyaalaat.	*sayyaaraat kathiira*
This is 10 riyals.	many cars

Drill 3: COUNTING EXERCISES

In this exercise, the teacher uses colored rods of various shapes and sizes in orderly patterns.

a. With ten rods lined up in sequence, the teacher assigns each color a different number. First the teacher counts and then the students take turns counting.

b. Using the same colors to represent the same numbers, the teacher next arranges exercises in addition for students.

c. Teacher does steps *a* and *b* for numbers 11 through 20.

Drill 4: COMPLETION

a. Practice the following sentences, using numbers 3 through 10.

1. _____ *riyaalaat kifaaya.*
2. *tafaDDal. haadhi* _____ *riyaalaat.*

b. Practice the following sentences, using numbers 11 through 20.

1. *il-ujra* _____ *riyaal.*
2. *tafaDDal. haadhi* _____ *riyaal.*

D. Negation

Most nouns, pronouns, adjectives, adverbial phrases, and equational sentences are negated with the word *mish*.

mish baʕiid min huna	*ana mish saakin huna.*
not far from here	I (*m*) don't live here.
mish haadhi l-ʕamaara	*mish inti*
not this building	not you (*f*)

Drill 5: NEGATION USAGE

Using the word *mish*, negate the ten sentences overleaf after you review the example below:

Example:

is-safaara qariiba min huna.   *is-safaara mish qariiba min huna.*

23

1. *haadhi hiya s-safaara l-ameerkiyya.*
2. *ana ʕarabi.*
3. *il-ʕinwaan baʕiid min huna.*
4. *haadha riyaal saʕuudi.*
5. *ana muwaDHDHafa ameerkiyya.*
6. *naHna ameerkaan.*
7. *hum ʕarab.*
8. *intu min is-safaara l-ameerkiyya?*
9. *hiya muwaDHDHafa huna.*
10. *huwa lubnaani.*

E. Subject pronouns: Summary

The forms of subject pronouns are summarized below:

huwa	*hiya*	*hum*
he	she	they

int (a)	*inti*	*intu*
you	you (*f*)	you (*pl*)

ana	*naHna*
I	we

F. Suffix (possessive) pronouns: Summary

The forms of the possessive pronouns are summarized below:

-uh	*-ha*	*-hum*
his	her	their

-ak / -k	*-ik / -ki*	*-kum*
your	your (*f*)	your (*pl*)

-i	*-na*
my	our

G. "Please" in Two Forms for Two Different Functions

There are two expressions in Arabic that are translated into English as "please," but these expressions serve two different functions: One (*min faDlak*) is used by a speaker requesting a favor or an action from someone else (e.g., asking to borrow a book); the other (*tafaDDal*) is used when the speaker is offering a favor or action to someone else (e.g., opening a door for someone, offering someone food or a cigarette).

Each of these expressions has three forms: masculine singular, feminine singular, and plural. They look like this:

As a Request: "please"	*As an Offering:* "please"
min faDlak (m)	*tafaDDal (m)*
min faDlik (f)	*tafaDDali (f)*
min faDilkum (pl)	*tafaDDalu (pl)*

IV. WORKING WITH VARIANTS

A. Translation from English into Arabic

Convert the following eight sentences into Arabic.

1. I want to go to the Kuwaiti Embassy.
2. How much is the fare from here to the American Embassy?
3. I want to know where the building is.
4. Is the embassy near here?
5. Do you (*m*) work on the third floor?
6. I want to go to this address, please.
7. This is not good.
8. He is not here.

B. Comprehension of Spoken Arabic

Listen to the Arabic sentences on Cassette 1 (side 2) and determine which version of the English sentences below best corresponds in meaning with the five spoken Arabic sentences. Mark the written English sentence you choose.

1. _____ I want to go to this building.
_____ I want to go to this address.
_____ I want to go to this embassy.

2. _____ I think the address is close to here.
_____ I think the address is far from here.
_____ I think this address is not far from here.

3. _____ How much is the fare, please?
_____ How much must I pay, please?
_____ Is the fare a lot, please?

4. _____ The building is ahead a little.
_____ This address is ahead a little.
_____ The ministry is ahead a little.

5. _____ Here's four riyals; keep the change.
_____ Here's six riyals; keep the change.
_____ Here's nine riyals; keep the change.

V. WORKING WITH THE SITUATION

Taking a taxi in an Arab country often involves bargaining, unless the taxi has a meter. You should always find out from the driver beforehand. Ask if there is a meter in the cab. If there is none, you should settle on a fare before you get in the cab. Once you get in, that's a signal to the driver that you've agreed to pay his price.

In general, taxi drivers will charge as much as they can, and foreigners should be especially careful not to agree to overpriced fares. Bargaining is a custom and an art in itself and needs to be practiced, both for psychological reasons (not giving in simply to be polite) and for linguistic and societal reasons (knowing what to say and when to say it).

Your teacher will engage you in this kind of dialogue, changing the lines of the Arab somewhat, but conversing essentially along the lines in the sample dialogues. Remember that you do not need to understand every word your teacher uses—you just need to get the general idea so that you can respond appropriately.

Before engaging in the simulation, spend some time discussing the situation with your teacher. Ask any questions you might have on how the process is handled (do you automatically cut the suggested fare in half, for example) and practice the "key lines" you know you will need.

الدرس الثالث

على التلفون

١. الاميركي : آلو ؟

٢. العربـــي : آلو ، ممكن اتكلم مع الملحق العسكري، لو سمحت ؟

٣. الاميركي : من فضلك ، مين حضرتك ؟

٤. العربـــي : انا العريف "نجيب سلام" من الجيش الأردني .

٥. الاميركي : نعم ، ليش تريد الملحق العسكري ؟

٦. العربـــي : احب اقابل حضرة الملحق حتى اسلمه رسالة من العقيد "الخياط" بخصوص سفري للولايات المتحدة .

٧. الاميركي : شوي شوي من فضلك انا ما افهم عربي كثير ايش تريد ، مرة ثانية ؟

٨. العربـــي : احب اشوف الملحق العسكري ، عندي رسالة اله .

٩. الاميركي : طيب من مين هذي الرسالة ؟

١٠. العربـــي : هذي الرسالة من العقيد مصطفى الخياط من وزارة الدفاع .

١١. الاميركي : مع الاسف ، الملحق مش موجود هلا .

١٢. العربـــي : ممكن اعمل معه موعد ؟

١٣. الاميركي : ليش لا ، ممكن بكرة الساعة ثلاثة بعد الظهر ؟

١٤. العربـــي : ايوه ممكن . نشوفكم بكرة ان شاء الله .

١٥. الاميركي : طيّب . مع السلامة .

١٦. العربـــي : الله يسلمك .

LESSON THREE: On the Phone

id-dars ith-thaalith: ʕala t-talifoon

Sample Dialogue:

AMERICAN says:

1: *aloo?*
Hello?

3: *min faDlak, miin HaDirtak?*
Who's calling, please? (*literally,*
Please, who are you?)

5: *naʕam, leesh turiid il-mulHaq
il-ʕaskari?*
Yes, why do you want
the military attaché?

7: *shwayy shwayy, min faDlak,
ana ma afham ʕarabi kathiir. eesh
turiid marra thaaniya?*
Slowly, please. I don't
understand much Arabic. What is
it that you want again?

9: *Tayyib, min miin haadhi r-risaala?*
All right. From whom is this letter?

11: *maʕ il-asaf, il-mulHaq mish mawjuud
halla.*
Unfortunately, the attaché isn't here
right now.

13: *leesh la? mumkin bukra is-saaʕa
thalaatha baʕd iDH-DHuhur?*
Why not? Perhaps tomorrow
at 3:00 p.m.?

15: *Tayyib. maʕ is-salaama.*
Fine. Good-bye.

ARAB says:

2: *aloo, mumkin atakallam maʕ
il-mulHaq il-ʕaskari law samaHti?*
Hello. May I speak with the
military attaché, please?

4: *ana l-ʕariif najiib salaam min
il-jeesh il-urduni.*
I am sergeant Najib Salam
from the Jordanian Army.

6: *aHibb uqaabil Hadrat il-mulHaq
Hatta usallimu risaala min
il-ʕaqiid il-xayyaaT bi-xuSuuS
safari li-l-wilaayaat il-muttaHida.*
I'd like to meet with the
attaché to deliver a letter to
him from Colonel Al-Khayyaat
regarding my trip to the U.S.

8: *aHibb ashuuf il-mulHaq
il-ʕaskari. ʕindi risaala ilu.*
I'd like to see the military
attaché. I have a letter for him.

10: *haadhi r-risaala min il-ʕaqiid
muSTafa il-xayyaaT, min wazaarat
id-difaaʕ.*
This letter is from Colonel
Mustafa Al-Khayyaat, of the
Ministry of Defense.

12: *mumkin aʕmil maʕu mawʕid?*
May I make an appointment
with him?

14: *aywa mumkin. nashuufkum
bukra in shaa' allaah.*
Okay. I'll see you tomorrow,
God willing.

16: *allaah yusallimik.*
Good-bye.

27

VOCABULARY

thaalith
third

mumkin
may, can, could, perhaps

atakallam
I speak, I talk

maʕ
with

il-mulHaq il-ʕaskari
military attaché

law samaHti
if you (*f*) please

miin
who

ʕariif
sergeant

jeesh
army

urduni
Jordanian

leesh
why

turiid
you (*m*) want

aHibb
I like, I'd like

uqaabil
I meet

Hatta
in order to

usallimu
I deliver [to] him

risaala
letter

ʕaqiid
colonel

bi-xuSuuS
regarding

safari
my trip

il-wilaayaat il-muttaHida
the U.S.

shwayy-shwayy
slowly

ma
not (*negates verbal expressions*)

afham
I understand

ʕarabi
Arabic

eesh
what

marra thaaniya
again; another time

ashuuf
I see

ʕindi
I have

ilu
for him, to him

difaaʕ
defense

maʕ il-asaf
regretfully, unfortunately

mawjuud
present, here

halla
now; right now

aʕmil
I make, I do

maʕu
with him

mawʕid
appointment

bukra
tomorrow

saaʕa
o'clock, hour, watch

baʕd
after

baʕd iDH-DHuhur
afternoon

leesh laʔ
why not?

nashuufkum
we (shall) see you

in shaa' allaah
God willing

SUPPLEMENTARY VOCABULARY

maktab
  office

talifoon
  telephone

in-numra ghalaT
  "wrong number"

safiir
  ambassador

sayyid
  Mr.

il-yoom
  today

iS-SubuH
  this morning

il-layla
  tonight

baʕd bukra
  day after tomorrow

usbuuʕ
  week

shahr
  month

baʕd shahr
  in a month

baʕd usbuuʕ
  in a week

sikriteer
  secretary (m)

sikriteera
  secretary (f)

mas'uul
  official (n)

ʕindak mawʕid?
  Do you (m) have an
  appointment?

I.WORKING WITH WORDS AND PHRASES

A. Matching English with the Arabic Equivalent
Match the ten English expressions on the left with their Arabic equivalents by writing the appropriate numbers in the blanks after the letters.

1. ministry of defense
2. why
3. slowly
4. I don't understand
5. again; another time
6. sorry
7. attaché
8. tomorrow
9. is not here
10. Okay. Good-bye.

a. _____ maʕ il-asaf
b. _____ Tayyib. maʕ is-salaama.
c. _____ wazaarat id-difaaʕ
d. _____ marra thaaniya
e. _____ bukra
f. _____ shwayy-shwayy
g. _____ leesh
h. _____ mish mawjuud
i. _____ ma afham
j. _____ mulHaq

B. Completion of the Arabic Dialogue

In the following version of the dialogue, some Arabic words are missing from the conversation. Complete each of the sixteen sentences by filling in with appropriate words.

AMERICAN says:

1: aloo?

*3: min _____, miin
HaDirtak?*

*5: naʕam, leesh _____
il-mulHaq il-ʕaskari?*

*7: shwayy-shwayy, min faDlak, ana ma
_____ ʕarabi kathiir. eesh
turiid _____ thaaniya?*

*9: Tayyib, min _____ haadhi
r-risaala?*

*11: maʕ il-asaf, il-mulHaq mish
_____ halla.*

*13: leesh la? mumkin is-saaʕa
thalaatha baʕd _____?*

15: Tayyib. maʕ _____.

ARAB says:

*2: aloo, mumkin _____ maʕ
il-mulHaq _____ law
samaHti?*

*4: ana il-ʕariif najiib salaam
min _____ il-urduni.*

*6: _____ uqaabil HaDrat
il-mulHaq Hatta usallimu
_____ min il-ʕaqiid
il-xayyaaT _____ safari
li-l-wilaayaat il-muttaHida.*

*8: aHibb _____ il-mulHaq
il-ʕaskari. _____ risaala ilu.*

*10: haadhi r-risaala _____
il-ʕaqiid muSTafa il-xayyaaT, min
wazaarat _____.*

*12: mumkin aʕmil maʕu
_____ ?*

*14: aywa mumkin. nashuufkum bukra in
_____ allaah.*

16: allaah _____.

II. WORKING WITH SENTENCES

A. Matching Spoken Arabic with English (listening)

Listen to Cassette 2 (side 1) or to your teacher, and match what is said in Arabic by writing the number of each Arabic sentence in the blank to the left of its English equivalent.

_____ May I speak with the military attaché?

_____ Who are you, please?

_____ Why do you want the military attaché?

_____ Slowly please, I don't understand much Arabic.

_____ Okay, from whom is this letter?

_____ What do you want, once again?

_____ Sorry, the attaché isn't here now.

_____ May I make an appointment with him?

B. Scrambled Arabic Dialogue

Reconstruct the Sample Dialogue by numbering the following sixteen sentences so they are in a meaningful sequence.

_____ aHibb ashuuf il-mulHaq il-ʕaskari. ʕindi risaala ilu.

_____ mumkin aʕmil maʕu mawʕid?

_____ Tayyib, min miin haadhi r-risaala?

_____ aywa mumkin. nashuufkum bukra in shaa' allaah.

_____ min faDlak, miin HaDirtak?

_____ aHibb uqaabil HaDrat il-mulHaq Hatta usallimu risaala min
il-ʕaqiid il-xayyaaT bi-xuSuuS safari li-l-wilaayaat il-muttaHida.

_____ shwayy-shwayy, min faDlak, ana ma afham ʕarabi kathiir.
eesh turiid marra thaaniya?

_____ naʕam, leesh turiid il-mulHaq il-ʕaskari?

_____ haadhi r-risaala min il-ʕaqiid muSTafa il-xayyaaT, min wazaarat
id-difaaʕ.

_____ allaah yusallimik.

_____ aloo, mumkin atakallam maʕ il-mulHaq il-ʕaskari law samaHti?

_____ leesh la? mumkin bukra is-saaʕa thalaatha baʕd iDH- DHuhur?

_____ ana l-ʕariif najiib salaam min il-jeesh il-urduni.

_____ Tayyib. maʕ is-salaama.

_____ maʕ il-asaf, il-mulHaq mish mawjuud halla.

_____ aloo?

C. Matching English with Arabic

Match the English sentences with their eight Arabic counterparts. Either draw a line to connect the two or write the "English" number next to its Arabic equivalent. You can also respond orally.

1. May I speak with the military attaché?

2. Who are you, please?

3. Why do you want the attaché?

4. I'd like to meet the attaché.

5. Sorry, the attaché isn't here.

6. I don't understand much Arabic.

7. I want to see the military attaché.

8. It's possible tomorrow at 3:00 pm.

a. aHibb uqaabil il-mulHaq.

b. maʕ il-asaf, il-mulHaq mish huna.

c. mumkin atakallam maʕ il-mulHaq il-ʕaskari?

d. leesh turiid il-mulHaq il-ʕaskari?

e. biddi ashuuf il-mulHaq il-ʕaskari.

f. mumkin bukra is-saaʕa thalaatha baʕd iDH-DHuhur.

g. min faDlak, miin HaDirtak?

h. ana ma afham ʕarabi kathiir.

D. Matching Arabic Remarks and Responses

Match the Arabic lines on the left with their responses on the right. Either draw a line to connect the two or write the matching number to the left of the appropriate letter. You may also respond orally.

1. min faDlak, miin HaDirtak?

2. leesh turiid il-mulHaq il-ʕaskari?

3. shwayy shwayy, min faDlak; eesh turiid?

4. Tayyib, min miin haadhi r-risaala?

5. mumkin aʕmil maʕu mawʕid?

6. Tayyib. maʕ is-salaama.

a. aHibb ashuuf il-mulHaq il-ʕaskari. ʕindi risaala ilu.

b. allaah yusallimak.

c. leesh laa, mumkin bukra is-saaʕa thalaatha?

d. ana l-ʕariif najiib salaam min il-jeesh il-urduni.

e. haadhi r-risaala min il-ʕaqiid muSTafa.

f. aHibb uqaabil il-mulHaq Hatta usallimu risaala.

E. Translation of English into Arabic

Convert the ten English phrases in Exercise **A** of Section I (p. 29) into Arabic.

III. WORKING WITH THE LANGUAGE

A. Verb strings

In Arabic, verbs can be strung together, as they are in the following three lines from the dialogue:

aHibb uqaabil HaDrat il-mulHaq.
I'd like to meet the attaché.

aHibb ashuuf il-mulHaq.
I'd like to see the attaché.

biddi aruuH ila haadha l-ʕinwaan.
I want to go to this address.

It is very common to string verbs together like this, especially after an expression of 'wanting' or 'liking.' In English, we follow the first verb with an infinitive (eg. 'to see'), but this is not necessary in Arabic. The second verb is a regular present tense verb, so that what is being said is, literally:

"I'd like I see the attaché," **or** "I'd like I meet with the attaché."

Drill 1: COMPREHENSION

Give the English equivalent of these sentences.

1. aHibb ashuuf HaDirtak.
2. biddi uqaabil il-mulHaq.
3. aHibb atakallam maʕ is-safiir.

4. biddi usallimu risaala.
5. turiid taʕmil mawʕid?
6. feen turiid taruuH?

Drill 2: TRANSLATION INTO ARABIC

1. I'd like to go to the American Embassy.
2. I want to speak with him.
3. I would like to see the letter.

4. I want to meet with you.
5. Do you want to speak with the Ambassador?
6. I want to see the secretary, please.

Drill 3: PHRASE-MAKING

Make your own sentences, stringing one of the first verbs (**a**, **b**, or **c**) with an appropriate second verb (**1** to **5**). First, study the two examples below:

aHibb aʕmil mawʕid.
I'd like to make an appointment.

biddi ashuuf is-safiir.
I want to see the Ambassador.

a. aHibb	**1.** atakallam
	2. aʕmil
b. biddi	**3.** ashuuf
	4. uqaabil
c. uriid	**5.** aruuH

33

B. Helping words (auxiliaries)

There are three very common Arabic words used together with verbs to indicate **necessity, possibility, and purpose.** These words are:

laazim	mumkin	Hatta
it is necessary;	it is possible;	in order to;
must;	may;	in order that;
have to	can	so that

These same words are normally followed by present tense verbs:

laazim adfaʕ.	mumkin afham.	Hatta ashuufu
I have to pay; it is necessary that I pay.	I can understand.	in order that I see him

These words are negated with *mish*:

mish laazim adfaʕ.	mish mumkin afham.
I do not have to pay.	I cannot understand.

The word *mumkin* when used by itself, can mean "maybe," "possibly" or "possible."

hiya mawjuuda?	mumkin atakallam maʕha?
Is she here?	May I speak with her?

mumkin.	mish mumkin.
Maybe.	It's not possible.

Drill 4: USE OF laazim AND mumkin

Use the words *laazim* and *mumkin* with the following six sentences. Then translate them into English.

1. _____ aruuH ila s-safaara.
2. _____ uqaabil il-mulHaq?
3. _____ atakallam ʕarabi.
4. _____ adfaʕ il-ujra?
5. _____ aʕmil mawʕid maʕ il-mulHaq.
6. _____ ashuuf is-safiir.

Drill 5: USE OF HELPING WORDS

Use the most appropriate helping word in the six blanks below:

1. biddi aruuH ila s-safaara _____ ashuuf il-mulHaq.
2. _____ atakallam maʕ il-ʕaqiid halla?
3. _____ ashuuf ir-risaala min faDlak?
4. aHibb ashuuf il-mulHaq _____ usallimu risaala.
5. _____ aʕmil mawʕid maʕ il-ʕariif? aHibb ashuufu.
6. _____ adfaʕ thamaan riyaalaat li-t-taksi.

C. Negation

The word *ma* is used to negate most Arabic verbal expressions:

ma biddi aruuH.
I don't want to go.

ma afham ʕarabi.
I don't understand Arabic.

ma ʕindi mawʕid.
I don't have an appointment.

Drill 6: USE OF ma

Use *ma* to negate these ten sentences, then put them into English.

1. *afham ʕarabi kathiir.*
2. *turiid tashuuf il-mulHaq?*
3. *aHibb usallimu r-risaala.*
4. *ʕindak mawʕid il-yoom?*
5. *ashtaghil huna.*

6. *aʕrif.*
7. *aHibb aruuH.*
8. *taʕrifi ween?*
9. *biddi ashuufu.*
10. *nashuufkum.*

Drill 7: USE OF mish

Use *mish* to negate these ten sentences, then put them into English.

1. *ana ameerki.*
2. *il-ujra kathiira.*
3. *haadha maʕquul.*
4. *is-safiir fi s-safaara.*
5. *huwa fi l-jeesh.*

6. *haadhi l-wazaara S-Saghiira.*
7. *hiya fi-T-Taabiq ith-thaalith.*
8. *laazim tadfaʕ.*
9. *mumkin uqaabil is-safiir?*
10. *huwa mawjuud.*

Drill 8: USE OF mish AND ma

Negate the following ten sentences with *mish* or *ma*, then translate them into English.

1. *inta taʕrif ween il-ʕamaara?*
2. *il-mulHaq fi s-safaara.*
3. *aHibb il-wilaayaat il-muttaHida.*
4. *atakallam ʕarabi kwayyis.*
5. *il-ʕaqiid ameerki.*

6. *is-safiir mawjuud.*
7. *is-sikriteera fi l-maktab.*
8. *laazim atakallam maʕu.*
9. *turiid mawʕid?*
10. *mumkin tashuufu bukra.*

D. ʕind- "to have"

Just like *bidd-*, the expression *ʕind-*, is not a verb, but it has verbal meaning. Like *bidd-*, *ʕind-* takes pronoun suffixes to conjugate:

ʕind-u	ʕind-ha	ʕind-hum
he has	she has	they have

ʕind-ak	ʕind-ik	ʕind-kum
you(*m*) have	you(*f*) have	you(*pl*) have

ʕind-i	ʕind-na
I have	we have

ʕind expressions are negated with *ma*:

ma ʕindi risaala.	ma ʕindna mawʕid.
I don't have a letter.	We don't have an appointment.

Drill 9: CONJUGATION

a. Teacher says forms of *ʕind-* on chart; students listen.
b. Teacher says forms of *ʕind-* and students repeat.
c. Students take turns reciting *ʕind-* forms, referring to chart if necessary.
d. Students conjugate the following sentences:

1. *ʕindi sayyaara.*   **2.** *ʕindi mawʕid.*   **3.** *ʕindi ʕinwaan is-safaara.*

E. Object Pronouns for Verbs and Prepositions

Verbs and prepositions in Arabic can take pronouns as objects:

maʕ-u	nashuuf-kum
with him	we see you (*pl*)

il-u	usallim-u
to him; for him	I deliver [to] him

These object pronouns are essentially the same as the possessive pronouns. The only exception is the first person singular, "me", used as object of a verb, in which case it is *-ni* instead of *-i*:

shaaf-ni.	taʕrif-ni.
He saw me.	You know me.

Arabic Object Pronouns

-(h)u / -h*	-ha	-hum
him	her	them

-ak / k*	-ik / -ki*	-kun
you (*m*)	you (*f*)	you (*pl*)

-ni / -i	-na
me / me	us
(*verb / prep.*)	

36 | *After long vowels

Just for review, the prepositions that have occurred in the text thus far are:

maʕ	min	ʕan	baʕd
with	from	from, away from	after

il, li-, la-	ila or li-	bi-	fi
to; for	to; toward	at, by, in	in, at

Example: Preposition + Pronoun

maʕ + _____

maʕ-u	maʕ-ha	maʕ-hum
with him	with her	with them

maʕ-ak	maʕ-ik	maʕ-kum
with you (m)	with you (f)	with you (p l)

maʕ-i	maʕ-na
with me	with us

Drill 10: SUBSTITUTION

Suffix the set of eight object pronouns to the following six prepositions:

1. baʕd   3. il-   5. fi
2. min   4. bi-   6. ʕan

Drill 11: VERB AND PRONOUN OBJECTS

Complete the following Arabic sentences by using pronouns as objects of the verbs, then translate the five sentences into English.

1. aHibb ashuuf _____ bukra.
2. biddak tuqaabil _____ il-yoom?
3. laazim ashuuf _____ halla.
4. mumkin tuqaabil _____ fi s-safaara.
5. laazim usallim _____ ir-risaala.

Drill 12: TRANSLATION

Translate the ten sentences below into Arabic.

1. I like him a lot.
2. Do I know her?
3. I'd like to meet you (m) tomorrow.
4. I don't know them.
5. I want to deliver (to you) the letter.
6. She is with us.
7. This (m) is from him.
8. May I go with you (pl)?
9. I don't understand you (f).
10. I see him in the office.

REVIEW DRILLS:

Drill 13: SUBSTITUTION AND COMPLETION

Use one of the phrases below, as appropriate, in each of the following four sentences.

il-mulHaq il-ʕaskari   *il-mas'uul*
il-ʕariif   *il-muwaDHDHaf*
il-ʕaqiid muSTafa   *is-safiir*

1. *mumkin atakallam maʕ _____?*
2. *mumkin uqaabil _____ il-yoom?*
3. *leesh turiid _____?*
4. *maʕ il-asaf_____ mish mawjuud halla.*

Drill 14: TRANSFORMATION OF PERSON AND NUMBER

Change the five sentences below from first person singular to second person singular (*masculine & then feminine*):

Examples:
mumkin atakallam maʕ il-mulHaq?
mumkin tatakallam maʕ il-mulHaq?
mumkin tatakallami maʕ il-mulHaq?

1. *uriid ashuuf is-sikriteer.*
2. *aHibb uqaabil il-mas'uul.*
3. *maa afham ʕarabi kathiir.*
4. *mumkin aʕmil maʕu mawʕid?*
5. *aHibb ashtaghil fi s-safaara l-ameerkiyya.*

IV. WORKING WITH VARIANTS

A. Translation into Arabic

Translate the seven sentences below into Arabic:

1. May I speak with an official at the Embassy?
2. Why do you want to work at the American Embassy?
3. You understand a lot of English.
4. I want to see the Colonel.
5. May I see the military attaché?
6. I am Colonel Smith from the American Embassy.
7. Colonel Smith is not at the Embassy now.

B. Comprehension

Listen to the Arabic sentences on Cassette 2 and determine which version of the following English sentences best corresponds in meaning with the taped Arabic. Mark the sentence you choose.

1. ____ Could I speak with Colonel Al-Khayyaat?
   ____ Could I speak with Sergeant Al-Khayyaat?
   ____ Could I see Colonel Al-Khayyaat?

2. ____ I don't speak much Arabic.
   ____ I don't understand much Arabic
   ____ I don't know much Arabic.

3. ____ I'd like to meet with the attaché regarding my trip.
   ____ I'd like to see the attaché regarding my trip.
   ____ I'd like to meet the attaché regarding the letter.

4. ____ Could you see the Colonel tomorrow?
   ____ Could you see the Colonel in the afternoon?
   ____ Could you see the Colonel tomorrow afternoon?

5. ____ The military attaché lives in this building.
   ____ The Ambassador lives in this building.
   ____ The Colonel lives in this building.

6. ____ I'd like to speak to the attaché regarding my trip to the U.S.
   ____ I want to speak to the attaché regarding my trip to the U.S.
   ____ I want to see the attaché regarding my trip to the U.S.

V. WORKING WITH THE SITUATION

Speaking on the phone in a foreign language is a special but necessary skill for anyone in a foreign country. Again, if you equip yourself with a set of "key lines," it will be very helpful for you in responding to almost any type of phone call.

Discuss the key lines you will need with your teacher and ask about any that do not occur in the dialogue, but which you might want and need to use (e.g., "Would you please wait a moment?" "Could you call back later?").

Also discuss with your teacher any questions you might have on how the phone system in the Arab world works, e.g., how many digits there are, if you have to know Arabic to speak with the operator, etc.

Your teacher will simulate the phone-call situation with you once you have your key lines ready. Remember that you don't need to understand every word that you hear—just get the general idea of what the Arab speaker is trying to say and respond appropriately.

الدرس الرابع

احتاج مساعدة

١. الاميركية : عن اذنك يا استاذ ، ممكن اسألك سؤال ؟

٢. العربـــي : تفضل ، أهلاً وسهلاً .

٣. الاميركية : كيف ممكن اوصل الى فندق السعادة من فضلك ؟

٤. العربـــي : ممكن تحتاجي تاكسي ، افتكر الفندق بعيد شوي من هنا .

٥. الاميركية : مش ضروري تاكسي ، احبّ أمشي .

٦. العربـــي : طيّب ، روحي دوغري حتي توصلي مكتب البريد ، حوالي ميتين متر .

٧. الاميركية : لازم اروح دوغري حتى اوصل مكتب البريد ، وبعدين ؟

٨. العربـــي : خذي يمينك على شارع خالد ابن الوليد وامشي لآخر الشارع ، وهناك لفّي عاليسار .

٩. الاميركية : لحظة من فضلك . لازم آخذ يميني على شارع خالد ابن الوليد ، وامشي لآخر الشارع ؟

١٠. العربـــي : وهناك لفي عاليسار وبعد حوالي مئة متر تشوفي محطة بنزين .

١١. الاميركية : محطة بنزين "شل" ؟ ايوه اعرفها .

١٢. العربـــي : الفندق قريب جداً من المحطة ، تقريباً مقابلها .

١٣. الاميركية : شكرا على مساعدتك . هلا اعرف كيف اوصل هناك .

١٤. العربـــي : عفواً ، مع السلامة .

١٥. الاميركية : الله يسلّمك .

LESSON FOUR: I Need Help

id-dars ir-raabiʕ: aHtaaj musaaʕada

Sample Dialogue:

AMERICAN says:

1: ʕan idhnak ya ustaadh, mumkin as'alak su'aal?
If you please, sir, may I ask you a question?

3: kiif mumkin uuSal ila funduq is-saʕaada, min faDlak?
How can I get to the Happiness Hotel, please?

5: mish Daruuri taksi, aHibb amshi.
A taxi isn't necessary. I'd like to walk.

7: laazim aruuH dughri Hatta uuSal maktab il-bariid, wa baʕdeen?
I have to go straight to the post office, and then?

9: laHDHa min faDlak. laazim aaxudh yamiini ʕala shaariʕ xaalid ibn-il-waliid, wa amshi li-aaxir ish-shaariʕ?
Just a moment, please. I have to take a right on Khalid ibn al-Walid Street and go to the end of the street?

11: maHaTTat banziin 'Shell?' aywa aʕrifha.
The Shell station? Yes, I know it.

13: shukran ʕala musaaʕadatak. halla aʕrif kiif uuSal hunaak.
Thanks for your help. Now I know how to get there.

15: allaah yusallimak.
Good-bye.

ARAB says:

2: tafaDDali, ahlan wa sahlan.
Sure, go ahead.

4: mumkin taHtaaji taksi, aftakir il-funduq baʕiid shwayy min huna.
You probably need a taxi. I think the hotel's a bit far from here.

6: Tayyib, ruuHi dughri Hatta tuuSali maktab il-bariid, Hawaali miiteen mitir.
All right. Go straight until you reach the post office, about 200 meters.

8: xudhi yamiinik ʕala shaariʕ xaalid ibn-il-waliid wa imshi li-aaxir ish-shaariʕ, wa hunaak liffi ʕa-l-yasaar.
Take your right on Khalid ibn al-Walid Street. Go to the end of the street, and there turn left.

10: wa hunaak liffi ʕa-l-yasaar wa baʕd Hawaali miit mitir tashuufi maHaTTat banziin.
And there, turn left. After about 100 meters you'll see a gas station.

12: il-funduq qariib jiddan min il-maHatta, taqriiban muqaabilha.
The hotel is very close to the station, practically across the street.

14: ʕafwan. maʕ is-salaama.
You're welcome. Good-bye.

41

VOCABULARY

raabiʕ
  fourth

aHtaaj
  I need

musaaʕada
  help, aid

ʕan idhnak
  pardon, with your permission

ya
  O, Oh

ustaadh
  Sir, Mr., professor

as'alak
  I ask you (*m*)

su'aal
  question

uuSal
  I reach, arrive

funduq
  hotel

taHtaaji
  you (*f*) need

Daruuri
  necessary, essential

amshi
  I go, I walk

ruuHi
  go (*imperative*)

dughri
  straight ahead

tuuSali
  you arrive at, reach

bariid
  mail

maktab il-bariid
  post office

Hawaali
  approximately

miiteen
  200

mitir
  meter

baʕdeen
  then, after that

xudhi
  take (*imperative*)

yamiinik
  your (*f*) right

shaariʕ
  street

imshi
  go, walk (*imperative*)

aaxir
  last, final; end

aaxir ish-shaariʕ
  end of the street

hunaak
  there; there is, there are

liffi
  turn (*imperative*)

ʕa-l-yasaar
  to the left

LaHDHa
  moment, second

aaxudh
  I take

yamiini
  my right

miit (or miya)
  100

tashuufi
  you (*f*) see

maHaTTa
  station

maHattat banziin
  gas station

aʕrif
  I know

aʕrifha
  I know it

qariib
  near

taqriiban
  approximately, about

muqaabil
  facing, across from

muqaabilha
  facing it, across from it

ʕafwan
  you're welcome

SUPPLEMENTARY VOCABULARY

sharq
  East

gharb
  West

shamaal
  North

januub
  South

zaawiya
  corner

ishaara
  sign

masaafa
  distance

ma aʕrif
  I don't know

xaariTa
  map

dillni ʕala
  show me

jadiid
  new

qadiim
  old

To the student: ask your teacher for any other vocabulary help that you think you may need in the kind of situations illustrated in the lesson's Sample Dialogue.

I. WORKING WITH WORDS AND PHRASES

A. Matching English with Arabic

Match one of the twelve English expressions below with its Arabic equivalent. Write the appropriate number to the right of the letters:

1.	a question	a. _____	*maktab*
2.	a hotel	b. _____	*laHDHa, min faDlak.*
3.	you (*m*) need	c. _____	*su'aal*
4.	not necessary	d. _____	*Hawaali*
5.	go straight (*m*)	e. _____	*maHaTTat banziin*
6.	office	f. _____	*funduq*
7.	approximately	g. _____	*shaariʕ*
8.	street	h. _____	*shukran ʕala musaaʕadatak.*
9.	take your right	i. _____	*taHtaaj*
10.	One moment, please.	j. _____	*xudh yamiinak*
11.	gas station	k. _____	*mish Daruuri*
12.	Thanks for your help.	l. _____	*ruuH dughri*

B. Completion of Arabic Dialogue

In the following version of the dialogue, certain words have been left out. Complete the fifteen sentences by filling in the missing Arabic words:

AMERICAN says:

1: *ʕan idhnak ya ustaadh, mumkin
_____ su'aal?*

3: *kiif mumkin _____ ila
funduq is-saʕaada, min faDlak?*

5: *mish Daruuri taksi, _____ amshi.*

7: *laazim aruuH _____ Hatta
uuSal maktab il-bariid, wa baʕdeen?*

9: *laHDHa min faDlak. laazim aaxudh
yamiini ʕala _____ xaalid
ibn-il-waliid, wa amshi li-
_____ ish-shaariʕ?*

11: *maHaTTat banziin "Shell?"
_____ aʕrifha.*

13: *_____ ʕala musaaʕadatak. halla
_____ kiif uuSal hunaak.*

15: *_____ yusallimak.*

ARAB says:

2: _____*, ahlan wa sahlan.*

4: *mumkin taHtaaji taksi, _____
il-funduq baʕiid shwayy min huna.*

6: *Tayyib, ruuHi dughri Hatta tuuSali
_____ il-bariid, Hawaali
_____ mitir.*

8: *xudhi _____ ʕala shaariʕ xaalid
ibn-il-waliid wa imshi li-aaxir ish-
shaariʕ, wa hunaak ____ ʕa-l-yasaar.*

10: *wa hunaak liffi _____
wa baʕd Hawaali _____ mitir
tashuufi _____ banziin.*

12: *il-funduq _____ jiddan min
il-maHaTTa, taqriiban _____.*

14: *ʕafwan; maʕ _____.*

II. WORKING WITH SENTENCES

A. Matching Spoken Arabic with English (listening)

Listen to Cassette 2 (side 2) or to your teacher, and match what is said in Arabic with the written English below by writing the number of each Arabic sentence to the left of the eight English sentences:

_____ Excuse me, sir. May I ask you a question?

_____ I have to go straight until I get to the post office?

_____ One moment, please. I have to take a right on _____ street?

_____ Thanks for your help. Now I know how to get there.

_____ How can I get to the Hilton Hotel, please?

_____ Maybe you need a taxi. I think the hotel is far from here.

_____ Turn left there, and after about 100 meters you'll see a gas station.

_____ The hotel is very close to the station.

B. Scrambled Arabic Dialogue

Reconstruct the dialogue below by numbering the fifteen Arabic sentences so they are in a meaningful sequence.

_____ il-funduq qariib jiddan min il-maHaTTa, taqriiban
muqaabilha.

_____ LaHDHa min faDlak. laazim aaxudh yamiini ſala shaariſ xaalid
ibn-il-waliid, wa amshi li-aaxir ish-shaariſ?

_____ kiif mumkin uuSal ila funduq is-saſaada, min faDlak?

_____ maHaTTat banziin "Shell"? aywa aſrifha.

_____ laazim aruuH dughri Hatta uuSal maktab il-bariid, wa baſdeen?

_____ ſafwan. maſ is-salaama.

_____ mumkin taHtaaji taksi, aftakir il-funduq baſiid shwayy min huna.

_____ xudhi yamiinik ſala shaariſ xaalid ibn-il-waliid wa imshi li-aaxir
ish-shaariſ, wa hunaak liffi ſa-l-yasaar.

_____ tafaDDali, ahlan wa sahlan.

_____ wa hunaak liffi ſa-l-yasaar wa baſd Hawaali miit mitir tashuufi
maHaTTat banziin.

_____ Tayyib, ruuHi dughri Hatta tuuSali maktab il-bariid, Hawaali
miiteen mitir.

_____ ſan idhnak ya ustaadh, mumkin as'alak su'aal?

_____ shukran ſala musaaſadatak. halla aſrif kiif uuSal hunaak.

_____ mish Daruuri taksi, aHibb amshi.

_____ allaah yusallimak.

C. Matching English with Arabic

Match each of the eight English sentences with its Arabic counterpart. Either draw a line to connect the two or write the correct English number to the left of the Arabic letter. You can also respond orally.

1. The hotel is very close to the station.

a. ruuH dughri Hatta tuuSal ila maktab il-bariid.

2. The hotel is almost opposite the gas station.

b. il-funduq qariib jiddan min il-maHaTTa.

3. Thanks for your help.

c. ʕan idhnak ya ustaadh.

4. You may need a taxi.

d. shukran ʕala musaaʕadatak.

5. One moment, please. I must take a right?

e. il-funduq taqriiban muqaabil maHaTTat il-banziin.

6. Excuse me, sir.

f. halla aʕrif kiif uuSal hunaak.

7. Go straight till you get to the post office.

g. laHDHa min faDlak, laazim aaxudh yamiini?

8. Now I know how to get there.

h. mumkin taHtaaj taksi.

D. Matching Arabic

Match each Arabic sentence on the left with its appropriate Arabic response on the right.

1. mumkin as'alak su'aal?

a. ʕafwan, maʕ is-salaama.

2. mumkin taHtaaj taksi.

b. allaah yusallimak.

3. baʕd Hawaali miit mitir tashuufi maHaTTat banziin.

c. maHattat banziin 'Shell?' aywa aʕrifha.

4. shukran ʕala musaaʕadatak.

d. tafaDDali, ahlan wa sahlan.

5. maʕ is-salaama.

e. mish Daruuri taksi, aHibb amshi.

E. Translation into Arabic

Translate the twelve English sentences in Exercise **A** of this Section (p. 43) into Arabic.

III. WORKING WITH THE LANGUAGE

A. Imperatives in Arabic

Imperative forms are used for making requests, giving directions, and / or commands. Four imperative verbs occur in the text of this lesson, all in the feminine form below because the person addressed is a woman:

ruuHi	imshi	xudhi	liffi
go	walk, go	take	turn

The masculine equivalents for these same imperatives are given below:

ruuH	imshi	xudh	liff
go	walk, go	take	turn

Drill 1: TRANSFORMATION OF IMPERATIVES

Change the following sentences from feminine imperative to masculine imperative. Make any other necessary changes to the six sentences below the example:

Example: *ruuHi maʕu.* -----> *ruuH maʕu.*
Go with him.

1. *ruuHi dughri.*
2. *liffi ʕa-l-yamiin.*
3. *imshi Hawaali miit mitir.*
4. *xudhi yamiinik ʕind maHaTTat il-banziin.*
5. *ruuHi ila funduq.*
6. *liffi ʕa-l-yasaar fi aaxir ish-shaariʕ.*

B. Construct Phrases: Differences between English and Arabic

English often joins two nouns together to make a phrase, as in the six phrases below:

gas station	Happiness Hotel	army officer
post office	embassy official	taxi fare

Sometimes English joins two nouns together by using the word "of," indicating a broad possessive relationship:

cup of coffee	end of the road	the address of the embassy
Ministry of the Interior	days of the week	the city of Cairo

And sometimes English puts an "s" on the first word of a two-noun phrase to indicate similar possessiveness:

the teacher's book	the ambassador's secretary
Ahmad's car	the employee's office

Arabic handles all these construction relationships by putting two nouns together in what is called a "construct" phrase (in Arabic, *iDaafa*, or "annexation" structure). These nouns are typically referred to as the first "term" or second "term" of the construct, depending on their order. Five examples are given below:

maktab il-bariid	maktab il-mulHaq	aaxir ish-shaariʕ
the post office	the attaché's office	the end of the road

muwaDHDHaf is-safaara	finjaan qahwa
embassy employee	a cup of coffee

46

RULES FOR CONSTRUCT PHRASES:

*1.*When the second term of the construct has a definite article, the construct is considered definite. **The first noun in the construct never has the definite article.**

*2.*When the first term of a construct is a feminine noun ending in *-a*, then a *-t* sound is usually suffixed to that word:

maHaTTa(t) banziin	wazaara(t) id-daaxilyya	sayyaara(t) is-safaara
a gas station	the Ministry of the Interior	the embassy car

Reminder: This rule of *-t* insertion applies also to feminine nouns that get a posses-sive pronoun suffix, as in the four examples below:

ʕamaara	sayyaara
building	car
ʕamaarati	sayyaaratak
my building	your car

Drill 2: CONSTRUCT FORMATION
Create as many constructs as you can, using one of the eleven lettered words on the left as the first term of the construct and the appropriate numbered words on the right as the second term.

a.	maktab	*1.*	id-difaaʕ
b.	maHaTTa(t)	*2.*	xaalid ibn il-waliid
c.	safaara(t)	*3.*	is-saʕuudiyya
d.	funduq	*4.*	il-baaS
e.	shaariʕ	*5.*	il-bariid
f.	wazaara(t)	*6.*	il-kuweet
g.	ʕinwaan	*7.*	il-mulHaq
h.	sikriteera(t)	*8.*	baladna
i.	ʕamaara(t)	*9.*	ameerka
j.	ism	*10.*	is-safiir
k.	xaariTa(t)	*11.*	banziin

Drill 3: REVIEW OF VERBS
Study the example below, then change the following ten sentences from the first person singular to the second person singular, masculine and feminine.

Example:

aHibb as'al su'aal. ----->   taHibb tas'al su'aal. ---->   taHibbi tas'ali su'aal.

1. kiif mumkin uuSal ila l-maHaTTa?
2. mumkin aHtaaj taxi?
3. ana aHibb amshi.
4. laazim aruuH dughri Hatta uuSal maktab il-bariid.
5. halla aʕrif kiif uuSal hunaak.
6. aHibb aʕrif kiif uuSal ila l-funduq.
7. laazim ashtaghil bukra.
8. maa afham kathiir.
9. aHibb ashuuf is-sikriteer.
10. maa aʕrif il-ʕinwaan.

47

Drill 4: REVIEW OF SUFFIX PRONOUNS
Replace the possessive pronoun "my" (-*i*) with "your" (*m* & *f*) (-*ak* & -*ik*).

Example: yamiini ---> yamiinak ---> yamiinik

1. ʕamaarati
2. xaariTati
3. yasaari
4. Haali
5. ismi
6. ʕinwaani
7. baladi
8. su'aali
9. sayyaarati
10. maktabi
11. funduqi

Drill 5: COMPLETION OF ARABIC SENTENCES
Complete each sentence, one at a time, by using one of the appropriate lettered phrases from among the five examples listed below the three sentences:

1. *kiif mumkin uuSal ila _____?*
2. *il-funduq mish baʕiid ʕan _____, mish heek?*
3. *il-maHaTTa qariiba min _____, mish heek?*

a. *is-safaara l-ameerkiyya*
b. *wazaarat id-difaaʕ*
c. *maktab il-bariid*
d. *shaariʕ xaalid ibn il-waliid*
e. *haadha l-ʕinwaan*

IV. WORKING WITH VARIANTS

A. Translation of English into Arabic
Give the Arabic for each of the following ten sentences.

1. How do I get to the embassy from here?
2. Do I go right or left?
3. I don't know where it is.
4. Is it near here?
5. What's the distance, approximately?
6. Could you show me on the map?
7. Do you (*m*) know where this address is?
8. May I ask you a question?
9. Could I see him tomorrow?
10. Do you (*f*) understand?

B. Comprehension of Spoken Arabic

Listen to the six Arabic sentences on the Cassette 2 (side 2) and determine which version among the following English sentences corresponds in meaning with the taped Arabic sentences. Mark the sentence you choose.

1. _____ You have to go north.
_____ You have to go south.
_____ You have to go right.

2. _____ Go to the corner and turn left.
_____ Go to the corner and turn right.
_____ Go to the sign and turn left.

3. _____ It's about 100 meters west of here.
_____ It's about 100 meters east of here.
_____ It's about 200 meters east of here.

4. _____ Walk straight down this street.
_____ Walk straight to the end of the street.
_____ Walk with me down the street.

5. _____ It's not far from here.
_____ It's a little far from here.
_____ It's very far from here.

6. _____ One moment, please. I must turn left?
_____ One moment, please. I must take a left?
_____ One moment, please. I must turn right?

V. WORKING WITH THE SITUATION

It is difficult to predict what kind of answer you will get if you ask someone for directions. Before you start role-playing situations with your teacher, ask him or her to tell you what kind of answers you might expect. For example, do answers tend to be very detailed and precise, or are they usually simple and approximate? What are polite ways to approach someone for information? What are some ways you can slow people down if they are talking too fast? If you show the person a map, does that help?

As always, it is helpful to have a set of communication strategies and key lines ready. For instance, in this kind of situation it is especially important that you understand the directions clearly, so practice repeating and paraphrasing in Arabic what you hear from your informant in order to confirm your comprehension.

الدرس الخامس

في محطة البنزين

١. الاميركي : مرحبا.

٢. العربـــي : أهلاً ، اي خدمة ؟

٣. الاميركي : ممكن تُعبي الخزّان بنزين ، من فضلك ؟

٤. العربـــي : تكرم. تريد اكشف على الزيت ؟

٥. الاميركي: ايوه من فضلك .

٦. العربـــي : لازمك علبة زيت .

٧. الاميركي : طيّب ، حُط علبة. ممكن تشوف المي كمان ؟

٨. العربـــي : حاضر... (بعد دقيقتين) هلا الزيت تمام والمي عندك كفاية .

٩. الاميركي: من فضلك ، شوف اذا ضغط الهوا كافي في العجال .

١٠. العربـــي: طيّب . (بعد دقيقة) فيه عجل منفس شوي .

١١. الاميركي: ممكن تنفخ العجل من فضلك ؟

١٢. العربـــي : على راسي. بدك شي ثاني ؟

١٣. الاميركي: لا، هذا كل شي. قديش الحساب ؟

١٤. العربـــي : البنزين اربعين لتر ثمنها خمس دنانير وعلبة الزيت نص دينار إذاً حسابك خمس دنانير ونص .

١٥. الاميركي: تفضل. هذي ست دنانير وخلي الباقي .

LESSON FIVE: At the Gas Station

id-dars il-xaamis: fi maHaTTat il-banziin

Sample Dialogue:

AMERICAN says:

1: marHaba.
Hello.

3: mumkin tuʕabbi l-xazzaan banziin,
min faDlak?
Would you please fill the tank
with gas?

5: aywa, min faDlak.
Yes, please.

7: Tayyib, HuTT ʕilba. mumkin
tashuuf il-mayy kamaan?
Okay, put (in) a can. Would
you check the water, too?

9: min faDlak, shuuf idha DaghT
il-hawa kaafi fi l-iʕjaal.
Please see whether the air
pressure in the tires is enough.

11: mumkin tanfux il-ʕajal min faDlak?
Would you please inflate it?

13: la, haadha kull shi. qaddeesh
il-Hisaab?
No. That's all. How much
is the bill?

ARAB says:

2: ahlan, ayy xidma?
Welcome. Can I help you?

4: tikram. turiid akshif ʕala z-zeet?
At your service. Do you want
me to check the oil?

6: laazimak ʕilbat zeet.
You need a can of oil.

8: HaaDir . . . (baʕd shwayy) halla
iz-zeet tamaam wa l-mayy ʕindak
kifaaya.
At your service. (After a while)
Now the oil is fine. And you
have water enough.

10: Tayyib . . . (baʕd shwayy) fii ʕajal
munaffis shwayy.
All right. (After a while) There's
a tire that's a little flat.

12: ʕala raasi. biddak shi thaani?
Right away. Do you want
anything else?

14: il-banziin arbaʕiin litir thamanha
xams danaaniir, wa ʕilbat iz-zeet
nuSS diinaar, idhan Hisaabak xams
danaaniir wa nuSS.
The gas is forty liters, costing
five dinars, and the can of oil
is half a dinar—So your bill is
five and a half dinars.

15: tafaDDal. haadhi sitt danaaniir wa
xalli l-baaqi.
Here's six dinars. Keep the
change.

VOCABULARY

xaamis
fifth

marHaba
hello

ayy xidma?
May I help you?
("any service")

tuʕabbi
you fill

xazzaan (-aat)
tank

banziin
gasoline

tikram
"at your service"

akshif (ʕala)
I check, inspect

laazimak
you (m) need

ʕilba (ʕilab)
can, box, container

zeet
oil

HuTT
put (imperative)

mayy (f)
water

kifaaya (n.)
enough

Haadir
"at your service"

tamaam
okay, fine

shuuf
look, look at
(*imperative*)

idha
if, whether

DaghT il-hawa
air pressure

kaafi (adj.)
adequate, enough

iʕjaal
tires

fiit
here is, there are

ʕajal
tire

munaffis
flat, deflated

tanfux
you (m) inflate

ʕala raasi
"at your service"

shi (ashyaa')
(some) thing

thaani
other, second

shi thaani
something else

kull
all; every

kull shi
everything

Hisaab (-aat)
bill, invoice

litir
liter

arbaʕiin
forty

thamanha
their price

nuSS
half

idhan
therefore; so

SUPPLEMENTARY VOCABULARY:

Numbers:

ʕishriin
twenty

thalaathiin
thirty

arbaʕiin
forty

xamsiin
fifty

sittiin
sixty

sabʕiin
seventy

thamaaniin
eighty

tisʕiin
ninety

miyya / miit
one hundred

alf
one thousand

Currency: Coins and Bills

diinaar (danaaniir)
dinar

fils (fuluus)
fils

riyaal (-aat)
riyal

liira (-aat)
lira (pound)

doolaar (-aat)
dollar

fuluus
money (in general)

I. WORKING WITH WORDS AND PHRASES

A. Matching English with Arabic
Match each of the twelve English expressions with its Arabic equivalent by writing the appropriate number after the letter which identifies the Arabic.

1.	hello	a.	_____	zeet
2.	May I help you?	b.	_____	ʕindak
3.	oil	c.	_____	marHaba
4.	can	d.	_____	iʕjaal
5.	water	e.	_____	ʕilba
6.	you have	f.	_____	qaddeesh
7.	air pressure	g.	_____	ayy xidma?
8.	tires	h.	_____	kamaan
9.	how much	i.	_____	laazimak
10.	half a dinar	j.	_____	mayy
11.	also	k.	_____	nuSS diinaar
12.	you need	l.	_____	DaghT il-hawa

B. Completion of Arabic Dialogue
In the following version of the dialogue, certain Arabic words have been left out. Complete the sentences by filling in the missing words.

AMERICAN says:

1: marHaba.

3: mumkin _____ l-xazzaan banziin, min faDlak?

5: aywa, min _____.

7: Tayyib, _____ ʕilba. mumkin tashuuf _____ kamaan?

9: min faDlak shuuf _____ DaghT il-hawa kaafi fi _____.

11: mumkin _____ il-ʕajal min faDlak?

13: la, haadha _____ shi. qaddeesh _____?

15: _____. haadhi sitt danaaniir wa _____ l-baaqi.

ARAB says:

2: ahlan, ayy _____?

4: tikram. turiid akshif ʕala _____?

6: laazimak _____ zeet.

8: HaaDir . . . (baʕd shwayy) _____ iz-zeet tamaam wa l-mayy ʕindak _____.

10: Tayyib . . . (baʕd shwayy) fii ʕajal _____ shwayy.

12: ʕala raasi. biddak _____ thaani?

14: il-banziin arbaʕiin litir _____ xams danaaniir, wa ʕilbat iz-zeet nuSS diinaar, idhan Hisaabak _____ danaaniir wa nuSS.

53

II. WORKING WITH SENTENCES

A. Matching Spoken Arabic to English (listening)

Listen to the Cassette 3 (side 1) or to your teacher, and match what is said in Arabic with the following eight English sentences.

_____ Welcome, may I help you?
_____ Could you please fill the tank with gas?
_____ You need a can of oil.
_____ Could you also check the water?
_____ Could you please inflate the tires?
_____ Here's six dinars and keep the change.
_____ You want me to check the oil?
_____ Please check the air pressure in the tires.

B. Scrambled Arabic Dialogue

Reconstruct the dialogue below by numbering the fifteen sentences so they are in a meaningful sequence.

_____ min faDlak, shuuf idha DaghT il-hawa kaafi fi
l-iʕjaal.
_____ tafaDDal. haadhi sitt danaaniir wa xalli l-baaqi.
_____ mumkin tuʕabbi l-xazzaan banziin, min faDlak?
_____ la, haadha kull shi. qaddeesh il-Hisaab?
_____ Tayyib . . . (baʕd shwayy) fii ʕajal munaffis shwayy.
_____ laazimak ʕilbat zeet.
_____ mumkin tanfux il-ʕajal min faDlak?
_____ Haadir . . . (baʕd shwayy) halla iz-zeet tamaam wa l-mayy ʕindak
kifaaya.
_____ marHaba.
_____ aywa, min faDlak.
_____ Tayyib, HuTT ʕilba. mumkin tashuuf il-mayy kamaan?
_____ ʕala raasi. biddak shi thaani?
_____ tikram. turiid akshif ʕala z-zeet?
_____ il-banziin arbaʕiin litir thamanha xams danaaniir, wa ʕilbat iz-zeet nuSS
diinaar, idhan Hisaabak xams danaaniir wa nuSS.
_____ ahlan, ayy xidma?

C. Matching English with Arabic

Match each of the eight English sentences with its correct Arabic counterpart. Either draw a line to connect the two, or write the number for the English next to the Arabic equivalent. You may also respond orally.

1. Hello.

2. You need a can of oil.

3. You want me to check the oil?

4. Could you inflate the tire?

5. Now the oil is fine and you have enough water.

6. Welcome. May I help you?

7. Could you also check the water?

8. Could you fill the tank with gas?

a. turiid akshif ʕala iz-zeet?

b. ahlan, ayy xidma?

c. marHaba.

d. mumkin tashuuf il-mayy kamaan?

e. mumkin tuʕabbi l-xazzaan banziin?

f. mumkin tanfux il-ʕajal?

g. laazimak ʕilbat zeet.

h. halla iz-seet tamaam wa l-mayy ʕindak kifaaya.

D. Matching Arabic

Match each of the seven Arabic sentences on the left with an appropriate response on the right. Either draw a line to connect the two, or write the number of the sentence next to the letter of the correct response. You may also respond orally.

1. ahlan, ayy xidma?

2. turiid akshif ʕala z-zeet?

3. laazimak ʕilbat zeet.

4. mumkin tashuuf il-mayy kamaan?

5. mumkin tanfux il-ʕajal?

6. qaddeesh il-Hisaab?

7. shuuf idha DaghT il-hawa kaafi fi l-ʕijaal.

a. tayyib. HuTT ʕilba.

b. fii ʕajal munaffis shwayy.

c. ʕala raasi.

d. aywa, min faDlak.

e. HaaDir.

f. mumkin tuʕabbi l-xazzaan banziin?

g. Hisaabak xams danaaniir wa nuSS.

E. Translation into Arabic

Translate the eight sentences in Exercise **A** on the facing page into Arabic.

III. WORKING WITH THE LANGUAGE

A. Plurals of nouns and adjectives

Spoken Arabic forms plurals in three different ways:

1. The masculine plural sound *(-iin)* Use of the suffix *-iin* or *-iyyiin* is one way of pluralizing a number of words in Arabic. These are words that generally refer to male human beings. They may be nouns, adjectives, or participles.

mawjuud	*mulHaq*	*muwaDHDHaf*
mawjuudiin	*mulHaqiin*	*muwaDHDHafiin*

saakin	*sikriteer*
saakiniin	*sikriteeriin*

When words ending in **-i** take this plural, the form of the suffix is *-iyyiin*:

kuweeti	*lubnaani*	*saʕuudi*
kuweetiyyiin	*lubnaaniyyiin*	*saʕuuudiyyiin*

2. The sound feminine plural (*-aat*) The suffix *-aat* is a way of pluralizing many nouns and adjectives in Arabic, especially feminine ones ending in *-a*, and borrowed words.

baaS	*doolaar*	*safaara*
baaSaat	*doolaaraat*	*safaaraat*

ʕamaara	*sayyaara*	*talifoon*
ʕamaaraat	*sayyaaraat*	*talifoonaat*

3. The "broken" or "internal" plural Many Arabic nouns and adjectives actually change their internal shape in order to become plural. Note that in general, the consonants stay the same but the vowels change.

kabiir	*maktab*	*Saghiir*
kibaar	*makaatib*	*Sighaar*

ʕajal	*ʕarabi*	*ʕilba*
iʕjaal	*ʕarab*	*ʕilab*

usbuuʕ	*yoom*	*zaawiya*
asaabiiʕ	*ayyaam*	*zawaayaa*

There is no easy way to specify what the plural of an Arabic noun or adjective will be. From this lesson forward, you will see the plural words noted along with the singular words in your vocabulary lists. Also, the plurals of all nouns and adjectives are listed in the glossaries at the end of this book.

Drill 1: IDENTIFICATION

Go back over the first four lessons and pick out the nouns and adjectives. Make a list of these with your teacher, and ask for the plural forms for each. Recall, pages 217 through 222 at the back of this book are reserved for your lists and notes.

Drill 2: PLURALS
Give the plurals of the following words.

1. ishaara	*5. jadiid*	*9. jeesh*
2. shaariʕ	*6. su'aal*	*10. risaala*
3. ism	*7. saaʕa*	*11. balad*
4. mas'uul	*8. kwayyis, kwayyisa*	*12. xaariTa*

B. Plural agreement
Arabic divides nouns into two basic categories: human and non-human. This is significant when dealing with plurals. The basic rule is that **human nouns take plural agreement and non-human nouns take feminine singular agreement**:

Human:
mas'uuliin ameerkaan
   American officials

muwaDHDHafaat jadiidaat
   new employees (f)

sufaraa' ʕarab
   Arab ambassadors

mulHaqiin judud
   new attachés

Non-Human:
makaatib Saghiira
   small offices

mawaaʕiid kathiira
   many appointments

ʕilab kabiira
   big cans

sayyaaraat jadiida
   new cars

This agreement rule applies to all words that refer to or go with the nouns involved. In addition to adjectives, these words include verbs and pronouns. For example:

ashuuf is-sufaraa'.
   I see the ambassadors.

ashuuf-hum.
   I see them.

ashuuf is-sayyaaraat.
   I see the cars.

ashuuf-ha.
   I see them (the cars).

Please note that this is a general rule based on the standard written language. However, there are places in the Arab world where you may hear people using plural adjectives, pronouns and verbs with non-human nouns. It is always acceptable, nevertheless, to use feminine singular agreement with non-human nouns.

Drill 3: TRANSFORMATION OF PHRASES TO PLURAL
Change the following phrases from singular to plural.

1. xariiTa qadiima	*7. ameerkiyya kwayyisa*
2. safaara ameerkiyya	*8. shi jadiid*
3. balad ʕarabi	*9. muwaDHDHafa urduniyya*
4. ʕilba jadiida	*10. shaariʕ qariib*
5. funduq kwayyis	*11. mas'uul saʕuudi*
6. masaafa baʕiida	

Drill 4: TRANSFORMATION OF NOUNS TO PLURAL
Change the underlined noun to plural and make any other necessary changes.

1. biddi <u>sayyaara</u> kabiira jiddan.	*5. haadhi <u>ʕamaarat</u> is-safaara.*
2. taʕrif <u>il-ʕinwaan</u>?	*6. aHibb ashuuf <u>is-safiir</u>.*
3. ʕindna <u>mawʕid</u> maʕu.	*7. ʕindi <u>ʕajal</u> munaffis.*
4. ʕindi <u>doolaar</u> ameerki.	

57

C. *kull* "every," "all"

The word *kull* is used in two ways. With a following definite noun, it means "all (of)" or "the whole." Used with a following indefinite noun, it means "every" or "each." Some definite examples are to the left below, and the indefinite examples are to the right:

kull il-yoom all day (long)	*kull yoom* every day	*kull shi* everything
kull is-safaaraat all the embassies	*kull safaara* every embassy	
kull il-ameerkaan all the Americans	*kull ameerki* every American	

Drill 5: MATCHING ENGLISH WITH ARABIC
Match the English phrases on the left with their Arabic equivalents on the right.

1. every embassy	_____ *kull ʕamaara*
2. all the cars	_____ *kull il-mas'uuliin*
3. the whole building	_____ *kull balad*
4. every official	_____ *kull safaara*
5. the whole embassy	_____ *kull sayyaara*
6. every country	_____ *kull il-balad*
7. all the officials	_____ *kull is-safaara*
8. every building	_____ *kull mas'uul*
9. every car	_____ *kull il-ʕamaara*
10. the whole country	_____ *kull is-sayyaaraat*

REVIEW DRILLS:

Drill 1: SUBSTITUTION OF PHRASES
Change Sentences *a* and *b* by substituting the phrases below for the underlined words:

a. *laazim taruuH ila l-funduq.*   **b.** *mumkin taʕmil mawʕid min faDlak?*

1. *tuʕabbi l-xazzaan*	5. *takshif ʕala z-zeet*
2. *tashuuf il-mayy*	6. *atakallam maʕ il-mulHaq*
3. *tashuuf DaghT il-hawa fi* *l-iʕjaal*	7. *ashuuf is-sayyid muSTafa*
4. *tanfux il-ʕajal*	8. *aruuH ila s-safaara*

Drill 2: CONSTRUCT PHRASE CREATION
Make as many construct phrases as possible, using the eight words in the left lettered column as the first term and those in the right numbered column as the second term.

a. ism	*1. banziin*
b. sayyaara	*2. is-safiir*
c. nuSS	*3. litir*
d. ʕilba	*4. dinaar*
e. maktab	*5. il-mayy*
f. maHaTTa	*6. zeet*
g. xaariTa	*7. is-safaara*
h. Haal	*8. il-balad*

IV. WORKING WITH VARIANTS

A. Translation into Arabic
Translate the following eight sentences into Arabic.

1. You need thirty liters of gasoline.
2. Do you work at this gas station?
3. What is the name of this oil?
4. Is there enough air pressure in the tires?
5. Thirty-five liters costs four and half dinars!?
6. How much is a can of oil?
7. I'd like to pay, please.
8. Is the bill seven dinars?

B. Comprehension of Spoken Arabic
Listen to the six Arabic sentences on this lesson's cassette and determine which among the following English sentences best corresponds in meaning with the taped Arabic sentences.

1. _____ Could you please fill the tank with water?
   _____ Could you please fill the tank with oil?
   _____ Could you please fill the tank with gas?

2. _____ You want me to check the oil?
   _____ You want me to fill the oil tank?
   _____ You want me to fill the oil can?

3. _____ You have enough gasoline.
   _____ You have enough water.
   _____ You have enough air pressure.

4. _____ Here is eight dinars and keep the change.
   _____ Here is nine dinars and keep the change.
   _____ Here is twenty dinars and keep the change.

5. _____ Is there a gas station nearby?
   _____ Is there a hotel nearby?
   _____ Is there a big building nearby?

6. _____ Is this address near the American Embassy?
   _____ Is this address far from the Ministry of Interior?
   _____ Is this address near the gas station?

V. WORKING WITH THE SITUATION

Getting service in a gas station in an Arab country involves many of the same things related to similar service in America, so you know pretty well what you will want to ask for. There may also be conventions governing tips for extra service, whether or not you ask for it. Check these things out with your teacher so you know what to expect. Your teacher will then simulate the situation with you.

الدرس السادس

في السوق

١.   الاميركية : صباح الخير .

٢.   العربـــي : صباح النور اهلاً وسهلاً . تفضلي . اي خدمة ؟

٣.   الاميركية : عندك عنب اليوم ؟

٤.   العربـــي : عندي عنب طازة يعجبك، عنب اخضر وعنب اسود .

٥.   الاميركية : وعندك بندورة كويسة .

٦.   العربـــي : ايوه، فيه بندورة على كيفك .

٧.   الاميركية : بكم كيلو البندورة ؟

٨.   العربـــي : البندورة بليرتين الكيلو ، والعنب بثلاث ليرات وربع بس .

٩.   الاميركية : يا سلام ! العنب غالي كثير !

١٠. العربـــي : لا والله مش غالي ، لكن معليش كرمالك بثلاث ليرات .

١١. الاميركية : من فضلك اعطيني كيلو عنب ونص كيلو بندورة .

١٢. العربـــي : على راسي . تؤمري شي ثاني ؟

١٣. الاميركية : عندك جبنة بيضا ؟

١٤. العربـــي : ايوه، عندي جبنة بيضا وجبنة صفرا .

١٥. الاميركية : من فضلك اعطيني وقية جبنة بيضا .

١٦. العربـــي : حاضر .

١٧. الاميركية : قديش الحساب ؟

١٨. العربـــي : ثمان ليرات .

١٩. الاميركية : طيّب . تفضّل ، هذي ثمان ليرات .

LESSON SIX: At the Market Place

id-dars is-saadis: fi s-suuq

Sample Dialogue:

AMERICAN says:

ARAB says:

1: SabaaH il-xeer.
Good morning.

2: SabaaH in-nuur, ahlan wa sahlan, tafaDDali. ayy xidma?
Good morning. Welcome, please. May I help you?

3: ʕindak ʕinab il-yoom?
Do you have grapes today?

4: ʕindi ʕinab Taaza yuʕjibik, ʕinab axDar wa ʕinab aswad.
I have fresh grapes that you'll like, green grapes and black ones.

5: wa ʕindak banaduura kwayyisa?
And do you have nice tomatoes?

6: aywa, fii banaduura ʕala keefik.
Yes, there are tomatoes (that will be) to your liking.

7: bi-kam kiilo l-banaduura?
How much is a kilo of tomatoes?

8: il-banaduura bi-liirateen il-kiilo, wa l-ʕinab bi-thalaath liiraat wa rubuʕ bass.
Tomatoes are two pounds a kilo, and grapes are only three and a quarter pounds.

9: ya salaam! il-ʕinab ghaali kathiir!
My goodness! The grapes are very expensive!

10: la, wallaah, mish ghaali laakin maʕaleesh kirmaalik bi-thalaath liiraat.
No, not really, they're not expensive, but never mind—for your sake, three pounds.

11: min faDlak, aʕTiini kiilo ʕinab wa nuSS kiilo banaduura.
Please give me a kilo of grapes and half a kilo of tomatoes.

12: ʕala raasi. ta'muri shi thaani?
At your service. Would you like something else?

13: ʕindak jibna bayDa?
Do you have white cheese?

14: aywa, ʕindi jibna bayDa wa jibna Safra.
Yes, I've got white cheese and yellow cheese.

15: min faDlak aʕTiini waqiyyat jibna bayDa.
Please give me a *waqiyya* of white cheese.

16: Haadir.
At your service.

17: qaddeesh il-Hisaab?
How much is the bill?

18: thamaan liiraat.
Eight pounds.

19: Tayyib. tafaDDal, haadhi thamaan liiraat.
Okay. Here, this is eight pounds.

VOCABULARY

saadis
  sixth

suuq (aswaaq)
  market place

ʕinab
  grapes

Taaza
  fresh

yuʕjibik
  you like it,
  "it pleases you"

axDar
  green (*m*)

aswad
  black (*m*)

banaduura
  tomatoes

ʕala keefik
  to your (*f*) liking

bi-kam
  how much

kiilo
  kilogram

liira (-aat)
  pound (currency)

liirateen
  two pounds

rubʕ
  quarter

bass
  only, just

ya salaam!
  "My goodness!"
  (a mild oath)

ghaali
  expensive

la wallaah
  not really

laakin
  but

kirmaalik
  for your (*f*) sake

aʕTiini
  give me (*m & f*)

tu'muri
  you (*f*) order, ask

jibna
  cheese

bayDa
  white (*f*)

Safra
  yellow (*f*)

waqiyya
  a unit of weight
  (*from 200 to 320
  grams / varies by
  country*)

SUPPLEMENTARY VOCABULARY

raxiiS
  cheap

loon (alwaan)
  color

xaDra
  green (*f*)

sawda
  black (*f*)

abyaD
  white (*m*)

aSfar
  yellow (*m*)

aHmar
  red (*m*)

Hamra
  red (*f*)

azraq
  blue (*m*)

zarqa
  blue (*f*)

burtuqaali
  orange

bunni
  brown

faakiha (fawaakih)
  fruit

tuffaaH
  apples

mishmish
  apricots

mooz
  bananas

tamr
  dates

tiin
  figs

leemuun
  lemons

baTTiix
  melon

burtuqaal
  oranges

rummaan
  pomegranates

zabiib
  raisins

mandaliina
  tangerines

durraaq
  peaches

injaaS
  pears

ananaas
  pineapple

manga
  mangos

xuDaar (xuDra)
  vegetables

xass
  lettuce

lift
  turnips

faSuulya
  beans (green)

baamya
  okra

zahra (qarnabiit)
  cauliflower

fuul
  fava beans

zeetuun
  olives

bazeella
  peas

malfuuf
  cabbage

baSal
  onions

albaan
  dairy products

jazar
  carrots

baTaaTa
  potatoes

Haliib
  milk

xiyaar
  cucumber

fijil
  radishes

zibda
  butter

baadhinjaan
  eggplant

sabaanix
  spinach

bayD
  eggs

filfil
  peppers

kuusa
  squash

laban
  yoghurt

laHm
  meat

laHm ʕijil
  veal

dajaaj
  chicken

laHm baqar
  beef

laHm xanziir
  pork

samak
  fish

laHm ghanam
  lamb

munawwaʕaat
  miscellaneous

qahwa
  coffee

ʕadas
  lentils

baqduunis
  parsley

taHiin
  flour

simsim
  sesame seed

naʕnaʕ
  mint

thuum
  garlic

looz
  almonds

milH
  salt

xubz
  bread

fustuq
  peanuts

sukkar
  sugar

zeet zeeytuun
  olive oil

fustuq Halabi
  pistachios

xall
  vinegar

ruzz
  rice

jooz
  walnuts

shaay
  tea

Note to the Student: Certain foods that are very common in the Middle East are not so common in many parts of America (okra, for example). Conversely, certain foods common in America are hard to find in the Middle East. With your teacher, go through the list of foods in this lesson and ask about things that may or may not be available in the country of your assignment. And, if you have never been exposed to Middle Eastern food, take a trip to a Middle Eastern grocery store and explore.

I. WORKING WITH WORDS AND PHRASES

A. Matching English with Arabic

Match the English expressions with their Arabic equivalents by writing the appropriate number after the letter of the correct Arabic.

1.	grapes	a. _____	banaduura
2.	fresh	b. _____	shi
3.	green	c. _____	Ɛinab
4.	tomatoes	d. _____	rubɛ
5.	quarter	e. _____	aswad
6.	expensive	f. _____	maɛaleesh
7.	give me	g. _____	Taaza
8.	thing	h. _____	kirmaalak
9.	white cheese	i. _____	aɛTiini
10.	black	j. _____	axDar
11.	for your sake	k. _____	jibna bayDa
12.	it's all right	l. _____	ghaali

B. Completion of Arabic Dialogue

In the dialogue below, certain words in the conversation have been left out. Complete the sentences by filling in the missing words.

AMERICAN says:

1: SabaaH il-_____.

3: ɛindak _____ il-yoom?

5: wa ɛindak _____ kwayyisa?

7: _____ kiilo l-banaduura?

9: ya salaam! il-ɛinab _____
kathiir!

11: min faDlak, _____ kiilo
ɛinab wa nuSS kiilo banaduura.

13: ɛindak _____ bayDa?

15: min faDlak aɛTiini_____
jibna bayDa.

17. qaddeesh _____?

19. _____. tafaDDal, haadhi
thamaan liiraat.

ARAB says:

2: _____ in-nuur, ahalan wa
sahlan, _____.
ayy xidma?

4: ɛindi ɛinab _____ yuɛjibik,
ɛinab axDar wa ɛinab _____.

6: _____, fii banaduura ɛala keefik.

8: il-banaduura _____ il-kiilo,
wa l-ɛinab bi-thalaath liiraaat wa
_____ bass.

10: la wallaah _____ ghaali
laakin _____ kirmaalik
bi-thalaath liiraat.

12: ɛala raasi. tu'muri _____
thaani?

14: aywa, ɛindi jibna bayDa wa jibna
_____.

16. HaaDir.

18. thamaan liiraat.

II. WORKING WITH SENTENCES

A. Matching Spoken Arabic to English (listening)

Listen to Cassette 3 (side 1) or to your teacher, and match what is said in Arabic with the following English sentences.

_____ Here's eight liras.

_____ Do you have white cheese?

_____ The grapes are very expensive!

_____ Yes, we have tomatoes that you'll like.

_____ I have fresh grapes: green grapes and black grapes.

_____ How much is a kilo of tomatoes?

_____ Please give me 200 grams of white cheese.

_____ How much is the bill?

B. Scrambled Arabic Dialogue

Reconstruct the dialogue below by numbering the nineteen sentences so they are in a meaningful sequence.

_____ *aywa, ʕindi jibna bayDa wa jibna Safra.*

_____ *yaa salaam! il-ʕinab ghaali kathiir!*

_____ *ʕindak ʕinab il-yoom?*

_____ *HaaDir.*

_____ *wa ʕindak banaduura kwayyisa?*

_____ *Tayyib. tafaDDal, haadhi thamaan liiraat.*

_____ *min faDlak, aʕTiini kiilo ʕinab wa nuSS kiilo banaduura.*

_____ *il-banaduura bi-liirateen il-kiilo, wa l-ʕinab bi-thalaath liiraat wa rubuʕ bass.*

_____ *SabaaH in-nuur, ahalan wa sahlan, tafaDDali. ayy xidma?*

_____ *laa wallaah mish ghaali laakin maʕaleesh kirmaalik bi-thalaath liiraat.*

_____ *bi-kam kiilo l-banaduura?*

_____ *thamaan liiraat.*

_____ *ʕindak jibna bayDa?*

_____ *SabaaH il-xeer.*

_____ *min faDlak aʕTiini waqiyyat jibna bayDa.*

_____ *ʕindi ʕinab Taaza yuʕjibik, ʕinab axDar wa ʕinab aswad.*

_____ *qaddeesh il-Hisaab?*

_____ *ʕala raasi. tu'muri shii thaani?*

_____ *aywa, fii banaduura ʕala keefik.*

C. Matching English with Arabic

Match the English sentences with their Arabic counterparts. Either draw a line to connect the two, or write the number of the English next to its Arabic equivalent. You may also respond orally.

1. Good morning, welcome.

2. Yes, there are tomatoes just the way you like them.

3. Do you have grapes today?

4. How much is the bill?

5. Please give me half a kilo of tomatoes.

6. Grapes are three liras.

7. Do you need anything else?

a. ʕindak ʕinab il-yoom?

b. min faDlak aʕTiini nuSS kiilo banaduura.

c. SabaaH il-xeer ahlan wa sahlan.

d. tu'muri shi thaani?

e. il-ʕinab bi-thalaath liiraat.

f. aywa, fii banaduura ʕala keefik.

g. qaddeesh il-Hisaab?

D. Matching Arabic Remarks and Responses

Match each of the Arabic sentences on the left with an appropriate response on the right.

1. bi-kam kiilo l-banaduura?

2. min faDlak aʕTiini waqiyyat jibna.

3. ʕindak ʕinab il-yoom?

4. qaddeesh il-Hisaab?

5. ʕindak jibna bayDa?

6. il-ʕinab ghaali kathiir.

7. ʕindak banaduura kwayyisa?

a. ʕindi ʕinab Taaza yuʕjibik.

b. thamaan liiraat.

c. la wallaah mish ghaali.

d. il-banaduura bi-liirateen il-kiilo.

e. HaaDir.

f. aywa, fii banaduura ʕala keefik.

g. aywa, ʕindi jibna bayDa wa jibna Safra.

E. Translation of English into Arabic

Translate the sentences in Exercise **A** (p. 65) into Arabic.

III. WORKING WITH THE LANGUAGE

A. Dual Suffixes

Instead of two basic number categories (singular and plural), Arabic has three: singular, dual, and plural. When referring to two of anything, a dual suffix, -een, is attached to the (singular) noun instead of using the number "two" (*ithneen*):

darseen	*diinaareen*	*funduqeen*
two lessons	two dinars	two hotels

The dual suffix for most feminine words ending in an -a sound is -teen:

Silbateen	*maHattateen*
two cans	two stations

miiteen	*sayyaarateen*
two hundred	two cars

Borrowed words, such as *kiilo* do not normally form the dual this way. They are usually counted with the number "two," *ithneen*.

ithneen kiilo
two kilos

Drill 1: TRANSFORMATION FROM SINGULAR TO DUAL

Change the following words from singular to dual by adding the suffix.

1. *liira*	**5.** *muwaDHDHaf*	**9.** *taabiq*
2. *Samaara*	**6.** *ism*	**10.** *wazaara*
3. *maktab*	**7.** *balad*	
4. *mawSid*	**8.** *taksi*	

B. Unit Nouns and Collective Nouns

Most of the words for fruits, nuts, and vegetables have the collective concept as their base or simple form. For example, the word *Sinab* meaning "grapes", refers to grapes in general. The word for "a grape" or "grape" would be *Sinaba*. Adding the -a, or feminine suffix, makes a collective noun into a unit noun:

tuffaaHa	*baSala*	*mooza*
an apple	an onion	a banana

Drill 2: TRANSFORMATION INTO UNIT NOUNS

Change each underlined word in the seven sentences below the example into a unit noun and make any other necessary changes.

Example:

biddi <u>tuffaH</u>. -------> biddi tuffaaHa.
I want apples. ------> I want an apple.

1. *Sindak <u>injaaS</u> kwayyis?*	**5.** *ween <u>il-mooz</u>?*
2. *aSTiini <u>tuffaaHateen</u>.*	**6.** *aStiini kiilo <u>burtuqaal</u>.*
3. *biddi <u>baSal</u> axDar.*	**7.** *taHibb <u>durraaq</u> Taaza?*
4. *biddik <u>xiyaarateen</u> bass?*	

67

Drill 3: COMPLETION OF ARABIC
    Complete the following four sentences, choosing the correct word from those listed below:

ʕinab	banaduura	burtuqaal	xuDra	fawaakih	filfil
tuffaaH	baTTiix	bayD	leemuun	kuusa	

    1. min faDlak aʕTiini kiilo _____.
    2. ya salaam! _____ ghaali kathiir!
    3. ʕindak _____ Taaza?
    4. bi-kam kiilo _____?

REVIEW DRILLS:

Drill 4: REVIEW POSITIVE AND NEGATIVE ANSWERS TO QUESTIONS
    Read the ten questions below and then answer them, first in the positive and then in the negative.

    1. ʕindkum xuDra Taaza?
    2. ʕindkum tuffaaH kwayyis?
    3. ʕindak banaduura kwayyisa?
    4. ʕindik fawaakih Taaza?
    5. ʕindkum jibna Safra?
    6. ʕindik ʕinab aswad?
    7. ʕindu baTaaTa Taaza?
    8. ʕindha faSuulya xaDra?
    9. ʕindhum baadhinjaan?
    10. ʕindak zeetuun aswad?

Drill 5: SUBSTITUTION
    Study the example below which substitutes *qaddeesh* for *bi-kam* (both mean "how much"). Then do the same in the following sentences; answer the five questions afterwards.

Example:

    bi-kam kiilo l-ʕinab? ----> qaddeesh kiilo l-9inab?
    il-9inab bi-liirateen wa nuSS il-kiilo.

    1. bi-kam kiilo l-faSuulya?
    2. bi-kam kiilo t-tuffaaH?
    3. bi-kam kiilo l-banaduura?
    4. bi-kam kiilo l-burtuqaal?
    5. bi-kam kiilo l-baTaaTa?

IV. WORKING WITH VARIANTS

A. Translation into Arabic
Translate the following six sentences into Arabic.

1. Please give me a kilo of green beans and 200 grams of cheese.
2. Fruit and vegetables are very expensive in Kuwait.
3. Black grapes are not cheap here.
4. Do you like potatoes?
5. Is there fresh lemon here?
6. Do you have fresh parsley?

B. Comprehension of Spoken Arabic
Listen to the Arabic sentences on the cassette and determine which among the following English sentences best corresponds in meaning with the Arabic sentences.

1. _____ Please give me a kilo of green beans.
   _____ Please give me half a kilo of green grapes.
   _____ Please give me a kilo of black grapes.

2. _____ O.K., here's eight liras.
   _____ O.K., here's six dinaars.
   _____ O.K., here's six riyals.

3. _____ I have fresh tomatoes.
   _____ I have good potatoes.
   _____ Do you have fresh tomatoes?

4. _____ Goodness! Apples are very expensive.
   _____ Goodness! Oranges are very expensive.
   _____ Goodness! Bananas are very expensive.

5. _____ Please give me 100 grams of white cheese.
   _____ Please give me 400 grams of yellow cheese.
   _____ Please give me 200 grams of yellow cheese.

6. _____ How much is a kilo of eggplant?
   _____ How much is a kilo of cauliflower?
   _____ How much is a kilo of cucumbers?

V. WORKING WITH THE SITUATION

When buying fresh food in the Arab world, you may have to deal with merchants who do not speak English and who will sometimes try to get a high price from you. Vegetable and fruit sellers, in particular, tend to have small stores or stalls located throughout the city. It is usually a good idea to become a regular customer at one or two of them so they know you, and so you will have an easier time talking to them and bargaining with them.

Before acting out this scenario, check with your teacher about how to deal with the situation. Should you always bargain, for example? Should you tell the merchant to give you a discount because the food does not look fresh? Where is the line between driving a hard bargain and insulting the merchant's goods? Do they really mean it when they tell you they will have something *bukra in shaa' allaah*?

الدرس السابع

في المطعم

١. العربـــي : اهلاً وسهلاً، شو تؤمر ؟

٢. الاميركي : شو عندكم اليوم ؟

٣. العربـــي : عندنا فراريج محمرة وكبة بالصينية وكوسا محشي .

٤. الاميركي : ما عندكم حمص ؟

٥. العربـــي : طبعاً عندنا كل انواع المقبلات، حمص وباباغنوج وسلطة ومخلل وغيره .

٦. الاميركي : اعطيني صحن كوسا محشي وصحن حمص صغير من فضلك .

٧. العربـــي : على عيني . شو تحب تشرب ؟

٨. الاميركي : فيه عصير تفاح او عصير جزر ؟

٩. العربـــي : لا والله ما في، لكن عندنا عصير برتقال وليمونادا وشاي وطبعا ميّ معدنية .

١٠. الاميركي : طيَب، جيب لي عصير برتقال لو سمحت .

١١. العربـــي : تكرم . على راسي .

(بعد شوي)

١٢. العربـــي : ان شاء الله اعجبك الأكل ؟

١٣. الاميركي : كل شي كان ممتاز . شكراً .

١٤. العربـــي : صحتين، تحب حلويات بعد الاكل ؟

١٥. الاميركي : شكراً، لا مؤاخذة، انا مستعجل . ممكن الفاتورة ؟

١٦. العربـــي : على راسي، دقيقة واحدة .

LESSON SEVEN: At the Restaurant

id-dars is-saabiʕ: fi l-maTʕam

Sample Dialogue:

ARAB says:

1: ahlan wa sahlan, shu tu'mur?
Welcome, what would you like?

3: ʕindna faraariij muHammara wa kubba bi-S-Siiniyya wa kuusa maHshi.
We have roast chicken, kibbee in-a-tray, and stuffed squash.

5: Tabʕan. ʕindna kull anwaaʕ il-muqabbilaat, HummuS wa baaba ghannuuj wa salaTa wa muxallal wa gheeru.
Of course, we have all sorts of appetizers, hummus, baba ghannuuj, salad, pickled vegetables, and other things.

7: ʕala ʕeeni. shu taHibb tashrab?
Right away. What would you like to drink?

9: la wallaah ma fii, laakin ʕindna ʕaSiir burtuqaal wa leemonaada wa shaay wa Tabʕan mayy maʕdaniyya.
No, there isn't any, but we have orange juice, lemonade, tea, and, of course, mineral water.

11: tikram, ʕala raasi.
At your service.

AMERICAN says:

2: shu ʕindkum il-yoom?
What do you have today?

4: ma ʕindkum HummuS?
Don't you have hummus?

6: aʕTiini SaHn kuusa maHshi wa SaHn HummuS Saghiir, min faDlak.
Give me a plate of stuffed squash and a small dish of hummus, please.

8: fii ʕaSiir tuffaaH aw ʕaSiir jazar?
Is there apple juice or carrot juice?

10: Tayyib. jiib lii ʕaSiir burtuqaal, law samaHt.
All right. Bring me orange juice, please.

[*baʕd shwayy*   AFTER A WHILE]

12: in shaa' allaah aʕjabak il-akil?
I hope you liked the food.

14: SaHteen, taHibb Hilwayaat baʕd il-akil?
To your health. Would you like dessert after the meal?

16: ʕala raasi. daqiiqa waaHida.
Right away. One minute.

13: kull shi kaan mumtaaz. shukran.
Everything was excellent. Thanks.

15: shukran. la mu'aaxadha. ana mustaʕjil. mumkin il-faatuura?
Thanks, but if you'll excuse me, I'm in a hurry. May I have the bill?

71

VOCABULARY

saabiʕ
seventh

maTʕam (maTaaʕim)
restaurant

faraariij
chicken(s)

muHammar
roasted

kubba
kibbee
(roast ground lamb)

Siiniyya (Sawaani)
tray, pan

maHshi
stuffed

HummuS
chickpea purée
(appetizer)

Tabʕan
naturally, of course

nawʕ (anwaaʕ)
kind, sort

muqabbilaat
appetizers

baaba ghannuuj
eggplant purée
(appetizer)

salaTa
salad

muxallal
pickled vegetables

gheer
other(s)

wa gheeru
other things, etc.

SaHn (SuHuun)
plate, dish

ʕala ʕeeni
"at your service"

tashrab
you (m) drink

ʕaSiir
juice

aw
or

ma fii
there isn't any,
there aren't any

leemonaada
lemonade

mayy maʕdaniyya
mineral water

shaay
tea

jiib
bring (imperative)

jiib lii
bring (to) me

baʕd swayy
after a short time

aʕjabak
it pleased you

akil
food

kaan
it was, he was

mumtaaz
excellent

SaHteen
"to your health"

Hilwayaat
sweets

la mu'aaxadha
"pardon me,"
"excuse me"

mustaʕjil (-iin)
in a hurry

faatuura (fawaatiir)
bill, check

daqiiqa (daqaa'iq)
minute

SUPPLEMENTARY VOCABULARY

Terms for Utensils

shawka (shuwak)
 fork

sikkiin (sakaakiin)
 knife

milʕaqa (malaaʕiq)
 spoon

kaas (kaasaat)
 glass

finjaan (fanaajiin)
 cup

fuuTa (fuwaT)
 napkin

kursi (karaasi)
 chair

Taawila (-aat)
 table

Miscellaneous Terms

sandwiitsh
 sandwich

shoorba
 soup

falaafil
 falafil

dajaaj
 chicken

Haarr
 hot

baarid
 cold

mashwi
 broiled, grilled

fuTuur
 breakfast

ghada
 lunch

ʕasha
 dinner

garsoon
 waiter

liista
 menu

nabiidh
 wine

biira
 beer

thalj
 ice

jalas / yajlis
 to sit

sharib / yashrab
 to drink

akal / yaakul
 to eat

73

I. WORKING WITH WORDS AND PHRASES

A. Matching English with Arabic

Match each English expression with its Arabic equivalent by writing the appropriate number next to the correct letter.

1.	chicken	a.	_____	SaHn
2.	stuffed squash	b.	_____	faatuura
3.	appetizers	c.	_____	kull shi
4.	dish	d.	_____	faraariij
5.	juice	e.	_____	anwaaʕ
6.	bring me	f.	_____	mustaʕjil
7.	food	g.	_____	kuusa maHshi
8.	dessert	h.	_____	akil
9.	in a hurry	i.	_____	muqabbilaat
10.	bill	j.	_____	jiib lii
11.	everything	k.	_____	Hilwayaat
12.	kinds	l.	_____	ʕaSiir

B. Completion of Arabic Dialogue

In the following version of the dialogue, certain words have been left out. Complete the conversation by filling in the missing words, either in writing or orally.

ARAB says: **AMERICAN says:**

1: ahlan wa _____, shu tu'mur?   *2: shu ʕindkum _____?*

3: ʕindna _____ muHammara wa kubba bi-S-Siiniyya wa kuusa _____.   *4: ma ʕindkum _____?*

5: Tabʕan. ʕindna kull _____ il-muqabbilaat, HummuS wa baaba _____ wa salaTa wa muxallal wa gheeru.   *6: aʕTiini SaHn kuusa maHshi wa _____ HummuS Saghiir min faDlak.*

7: ʕala ʕeeni. shu _____ tashrab?   *8: fii ʕaSiir tuffaaH aw _____ jazar?*

9: la wallaah ma fii, laakin ʕindna ʕaSiir _____ wa leemonaada wa _____ wa Tabʕan mayy maʕdaniyya.   *10: Tayyib. _____ lii ʕaSiir burtuqaal law samaHt.*

11: _____, ʕala raasi.

12: in shaa' _____ aʕjabak il-akil?   *13: kull shi kaan _____. shukran.*

14: _____, taHibb Hilwayaat baʕd _____?   *15: shukran. la mu'aaxadha. ana _____. mumkin il-faatuura?*

16. ʕala raasi. _____ waaHida.

II. WORKING WITH SENTENCES

A. Matching Spoken Arabic with English (listening)

Listen to Cassette 4 (side 1) or to your teacher, and match what is said in Arabic with the eight English sentences below.

_____ We have broiled chicken and kibbee.

_____ Of course, we have all sorts of appetizers.

_____ Please give me a dish of stuffed squash.

_____ Do you have apple juice or carrot juice?

_____ Everything was excellent, thank you.

_____ Excuse me, I am in a hurry. May I have the bill?

_____ What would you like to drink?

_____ I hope you enjoyed the food.

B. Scrambled Arabic Dialogue

Reconstruct the dialogue below by numbering the sixteen sentences so they are in a meaningful sequence.

_____ *(baʕd shwayy) in shaa' allaah aʕjabak il-akil?*

_____ *ʕala ʕeeni. shu taHibb tashrab?*

_____ *ʕala raasi. daqiiqa waaHida.*

_____ *ʕindna faraariij muHammara wa kubba bi-S-Siiniyya wa kuusa maHshi.*

_____ *SaHteen, taHibb Hilwayaat baʕd il-akil?*

_____ *Tayyib. jiib lii ʕaSiir burtuqaal law samaHt.*

_____ *Tabʕan. ʕindna kull anwaaʕ il-muqabbilaat, HummuS wa baaba ghannuuj wa salaTa wa muxallal wa gheeru.*

_____ *kull shi kaan mumtaaz. shukran.*

_____ *ahlan wa sahlan, shu tu'mur?*

_____ *aʕTiini saHn kuusa maHshi wa SaHn HummuS Saghiir min faDlak.*

_____ *la wallaah ma fii, laakin ʕindna ʕaSiir burtuqaal wa leemonaada wa shaay wa Tabʕan mayy maʕdaniyya.*

_____ *shu ʕindkum il-yoom?*

_____ *tikram, ʕala raasi.*

_____ *ma ʕindkum HummuS?*

_____ *shukran. la mu'aaxadha. ana mustaʕjil. mumkin il-faatuura?*

_____ *fii ʕaSiir tuffaaH aw ʕaSiir jazar?*

C. Matching English with Arabic

Match each of the six English sentences with its Arabic counterpart in the right-hand-column.

1. What do you have today?

a. fii ʕaSiir tuffaaH?

2. Don't you have Hummus?

b. shu ʕindkum il-yoom?

3. Give me a dish of stuffed squash.

c. kull shi mumtaaz, shukran.

4. Do you have apple juice?

d. aʕTiini SaHn kuusa maHshi.

5. Everything is excellent, thank you.

e. ma ʕindkum Hummus?

6. Excuse me, I'm in a hurry; May I have the bill?

f. la mu'aaxaaha, ana mustaʕjil; mumkin il-faatuura?

D. Matching Arabic with English

Match the Arabic sentences in the left-hand column with the appropriate responses at the right.

1. shu ʕindkum il-yoom?

a. ʕala raasi, daqiiqa waaHida.

2. aʕTiini SaHn kuusa maHshi.

b. SaHteen.

3. la mu'aaxadha. ana mustaʕjil. mumkin il-faatuura?

c. la wallaah ma fii, lakin ʕindna ʕaSiir jazar.

4. ma ʕindkum HummuS?

d. ʕala ʕeeni, shu taHibb tashrab?

5. kull shi mumtaaz, shukran.

e. TabʕAn, ʕindna kull anwaaʕ il-muqabbilaat.

6. fii ʕaSiir tuffaaH?

f. ʕindna faraariij muHammara wa kubba wa kuusa maHshi.

E. Translation into Arabic

Translate the sentences in Exercise **A** of this lesson into Arabic.

III.   WORKING WITH THE LANGUAGE

A. *kaan:* Conjugation in the Past Tense

The verb "to be" is not used in simple present tense sentences in Arabic, but *kaan* is used in the past tense and is conjugated as follows:

kaan	*kaanat*	*kaanu*
he was	she was	they were
kunt	*kunti*	*kuntu*
you were	you were	you were

kunt	*kunna*
I was	we were

Drill 1: CONJUGATION OF "kaan" IN THE SINGULAR AND PLURAL

First: Teacher goes over forms of *kaan* while students listen.
Then: Teacher goes over forms of *kaan* and students repeat.

Second: Students take turns conjugating *kaan.*
Then: Students conjugate *kaan* using the following sentences:

1. *kaan fi-l-maTʕam.*
2. *ween kaan?*
3. *kaan hunaak.*

Drill 2: TRANSLATION OF "Was" AND "Were" INTO ARABIC

Convert the ten sentences below into Arabic.

1. Where was he?
2. I was at the embassy.
3. Where were you (*f*)?
4. We were at the market.
5. They were with us.
6. She was here twenty minutes ago.
7. Were you (*pl*) there?
8. I don't know where you (*m*) were.
9. Was the restaurant good?
10. Was the car there?

B. Construct Phrases with Adjectives

The phrase *SaHn HummuS Saghiir* appears in the dialogue. It means "a small dish of Hummus." The Arabic structure, however, is: "a dish (of) Hummus small." The rule is that a construct phrase cannot be interrupted by an adjective. Therefore any adjectives must come **after** the construct, whether they modify the first term or the second term. If the construct is definite, the adjectives have the definite article.

Examples:

kaas mayy kabiir
  a big glass of water

finjaan qahwa Saghiir
  a small cup of coffee

ʕilbat zeet Saghiira
  a small can of oil

Drill 3: TRANSLATION OF ARABIC INTO ENGLISH

1. *ʕamaarat il-funduq*
2. *ʕamaarat il-funduq il-kabiira*
3. *kaas ʕaSiir Taaza*
4. *shoorbat dajaaj Haarra*
5. *sayyaarat is-safiir il-jadiid*
6. *sayyaarat is-safiir il-jadiida*
7. *maktab il-bariid il-qadiim*
8. *xaariTat il-balad iS-Saghiir*

C. Verbs: Citation Forms

Arabic verbs have no infinitive form. In lists, the third person masculine singular past tense is the cited form for verbs:

kaan
  ("he was" for "to be")

akal
  ("he ate" for "to eat")

sharib
  ("he drank" for "to drink")

Usually the present tense is also cited along with the past tense of the verb:

kaan / yakuun
  ("he was" / "he is" for "to be")

akal / yaakul
  ("he ate" / "he eats" for "to eat")

sharib / yashrab
  ("he drank" / "he drinks" for "to drink")

Drill 4: IDENTIFICATION OF VERBS

Go back over the verbs you have encountered so far in this *FAST* text. Make a list of them in whatever form they occur (imperative, first person singular, etc.).

Then, with your teacher, work out the citation forms of these verbs. As you progress in this course, add verbs to this list on the pages reserved for them in the back matter of this book (pp. 217–22).

REVIEW DRILLS:

Drill 5: TRANSFORMATION OF STATEMENTS INTO QUESTIONS

Change the six statements below to questions, and then answer them in the negative, as in the example given here. Write the transformation next to each or respond orally.

Example: ʕindkum kubba. -----> ʕindkum kubba? -----> la, ma ʕindna kubba.

1. ʕindna samak Tayyib.
2. ʕindu ʕaSiir jazar.
3. ʕindha kabaab.
4. ʕindak HummuS.
5. ʕindkum faraariij.
6. ʕindik Hilwayaat.

Drill 6: ANSWERS TO QUESTIONS , WITH "ma fii"

Answer the ten questions below, using **ma fii**:

Example: ma ʕindkum HummuS? -----> ma fii HummuS.

1. ma ʕindkum ʕaSiir burtuqaal?
2. ma ʕindkum muxallal?
3. ma ʕindkum laHm mashwi?
4. ma ʕindkum biira?
5. ma ʕindkum salaTa?
6. ma ʕindkum falaafil?
7. ma ʕindkum nabiidh?
8. ma ʕindkum shoorba?
9. ma ʕindkum fuul?
10. ma ʕindkum muqabbilaat?

IV. WORKING WITH VARIANTS

A. Translation into Arabic

Translate the following eight English sentences into Arabic:

1. The baba ghannuuj is very good.
2. Do you have grilled fish?
3. Do you like to drink coffee?
4. Where is there a good Arab restaurant?
5. Give me a dish of rice and beans.
6. Excuse me, I am in a hurry. Do you have falaafil sandwiches?
7. Do you like to drink water with your food?
8. Bring me the bill please, I'm in a hurry.

B. Comprehension of Spoken Arabic

Listen to the Arabic sentences on the cassette and determine which among the following English sentences best corresponds in meaning to the taped Arabic sentences.

1. _____ The restaurant has good food.
   _____ The restaurant has Arabic food.
   _____ The restaurant doesn't have Arabic food.

2. _____ I like to drink coffee in this restaurant.
   _____ I'd like to drink something cold.
   _____ I like to eat lunch in this hotel.

3. _____ Do you like dessert after your food?
   _____ Do you want coffee after your food?
   _____ Do you like to walk after your food?

4. _____ Please give me a dish of appetizers.
   _____ Please give me a dish of salad.
   _____ Please give me a dish of stuffed squash.

5. _____ If you'll excuse me, I'm in a hurry. May I have the bill?
   _____ If you'll excuse me, I must go. May I have the bill?
   _____ If you'll excuse me, that's everything. May I have the bill?

6. _____ Do you have chicken soup?
   _____ Do you have lentil soup?
   _____ Do you have vegetable soup?

7. _____ Do you like butter with your bread?
   _____ Do you like bread with your food?
   _____ Do you like sugar with your coffee?

V. WORKING WITH THE SITUATION

Eating in a restaurant is a cultural experience that you can look forward to and will probably enjoy if you are prepared. While restaurant behavior is pretty standard from one country to another, there are cultural and linguistic strategies or customs that may be quite different from what you know or expect. How do you get the waiter's attention, for example, and how should you address him? How do you complain politely, or send something back to the kitchen? Should you always ask for bottled water? When and where can you expect that you can order alcoholic drinks?

Discuss these and other questions, including typical dishes, with your instructor before role-playing this situation.

الدرس الثامن

في بيت عربي

١. العربية : تفضلوا. الأكل حاضر.

٢. الاميركي : ما شاء الله! فيه اكل كثير! اكيد تعبنا المدام.

٣. العربية : ابداً، ما في شي من واجبكم. تفضلوا.

٤. الاميركي : ما اطيب هالاكل!

٥. العربي : صحتين. لسا ما جربت هالاكلة. قرب صحنك.

٦. الاميركي : قطعة صغيرة من فضلك. شو اسمها؟

٧. العربي : هذي كبة، رح تعجبك.

٨. الاميركي : فعلا، طيبة الكبة. من شو معمولة يا ترى؟

٩. العربية : برغل ولحمة هبرة وبصل وصنوبر وسمنة وبهارات.

١٠. الاميركي : يا ريت اقدر اتعلم كيف اعملها.

١١. العربية : عملها سهل، رح اكتب لك الوصفة على ورقة.

١٢. الاميركي : هذا من لطفك. كل شي لذيذ.

١٣. العربي : شو تحب اقدم لك.

١٤. الاميركي : اكلت كثير، شكراً. سفرة دايمة.

١٥. العربي : صحتين. شو رأيك ياسعاد تجيبي الحلويات والقهوة؟
(سعاد تقدم الحلويات والقهوة)

١٦. الاميركي : انا فعلا شبعان، ممكن قطعة صغيرة بس، من فضلك.

١٧. العربية : كيف تحب القهوة؟ سادة او مع سكر.

١٨. الاميركي : سادة من فضلك.

١٩. العربي : اهلاً وسهلاً بالسيد فرانك.

٢٠. الاميركي : اهلاً بيكم.

LESSON EIGHT: At an Arab Home

id-dars ith-thaamin: fi beet ʕarabi

Sample Dialogue (Arab Hosts & Their Guest):

SUʕAD says:

1: *tafaDDalu, il-akil HaaDir.*
Please help yourselves, the food is ready.

3: *abadan, ma fii shi min waajibkum. tafaDDalu.*
Not at all. It was my pleasure. Please (be seated).

NABIL says:

5: *SaHteen. lissa ma jarrabt ha-l-akla. qarrib SaHnak.*
Bon appétit! You still haven't tried this dish. Bring your plate near.

7: *haadhi kubba, raH tuʕjibak.*
That's kibbee. You'll like it.

SUʕAD says:

9: *burghul wa laHma habra wa baSal wa Snoobar wa samna wa bahaaraat.*
Bulgur wheat, ground meat, onions, pine nuts, shortening, and spices.

11: *ʕamilha sahl, raH aktub lak il-waSfa ʕala waraqa.*
It's easy to make. I'll write the recipe for you on a piece of paper.

NABIL says:

13: *shu taHibb uqaddim lak?*
What may I offer you?

15: *SaHteen. shu ra'yik yaa suʕaad tajiibi l-Hilwayaat l-qahwa?*
Thank you. To your health. What do you think, Suad, should you bring dessert and coffee?

FRANK says:

2: *ma shaa' allaah! fii akil kathiir! akiid taʕʕabna l-madaam.*
How wonderful! What a lot of food! You must have gone to a great deal of trouble, Madam.

4: *maa aTyab ha-l-akil!*
What good food!

6: *qiTʕa Saghiira min faDlak. shu ismha?*
Just a small piece, please. What is it called?

8: *fiʕlan, Tayyiba l-kubba. min shu maʕmuula ya tura?*
Really, the kibbee is good. What is it made from?

10: *ya reet aqdar ataʕallam kiif aʕmalha!*
I wish I could learn how to make it.

12: *haadha min luTfik. kull shi ladhiidh.*
That's kind of you. Everything is delicious.

14: *akalt kathiir, shukran. sufra daayma.*
I've eaten a lot, thanks. "May your food be everlasting."

[suʕaad tuqaddim il-Hilwayaat wa l-qahwa.   SUʕAD OFFERS DESSERT AND COFFEE.]

FRANK says:
16: ana fiʕlan shabʕaan, mumkin qiTʕa
Saghiira bass, min faDlik.
  I'm really full. Perhaps just
  a small piece, please.

SUʕAD says:
17: kiif taHibb il-qahwa, saada aw maʕ
sukkar?
  How do you like your coffee—
  black or with sugar?

18: saada min faDlik.
  Black, please.

NABIL says:
19: ahlan wa sahlan bi-s-sayyid "Frank."
  We are pleased to have you
  here, Frank.

20: ahlan bi-kum.
  Thank you. I'm pleased to
  be here.

VOCABULARY

thaamin
  eighth

beet (buyuut)
  house, home

HaaDir
  ready

ma shaa' allaah
  "how wonderful!"
  "goodness!"

akiid
  surely, for sure

taʕʕabna
  we tired (s.o.) out,
  put to trouble

madaam
  Madam

abadan
  not at all, never

maa fii shi min waajib-
kum
  "It's a pleasure"
  (response to a "thank
  you" for something
  done)

ma aTyab
  "how good!"

ha-
  (abbreviation for pro-
  nouns haadha, haadhi, &
  haadhool)
  this

lissa
  still, not yet

jarrabt
  you tried out, tested

akla (-aat)
  dish (of food)

qarrib
  bring near

qiTʕa (qiTaʕ)
  piece, morsel

fiʕlan
  really

Tayyib
  delicious; fine; good

maʕmuul
  made

ya tura
  I wonder
  (question marker)

burghul
  bulgur wheat

laHma habra
  lean meat

Snoobar
  pine nuts

samna
  shortening

bahaaraat
  spices

ya reet
  would that, I wish,
  if only

aqdar
  I am able, can, could

ataʕallam
  I learn

aqdar ataʕallam
  I could learn

ʕamil
  making (n.)

ʕamilha
  making it

sahl
  easy

raH (+ present tense verb)
  will, shall
  (future marker)

aktub
  I write

raH aktub
  shall write

lak
  for you, to you

waSfa (-aat)
  recipe

waraqa (awraaq)
  (piece of) paper

haadha min luTfik
  "that's nice of you (f)"

ladhiidh
  delicious

uqaddim
  I offer, present

sufra daayma
  "may your food be
  everlasting"
  (said by guest at the
  meal's end)

SaHteen
  "bon appétit"
  (traditional response
  to "sufra daayma")

ra'yik
  your opinion

shu ra'yik?
  What do you think?
  ("What is your
  opinion?")

tajiibi
  you (f) bring

shabʕaan (-iin)
  full (no longer hungry)

saada
  black (of coffee)

85

SUPPLEMENTARY VOCABULARY

ʕaTshaan (-iin)
  thirsty

naʕsaan (-iin)
  sleepy

xarbaan (-iin)
  out of order, broken

jawʕaan (-iin)
  hungry

taʕbaan (-iin)
  tired

zaʕlaan (-iin)
  angry

shabʕaan (-iin)
  full

kaslaan (-iin)
  lazy

farHaan (-iin)
  happy

bardaan (-iin)
  cold, chilly (of persons)

sakraan (-iin)
  drunk

majnuun (majaaniin)
  crazy

shawbaan (-iln)
  hot

I. WORKING WITH WORDS AND PHRASES

A. Matching English with Arabic

Match the English expressions with their Arabic equivalents by writing the appropriate numbers in the blanks provided.

1.	food	a.	_____	HaaDir
2.	ready	b.	_____	qiTʕa
3.	piece	c.	_____	waSfa
4.	I wish	d.	_____	shabʕaan
5.	recipe	e.	_____	abadan
6.	sweets	f.	_____	ya reet
7.	for sure	g.	_____	ataʕallam
8.	full	h.	_____	SaHteen
9.	really	i.	_____	lissa
10.	I learn	j.	_____	akil
11.	to your health	k.	_____	sufra daayma
12.	made	l.	_____	akiid
13.	"may your food be everlasting"	m.	_____	fiʕlan
14.	still	n.	_____	Hilwayaat
15.	not at all	o.	_____	maʕmuul

B. Completion of Arabic Dialogue

In the following dialogue between the two Arabs and their guest, certain words have been left out. Complete each of the twenty sentences by filling in the missing words.

SUʕAD says:

1: *tafaDDalu, il-_____ HaaDir.*

FRANK says:

2: *ma _____! fii akil kathiir! _____ taʕʕabna l-madaam.*

3: *abadan, _____ fii _____ min waajibkum. tafaDDalu.*

4: *ma _____ ha-l-akil!*

NABIL says:

5: *SaHteen. lissa ma _____ ha-l-akla. qarrib SaHnak.*

6: *_____ Saghiira min faDlak. shu ismha?*

7: *haadhi _____, raH tuʕjibak.*

8: *fiʕlan, Tayyiba l-kubba. min shu _____ ya tura?*

SUʕAD says:

9: *burghul wa _____ habra wa baSal wa Snoobar wa _____ wa bahaaraat.*

10: *ya reet aqdar _____ kiif aʕmalha!*

11: *ʕamilha sahl, raH aktub lak _____ ʕala waraqa.*

12: *haadha min _____. kull shi ladhiidh.*

NABIL says:

13: *shu _____ uqaddim lak?*

14: *akalt kathiir, shukran. _____ daayma.*

15: *SaHteen. shu ra'yik yaa suʕaad _____ l-Hilwayaat wa l-qahwa?*

16: *ana fiʕlan _____, mumkin qiTʕa Saghiira _____, min faDlik.*

SUʕAD says:

17. *kiif taHibb il-qahwa: _____ aw maʕ sukkar?*

18: *saada _____ faDlik.*

19. *_____ wa sahlan bi-s-sayyid "Frank."*

20: *ahlan bi-_____.*

87

II. WORKING WITH SENTENCES

A. Matching Spoken Arabic with English (listening)

Listen to Cassette 4 (side 2) or to your teacher and match what is said in Arabic with the appropriate English sentence among the eight below:

_____ Just a small piece, please.

_____ I'll write the recipe on a piece of paper for you.

_____ You haven't tried this dish yet.

_____ How do you like your coffee—with sugar or black?

_____ I am really full. Could I have just a small piece, please?

_____ The kibbee is really delicious. What is it made of?

_____ I wish I could learn how to make it.

_____ I have eaten a lot, thank you.

B. Scrambled Arabic Dialogue

Reconstruct the dialogue below by numbering the twenty sentences so they are in a meaningful sequence.

_____ ʕamilha sahl, raH aktub lak il-waSfa ʕala waraqa.

_____ qiTʕa Saghiira min faDlik. shu ismha?

_____ abadan, maa fii shi min waajibkum. tafaDDalu.

_____ shu taHibb uqaddim lak?

_____ SaHteen. lissa ma jarrabt ha-l-akla. qarrib SaHnak.

_____ SaHteen. shu ra'yik ya suʕaad tajiibi l-Hilwayaat wa l-qahwa?

_____ haadhi kubba, raH tuʕjibak.

_____ ahlan bi-kum.

_____ burghul wa laHma habra wa baSal wa Snoobar wa samna wa bahaaraat.

_____ ya reet aqdar ataʕallam kiif aʕmalha!

_____ tafaDDalu. il-akil Haadir.

_____ haadha min luTfik. kull shi ladhiidh.

_____ ma aTyab ha-l-akil!

_____ akalt kathiir, shukran. sufra daayma.

_____ saada min faDlik.

_____ ana fiʕlan shabʕaan, mumkin qiTʕa Saghiira bass, min faDlik.

_____ ma shaa' allaah! fii akil kathiir! akiid taʕʕabna l-madaam.

_____ ahlan wa sahlan bi-s-sayyid 'Frank.'

_____ fiʕlan, Tayyiba l-kubba. min shu maʕmuula ya tura?

_____ kiif taHibb il-qahwa: saada aw maʕ sukkar?

C. Matching English with Arabic

Match each of the eight English sentences with its Arabic counterpart.

1. You haven't tried this dish yet.

   a. haadhi kubba. raH tuʕjibak.

2. This is kibbee. You'll like it.

   b. akalt kathiir, shukran.

3. What would you like me to offer you?

   c. lissa maa jarrabt ha-l-akla.

4. I've eaten a lot, thanks.

   d. il-akil HaaDir.

5. How wonderful! What a lot of food!

   e. kiif taHibb qahwatak?

6. The food is ready.

   f. ma shaa' allaah! fii akil kathiir!

7. I'm really full. Could I have just a small piece?

   g. ana fiʕlan shabʕaan. mumkin bass qiTʕa Saghiira?

8. How do you like your coffee?

   h. shu taHibb uqaddim lak?

D. Matching Written Arabic

Match each of the Arabic sentences in the left-hand column with the appropriate response on the right.

1. *ma aTyab ha-l-akla!*

   a. burghul wa laHma habra wa baSal.

2. *min shu maʕmuula?*

   b. saada min faDlik.

3. *kiif taHibb il-qahwa?*

   c. SaHteen!

4. *ahlan wa sahlan bi-s-sayyid "Frank."*

   d. ahlan bi-kum.

5. *shu taHibb uqaddim lak?*

   e. raH aktub lak il-waSfa.

6. *ya reet aqdar ataʕallam kiif aʕmalha.*

   f. akalt kathiir, shukran.

E. Translation into Arabic

Translate the sentences in Exercise **A** (on the facing page) into Arabic.

III. WORKING WITH THE LANGUAGE

A. Verbs: Past Tense of Regular Verbs

The past tense conjugation consists of a set of **suffixes** which are attached to the past tense **stem** of the verb. This stem corresponds exactly to the third person masculine singular past tense form (he ___-ed), and is considered the most basic form of any verb. *katab* is the past tense of the verb "to write" and it is conjugated below. Please note that ' marks the syllable on which the word stress falls:

kátab	kátab-at	kátab-u
he wrote	she wrote	they wrote
katáb-t	katáb-ti	katáb-tu
you wrote	you wrote	you wrote

katáb-t	katáb-na
I wrote	we wrote

The nineteen verbs below, which were used in the text so far, are conjugated like *katab:*

axadh	jalas	qaddam	takallam
ʕaraf	ʕamal	sallam	ishtaghal
dafaʕ	sharib	jarrab	iftakar
fahim	waSal	qaabal	sa'al
akal	qadar	taʕallam	

Drill 1: PRONUNCIATION AND TRANSLATION

Read the following words aloud. As you pronounce them, make sure that the stress is on the right syllable. Then translate them into English.

1. akalna	*6.* jarrab
2. taʕallamt	*7.* ishtaghalti
3. dafaʕu	*8.* sharibat
4. ʕamaltu	*9.* fahimt
5. axadhat	*10.* iftakarna

Drill 2: CONJUGATION OF VERBS IN ALL PERSONS

Conjugate the three verbs used in the following sentences in all persons:

1. akal kathiir.
2. dafaʕ il-ujra.
3. ishtaghal fi s-safaara.

B. Verbs: Past Tense of "Hollow" Verbs

Some Arabic verbs are termed "hollow," and typically they have long vowels. Six of these are listed below:

kaan
  to be
	shaaf
	  to see
		araad
		  to want

raaH
  to go
	jaab
	  to bring
		iHtaaj
		  to need

As you can see above, these six verbs all have the long vowel *aa* in the citation form. This vowel changes in length and quality during conjugation in the first and second person (*see kaan* in Lesson 7, Section A). Note also that *kaan, shaaf,* and *raaH,* are conjugated with the short *u*:

raaH
  he went
	raaH-at
	  she went
		raaH-u
		  they went

ruH-t
  you went
	ruH-ti
	  you went
		ruH-tu
		  you went

ruH-t
  I went
	ruH-na
	  we went

The verb *jaab* "to bring" is conjugated with short *i* in the first and second person:

jaab he brought	*jaab-at* she brought	*jaab-u* they brought
jib-t you brought	*jib-ti* you brought	*jib-tu* you brought

jib-t I brought	*jib-na* we brought

Note: The *aa* remains in the third person for *jaab*, as it does for *kaan, raah,* and *arood.*

The verbs *araad* "to want" and *iHtaaj* "to need" are both conjugated with the short *a* in the first and second person. *araad* is shown below:

araad he wanted	*araad-at* she wanted	*araad-u* they wanted
arad-t you wanted	*arad-ti* you wanted	*arad-tu* you wanted

arad-t I wanted	*arad-na* we wanted

Drill 3: PRONUNCIATION AND TRANSLATION OF VERB FORMS
Read aloud and translate the following ten verb forms:

1. *kaanu*
2. *shufna*
3. *ruHti*
4. *jibtu*
5. *araadat*
6. *kunt*
7. *jaab*
8. *iHtaajat*
9. *shuft*
10. *ruHna*

Drill 4: CONJUGATION
Conjugate the verbs in the following four sentences.

1. raaH ila l-maktab.   *3. shaaf is-safiir.*
2. jaab il-akil.   *4. iHtaaj musaaʕada.*

IV. WORKING WITH VARIANTS

A. Translation into Arabic
Translate the following sentences into Arabic:

1. Goodness! The 'hummus' is delicious.
2. This dish is really good. What is it made of?
3. Would you like to drink anything with dessert?
4. Tabbuleh is made of bulgur wheat, parsley, tomatoes, lemon, mint, and olive oil.
5. Would you like to drink coffee afterwards?
6. Would you like to learn how to make this dish?
7. What are the names of these sweets?

B. Comprehension of Spoken Arabic
Listen to the Arabic sentences on the cassette and determine which of the seven English sentences corresponds in meaning with the Arabic.

1. _____ I'll write you the message on a piece of paper.
    _____ I'll write you the recipe on a piece of paper.
    _____ I'll write you the address on a piece of paper.

2. _____ What is this dish made of?
    _____ What is this dessert made of?
    _____ What is this appetizer made of?

3. _____ I wish I could learn how to make it.
    _____ I wish I could know how to make it.
    _____ I wish I could tell you how to make it.

4. _____ This dish has parsley, onions, lemon, and olive oil.
    _____ This dish has parsley, cucumber, lemon, and olive oil.
    _____ This dish has cucumber, cracked wheat, and olive oil.

5. _____ I am really full. I can't eat anything.
    _____ I am really full. Just give me one piece.
    _____ I am not really full. Give me two pieces.

6. _____ Would you like sugar with your coffee?
    _____ Would you like milk with your coffee?
    _____ Would you like anything with your coffee?

7. _____ Goodness! There's a lot of food.

_____ Goodness! There's a lot of dessert.

_____ Goodness! There's a lot of drinks.

V. WORKING WITH THE SITUATION

When dining as the guest of Arabs, you should be aware of two basic things: protocol and strategy. (You must understand protocol in order to observe standard courtesy conventions and you must plan your strategy in order not to wind up eating more than you really feel comfortable with.) For Arabs are extremely hospitable, and with food, in particular, will seem insistent on your taking helping after helping, and on getting you to try everything. There will usually be a substantial quantity of food, and also great variety. In order to be able to sample everything, therefore, and be able to accept seconds (or thirds), it is advisable to start with small portions. It is also expected that you will praise the food and compliment the host and / or hostess on its abundance and its quality.

Before you role-play this situation with your teacher, try to find out as much as you can about standard courtesy conventions: Does one compliment before, during, and after the meal? What are some of the standard formulas for showing appreciation and giving praise? Can you refuse something? If so, how can you do it politely? How many times will you be asked to partake of something? Is it considered polite or impolite to leave food on your plate? You can probably think of other questions along these lines. Do ask your teacher.

As for strategy, see if your teacher has advice on how to handle, for example: a situation where you simply are not hungry but feel obliged to participate, a situation where you are offered something that you really do not want, a situation where you need to ask for something special or have to express dietary restrictions.

You may also want to try reversing the situation and finding out from your teacher what Arabs will expect from you when you are hosting them.

الدرس التاسع

مع الخادم

١. الاميركية : يا سعيد !

٢. العربـي : امر يامدام " براون " .

٣. الاميركية : ممكن تجيب بدلة السيد براون وقمصانه من المصبغة ؟

٤. العربـي : الساعة هلا ثمانية وربع والمصبغة تفتح حوالي الساعة تسعة .

٥. الاميركية : افتكرت المصبغة تفتح الساعة ثمانية ونص .

٦. العربـي : يمكن انا غلطان . على كل حال انا رايح هلا . تؤمري شي ثاني ؟

٧. الاميركية : لما ترجع بدي اياك تغسل السيارة .

٨. العربـي : حاضر ، رح اغسلها لما أرجع ان شاء الله. اي شيء ثاني ؟

٩. الاميركية : ايوه ممكن تنظف حول البيت وتسقي الزهور قبلما تبدأ الحفلة ؟

١٠. العربـي : على راسي . ممكن امر على الصيدلية قبل المصبغة لان لازم اشتري دواء ؟

١١. الاميركية : مافيه مانع . ما دامك رح توصل للصيدلية ، مر على دكان ابو حبيب وجيب صندوق بيبسي .

١٢. العربـي : حاضر ، رح اكون هنا بعد حوالي ساعة . ان شاء الله .

١٣. الاميركية : انتظر دقيقة ، خليني اعطيك فلوس للمصبغة وللمشروب .

(سعيد يروح الى المصبغة ويرجع) .

١٤. العربـي : القمصان م اكانت حاضرة . مغسولة لكن بدها كوي .

١٥. الاميركية : هذا اللي كنت خايفة منه. السيد " براون " يحتاج واحد منها للحفلة .

١٦. العربـي : قالوا لي القمصان رح تكون حاضرة الساعة واحدة .

١٧. الاميركية : حاول تكون هناك قبل الساعة واحدة .

١٨. العربـي : من كل بد .

94

LESSON NINE: Before the Party

id-dars it-taasi؟: qabl il-Hafla

Sample Dialogue:

MRS. BROWN says:

1: ya sa؟iid!
  Oh, Said!

3: mumkin tajiib badlat is-sayyid
  "Brown" wa qumSaanu min
  il-maSbagha?
  Could you fetch Mr. Brown's suit
  and his shirts from the cleaner's?

5: iftakart il-maSbagha taftaH is-saa؟a
  thamaanya wa nuSS!
  I thought the cleaner's opens at
  8:30.

7: lamma tarja؟ biddi yyaak taghsil
  is-sayyaara.
  When you come back, I'd like you
  to wash the car.

9: aywa, mumkin tunaDHDHif Hawl
  il-beet wa tasqi z-zuhuur qablma
  tabda' l-Hafla?
  Yes. Could you clean around the
  house and water the flowers
  before the party starts?

11: ma fii maani؟. ma daamak raH
  tuuSal li-S-Saydaliyya, murr ؟ala
  dukkaan abu Habiib wa jiib Sanduuq
  bibsi.
  That's okay. As long as you're
  going to the pharmacy, stop by
  Abu Habiib's shop and pick up a
  case of Pepsi.

13: intaDHir daqiiqa, xalliini a؟Tiik fuluus li l-maSbagha wa li-l-mashruub.
  Wait a minute. Let me give you
  money for the cleaner's and the
  drinks.

SA؟ID says:

2: amr, ya madaam "Brown."
  At your service, Mrs. Brown.

4: is-saa؟a halla thamaanya wa rubu؟
  wa l-maSbagha taftaH Hawaali
  s-saa؟a tis؟a.
  It's 8:15 now and the cleaner's
  doesn't open until about 9:00.

6: yumkin ana ghalTaan. ؟ala kull Haal,
  ana raayiH halla. tu'muri shi thaani?
  Perhaps I'm wrong. At any rate, I'll
  go now. Do you need anything
  else?

8: HaaDir, raH aghsilha lamma arja؟, in
  shaa' allaah. ayy shi thaani?
  Okay, I'll wash it when I return,
  God willing. Anything else?

10: ؟ala raasi. mumkin amurr ؟ala
  S-Saydaliyya qabl il-maSbagha,
  li'ann laazim ashtari dawa.
  Sure. I may stop at the pharmacy
  before the cleaner's because I
  have to buy (some) medicine.

12: HaaDir, raH akuun huna ba؟d
  Hawaali saa؟a, in shaa' allaah.
  Okay. I'll be here in about an hour.

[saʕiid yaruuH ila l-maSbagha wa yarjaʕ.   SAʕID GOES TO THE CLEANER'S AND COMES BACK.]

SAʕID says:

*14: il-qumSaan maa kaanat HaaDira.
maghsuula laakin biddha kawi.*
The shirts weren't ready. (They
were) washed but they need
ironing.

MRS. BROWN says:

*15: haadha illi kunt xaayifa minnu.
is-sayyid "Brown" yaHtaaj waaHid
minha li-l-Hafla.*
That's what I was afraid of. Mr.
Brown needs one for the party.

*16: qaalu lii l-qumSaan raH takuun
HaaDira s-saaʕa waaHida.*
They told me the shirts would be
ready at 1:00.

*17: Haawil takuun hunaak qabl is-saaʕa
waaHida.*
Try to be there before 1:00.

18: min kull budd.
By all means.

96

VOCABULARY

taasiʕ
ninth

xaadim (xuddaam)
servant; hired help

amr
"at your service"

tajiib
you (m) bring, fetch

badla (-aat)
suit

qamiiS (qumSaan)
shirt

maSbagha
dry cleaner's

thamaanya wa rubuʕ
8:15

taftaH
it (f) opens

is-saaʕa tisʕa
9:00

iftakart
I thought

thamaanya wa nuSS
8:30

yumkin
maybe, perhaps

ghalTaan
wrong, mistaken

ʕala kull Haal
anyway, anyhow

raayiH (-iin)
going

ana raayiH
I'm (m) going

lamma
when

tarjaʕ
you (m) return

(i)yyaa-
(pronoun carrier for
direct object of verb)

(i)yyaak
you (m) (direct object)

taghsil
you (m) wash

aghsil
I wash

aghsilha
I wash it (f)

arjaʕ
I return

tunaDHDHif
you (m) clean

Hawl
around, about

tasqi
you (m) water

zahra (zuhuur)
flower

qablma
before (+ verb)

tabda'
it (f) begins

Hafla (-aat)
party

amurr (ʕala)
I pass (by)

Saydaliyya (-aat)
pharmacy

qabl
before (+ noun)

li'ann
because

ashtari
I buy

dawa (adwiya)
medicine

maaniʕ
objection

ma fii maaniʕ
"that's all right,"
"no problem"

ma daam
as long as

ma daamak
as long as you

tuuSal
you (m) go (to),
arrive at, reach

murr (ʕala)
stop by, pass by

dukkaan (dakaakiin)
store, shop

Sanduuq (Sanaadiiq)
box, case

bibsi
Pepsi

akuun
I am

raH akuun
I shall be

intaDHir
wait (m)

xalliini
let me

aʕTiik
I give you (m)

mashruub
drinks

maghsuula
washed

kawi
ironing

illi
which, who

xaa'if (-iin)
afraid

haadha illi kunt xaaifa
minnu.
"That's what I was
afraid of."

qaalú
they said

qaalúu lii.
They told me.

takuun
she is

raH takuun
she will be

is-saaʕa waaHida
1:00

Haawil
try (imperative)

min kull budd
by all means

97

Supplementary vocabulary

Hadiiqa (Hadaa'iq) garden	*shiqqa (shiqaq)* apartment	*SallaH / yuSalliH* to repair, fix
shajara (ashjaar) tree	*ghurfa (ghuraf)* room	*xarbaan* broken, out of order
Hashiish grass	*baab (abwaab)* door	*maksuur* broken
karaaj (-aat) garage	*shubbaak (shabaabiik)* window	*mata* when

Terms for Items of Clothing

banTaloon (-aat) pants	*zunnaar (zanaaniir)* belt	*shamsiyya* umbrella
fustaan (fasaatiin) dress	*tannuura (tanaaniir)* skirt	*saaʕa (-aat)* watch
kundara (kanaadir) shoes	*bluuza (bluwaz)* blouse	*juzdaan (jazaadiin)* purse
kalsaat socks	*kanza (-aat)* sweater	*thoob (thiyaab)* garment
jakeet (-aat) jacket	*zirr (azraar)* button	*malaabis* clothes
kabbuut (kabaabiit) coat		

I. WORKING WITH WORDS AND PHRASES

A. Matching English with Arabic
Match the English expressions with their Arabic equivalents by writing the appropriate numbers next to the correct Arabic terms.

1.	party	a.	_____	*ʕala kull Haal*
2.	God willing	b.	_____	*ma daam*
3.	anyway	c.	_____	*Saydaliyya*
4.	dry cleaner	d.	_____	*Hafla*
5.	flowers	e.	_____	*badla wa qumSaan*
6.	as long as	f.	_____	*kawi*
7.	ironing	g.	_____	*in shaa' allaah*
8.	around the house	h.	_____	*lamma tarjaʕ*
9.	pharmacy	i.	_____	*mashruub*
10.	(grocery) store	j.	_____	*intaDHir*
11.	when you return	k.	_____	*Hawl il-beet*
12.	suit and shirts	l.	_____	*fuluus*
13.	drink(s)	m.	_____	*maSbagha*
14.	money	n.	_____	*dukkaan*
15.	wait	o.	_____	*zuhuur*

B. Completion of Arabic Dialogue

In the following dialogue, certain Arabic words have been left out. Complete the conversation by filling in the missing words in the eighteen sentences.

MRS. BROWN says:

1: _____ saʕiid!

3: mumkin tajiib _____
is-sayyid "Brown" wa qumSaanu
min _____?

5: iftakart il-maSbagha taftaH
_____ thamaanya wa nuSS!

7: lamma tarjaʕ biddi _____
taghsil is-sayyaara.

9: aywa, mumkin tunaDHDHif Hawl
_____ wa tasqi z-zuhuur
qablma tabda' _____?

11: ma fii maaniʕ. maa _____
raH tuuSal li-S-Saydaliyya, murr ʕala
dukkaan abu Habiib wa jiib
_____ bibsi.

13: _____ daqiiqa, xalliini
aʕTiik_____ li-l-maSbagha
wa li-l-mashruub.

15: haadha illi kunt _____
minnu. is-sayyid "Brown"
_____ waaHid minha
li-l-Hafla.

_____ takuun hunaak qabl
17. is-saaʕa waaHida.

SAʕID says:

2: _____ ya madaam "Brown."

4: is-saaʕa halla thamaanya wa
_____ wa l-maSbagha
_____ Hawaali s-saaʕa tisʕa.

6: yumkin ana _____. ʕala
kull Haal, ana _____ halla.
tu'muri shi thaani?

8: HaaDir, raH aghsilha lamma arjaʕ in
shaa' allaah. ayy _____ thaani?

10: ʕala raasi. mumkin _____
ʕala S-Saydaliyya qabl il-maSbagha,
li'an _____ ashtari dawa.

12: HaaDir. raH _____ huna
baʕd Hawaali saaʕa, in shaa' allaah.

14: _____ ma kaanat
HaaDira. maghsuula laakin biddha
_____.

16: qaalu lii l-qumSaan raH takuun
_____ is-saaʕa waaHida.

18: min kull _____.

II.   WORKING WITH SENTENCES

A. Matching Spoken Arabic with English (listening)

Listen to Cassette 5 (side 1) or to your teacher, and then match what is said in Arabic with each one of the eight English sentences.

_____ Could you get Mr. Brown's suit from the dry cleaner's?

_____ Maybe I'm mistaken. In any case I'm going right now.

_____ When you return I want you to wash the car.

_____ Could you clean around the house before the party starts?

_____ Wait a minute, let me give you money for the cleaner's.

_____ The shirts weren't ready. They are washed but need ironing.

_____ They told me the shirts will be ready at 1:00.

_____ Try to be there before 1:00.

B. Scrambled Arabic Dialogue

Reconstruct the dialogue below by numbering the eighteen Arabic sentences so they are in a meaningful sequence.

_____ HaaDir, raH akuun huna baʕd Hawaali saaʕa, in shaa' allaah.

_____ Haawil takuun hunaak qabl is-saaʕa waaHida.

_____ is-saaʕa halla thamaanya wa rubuʕ wa l-maSbagha taftaH Hawaali s-saaʕa tisʕa.

_____ qaalu lii l-qumSaan raH takuun HaaDira is-saaʕa waaHida.

_____ yumkin ana ghalTaan. ʕala kull Haal, ana raayiH halla. tu'muri shi thaani?

_____ lamma tarjaʕ biddi yyaak taghsil is-sayyaara.

_____ amr, yaa madaam "Brown."

_____ aywa, mumkin tunaDHDHif Hawl il-beet wa tasqi z-zuhuur qablma tabda' l-Hafla?

_____ ʕala raasi. mumkin amurr ʕala S-Saydaliyya qabl il-maSbagha, li'ann laazim ashtari dawa.

_____ il-qumSaan maa kaanat HaaDira. maghsuula laakin biddha kawi.

_____ yaa saʕiid!

_____ intaDHir daqiiqa, xalliini aʕTiik fuluus li-l-maSbagha wa li-l-mashruub.

_____ iftakart il-maSbagha taftaH is-saaʕa thamaanya wa nuSS!

_____ haadha illi kunt xaa'ifa minnu. is-sayyid "Brown" yaHtaaj waaHid minha li-l-Hafla.

_____ mumkin tajiib badlat is-sayyid "Brown" wa qumSaanu min il-maSbagha?

_____ min kull budd.

_____ HaaDir, raH aghsilha lamma arjaʕ in shaa' allaah. ayy shi thaani?

_____ ma fii maaniʕ. ma daamak raH tuuSal li-S-Saydaliyya, murr ʕala dukkaan abu Habiib wa jiib Sanduuq bibsi.

C. Matching English with Arabic

Match the English sentences with their Arabic counterparts.

1. I thought the cleaner's opens at 8:30.

a. raH aghsilha lamma arjaʕ.

2. I'm going now. Do you need anything else?

b. iftakart il-maSbagha taftaH is-saaʕa thamaanya wa nuSS.

3. I'll wash it when I return.

c. mumkin tasqi z-zuhuur?

4. Wait a minute, let me give you some money.

d. ana raayiH halla. tu'muri shi thaani?

5. The shirts will be ready at 1:00.

e. intaDHir daqiiqa, xalliini aʕTiik fuluus.

6. Could you water the flowers?

f. raH akuun huna baʕd Hawaali saaʕa.

7. Try to be there before 1:00.

g. Haawil takuun hunaak qabl is-saaʕa waaHida.

8. I'll be here in about an hour.

h. il-qumSaan raH takuun HaaDira s-saaʕa waaHida.

D. Matching Arabic Remarks and Responses

Match the Arabic sentences on the left with the appropriate responses on the right.

1. *amr yaa madaam "Brown."*

a. maa fii maaniʕ.

2. *biddi yyaak taghsil is-sayyaara.*

b. yumkin ana ghalTaan.

3. *mumkin amurr ʕala S-Saydaliyya.*

c. min kull budd.

4. *iftakart il-maSbagha taftaH is-saaʕa waaHida.*

d. mumkin tajiib il-badla min il-maSbagha?

5. *Haawil takuun hunaak qabl is-saaʕa waaHida.*

e. intaDHir daqiiqa, xalliini aʕTiik fuluus.

6. *raH akuun huna baʕd Hawaali saaʕa.*

f. raH aghsilha lamma arjaʕ.

E. Translation into Arabic

Translate the sentences in Exercise **A** on the facing page into Arabic.

III. WORKING WITH THE LANGUAGE

A. Present tense: Regular verbs

As explained in Lesson One, present tense verbs consist of a prefix and a stem. Sometimes there is also a suffix.

The chart below covers the present tense forms of a regular verb, "to return." For this chart, dashes have been inserted between the stem and its prefix and / or suffix to clearly indicate the components to you.

ya-rjaʕ he returns	*ta-rjaʕ* she returns	*ya-rjaʕ-u* they return
ta-rjaʕ you return	*ta-rjaʕ-i* you return	*ta-rjaʕ-u* you return
	a-rjaʕ I return	*na-rjaʕ* we return

Drill 1: CONJUGATION

First: Teacher conjugates *rajaʕ* while students listen.
Second: Teacher conjugates *rajaʕ* and students repeat.
Then: Both repeat the first and the second drill with the following verbs:

fataH   *iftakar*

Drill 2: CONJUGATION OF VERBS IN SENTENCES

Conjugate the verbs in the following sentences.

1. *antaDHir taksi.*
2. *aHibb ha-l-balad.*
3. *ataʕallam ʕarabi.*

B. Present tense: "hollow" verbs

Hollow verbs have a long vowel in the present tense. That vowel may be *ii, uu,* or *aa.* Here is a chart of *shaaf* "to see" a typical hollow verb in the present tense:

ya-shuuf he sees	*ta-shuuf* she sees	*ya-shuuf-u* they see
ta-shuuf you see	*ta-shuuf-i* you see	*ta-shuuf-u* you see
	a-shuuf I see	*na-shuuf* we see

Below is a list of the six other hollow verbs that have occurred so far in the text. Each is cited in the third person masculine singular, both past and present:

raaH / yaruuH	*qaal / yaquul*	*araad / yuriid*
kaan / yakuun	*jaab / yajiib*	*iHtaaj / yaHtaaj*

Drill 3: CONJUGATION OF PRESENT TENSE VERBS

Conjugate the verbs in these sentences in the present tense:

1. *yajiib iS-Sanduuq.*
2. *yaruuH maʕha.*
3. *yaHtaaj fuluus.*

C. Future Tense for Verbs

The future tense is formed by using the particle *raH* before a present tense verb:

raH aʕtiik fuluus.
I'll give you money.

raH tarjaʕ baʕd shwayy?
Will you return soon?

raH amurr ʕala S-Saydaliyya.
I'll stop by the pharmacy.

Drill 4: CONJUGATION OF FUTURE TENSE VERBS

Using the sentences in Drills 2 and 3, conjugate the verbs in them in the future tense.

D. Telling the Time of Day

Telling time is not complicated in Arabic. The word "hour" is used (*is-saaʕa*), followed by the number:

is-saaʕa xamsa
5:00

is-saaʕa thalaatha
3:00

is-saaʕa sabʕa
7:00

The words *nuSS* "half," *rubuʕ* "quarter," and *thulth* "third" are used to indicate the half hour, the quarter hour, and the 20-minute divisions. The word *illa* means "except for," or "minus."

is-saaʕa arbaʕa wa nuSS
4:30

is-saaʕa waaHida wa thulth
1:20

is-saaʕa thinteen wa rubuʕ
2:15

is-saaʕa thamaanya illa thulth
7:40

is-saaʕa sitta illa rubuʕ
5:45

Drill 5: TELLING TIME IN ARABIC

Say the following times in Arabic:

1. 2:30
2. 7:05
3. 10:20
4. 5:10
5. 12:00
6. 8:15
7. 10:40
8. 6:45
9. 3:30
10. 9:55

IV. WORKING WITH VARIANTS

A. Translation into Arabic
Put the following sentences into Arabic.

1. Could you get the medicine from the pharmacy?
2. Do you know what time Abu Khalid's store opens?
3. I'll water the flowers when I return from the pharmacy.
4. Please try to buy the drinks before the party.
5. Could you give him money for the medicine?
6. Wait (m) for me.
7. Could you clean the house tomorrow morning?
8. Please wash Mr. Brown's shirts.
9. This is broken. Can you fix it?
10. Please take these clothes to the cleaner's.

B. Comprehension of Spoken Arabic
Listen to the Arabic sentences on the cassette and determine which of the English sentences corresponds in meaning with the spoken Arabic sentence.

1. _____ When does the pharmacy open in the morning?
   _____ When does the pharmacy open in the afternoon?
   _____ When do the dry cleaner's open in the afternoon?

2. _____ The shirts will be ready at 1:30.
   _____ The suit will be ready at 1:30.
   _____ The pants will be ready at 1:30.

3. _____ The store opens at 8:15 in the morning.
   _____ The store opens at 9:35 in the morning.
   _____ The store opens at 8:45 in the morning.

4. _____ Would you like to go to the embassy party?
   _____ Are you going to the embassy party?
   _____ Do you want to go to the embassy party?

5. _____ I want you to come to my house.
   _____ I want you to visit my house.
   _____ I want you to see my house.

6. _____ Could you tell me when you are coming back?
   _____ Could you tell him when you are coming back?
   _____ Could you tell us when you are coming back?

V. WORKING WITH THE SITUATION

Cross-cultural communication involves the understanding of a culture as well as a language. Americans sometimes find commonplace actions by nationals of other countries puzzling. Thus needless misunderstandings may arise if one is not informed about certain aspects of behavior in the foreign culture.

For instance, in the sample dialogue on the opening page of this lesson. Saʕid has been asked to wash the car. He replies that he will, "God willing." To an American this reply might seem either off-hand or lackadaisical, but it is standard practice for an Arabic speaker to append *in shaa' allaah* to any promise or commitment about the future, and this traditional qualification does not imply a lack of concern or intent.

Similar scenarios might involve any situation where you hire someone to do something for you, or where you are in a work situation where you are responsible for giving instructions to Arabic-speaking employees. Before you practice this type of scenario with your teacher, it is a good idea to discuss with him or her such aspects of cross-cultural communication in the situation likely to be presented.

الدرس العاشر

على التليفون مع الخادمة

١.   الاميركية : آلو، مين عم يتكلم ؟

٢.   العربية : آلو، انا فوزية عم احكي من القرية.

٣.   الاميركية : خير ان شاء الله ؟ !

٤.   العربية : ابني الصغير عيّان كثير.

٥.   الاميركية : عفواً، يافوزية شو يعني " عيان " ؟ مافهمت.

٦.   العربية : يعني مريض، مش مبسوط.

٧.   الاميركية : سلامته. ان شاء الله شيء بسيط.

٨.   العربية : والله خايفة عليه. حرارته عالية وعم يسعل وعنده وجع راس.

٩.   الاميركية : سلامته. يعني ما رح تقدري تيجي اليوم ؟

١٠.   الاربية : حقيقة انا مش متأكدة. لازم اخذه للعيادة.

١١.   الاميركية : مش ممكن بنتك الكبيرة تاخذه للعيادة.

١٢.   العربية : بنتي الكبيرة راحت امبارح تزور جدتها في قرية كروان، وراجعة اليوم المسا.

١٣.   الاميركية : بسيطة، لا تهتمي. ديري بالك على ابنك، وما فيه مشكلة.

١٤.   العربية : خايفة عنده رشح اخذه عدوى من ابن عمه.

١٥.   الاميركية : تعني مفكرة عنده نمونيا ؟

١٦.   العربية : مش متأكدة. رح اشوف شو يقول الطبيب.

١٧.   الاميركية : ان شاء الله لا. سلامته.

١٨.   العربية : الله يسلمك، ممكن ابعث لك بنتي بكره الصبح اذا تحبّي.

١٩.   الاميركية : طيب. قولي لها تكون هنا بكير من فضلك.

LESSON TEN: On the Phone

id-dars il-ʕaashir: ʕala t-talifoon

Sample Dialogue:

AMERICAN says:

1: *aloo, miin ʕam yatakallam?*
Hello, who's speaking?

3: *xeer in shaa' allaah?*
I hope nothing's wrong!

5: *ʕafwan, ya fawziyya, shu yaʕni "ʕayyaan"? ma fahimt.*
Pardon me, Fawziyya, what does ʕayyaan mean? I did not understand.

7: *salaamtu, in shaa' allaah shi basiiT.*
I hope he'll be all right. I hope it's nothing serious.

9: *salaamtu. yaʕni ma raaH taqdari tiiji l-yoom?*
I hope he'll be okay. Does this mean that you won't be able to come today?

11: *mish mumkin bintik il-kabiira taaxudhu li-l-ʕiyaada?*
Can't your older daughter take him to the clinic?

13: *basiiTa, la tahtammi. diiri baalik ʕala ibnik. ma fii mushkila.*
That's all right. Don't worry. Take care of your son. No problem.

ARAB says:

2: *aloo, ana fawziyya. ʕam aHki min il-qarya.*
Hello, this is Fawziyya. I'm speaking from the village.

4: *ibni S-Saghiir ʕayyaan kathiir.*
My little son is very sick.

6: *yaʕni mariiD, mish mabsuuT.*
It means sick, not well.

8: *wallaah xaa'ifa ʕaleeh. Haraaratu ʕaaliya wa ʕam yasʕul wa ʕindu wajaʕ raas.*
I'm really worried about him. His temperature is high. He's coughing, and he has a headache.

10: *Haqiiqatan ana mish muta'akkida. laazim aaxudhu li-l-ʕiyaada.*
Actually, I'm not sure. I have to take him to the clinic.

12: *binti l-kabiira raaHat imbaariH tazuur jadatha fi qaryat karwaan, wa raajiʕa l-yoom il-masa.*
My older daughter went yesterday to visit her grandmother in the village of Karwan and she's coming back this evening.

14: *xaa'ifa ʕindu rashH axadhu ʕadwa min ibn ʕammu.*
I'm afraid he might have a cold that he caught from his (paternal) cousin.

AMERICAN says:

15: *taʕni mufakkira ʕindu nimoonya?*
You mean you think he has
pneumonia?

17: *in shaa' allaah la. salaamtu.*
I hope not. I hope he gets well.

19: *Tayyib. quuli laha takuun huna
bakkiir min faDlik.*
Okay. Tell her to be here early,
please.

ARAB says:

16: *mish muta'akkida. raH ashuuf
shu yaquul iT-Tabiib.*
I'm not sure. I'll see what the
doctor says.

18: *allaah yusallimik, mumkin abʕath lik
binti bukra S-SubuH idha taHibbi.*
Thank you. I could send you my
daughter tomorrow morning, if
you like.

VOCABULARY

ʕaashir
   tenth

ʕam
   (progressive marker)

aHki
   I speak, talk

ʕam aHki
   I'm speaking

qarya (qura)
   village

xeer in shaa' allaah!
   "I hope nothing's
   wrong!"

ibn (abnaa')
   son

ʕayyaan (-iin)
   sick

yaʕni
   it means; that is
   to say

fahimt
   I understand,
   understood

mariiD (marDa)
   sick

mabsuuT (-iin)
   well, happy

salaamtu
   "I hope he gets well,"
   "has a speedy recov-
   ery" (said when some-
   one is sick)

basiiT
   simple, uncomplicated

wallaah
   (a mild oath)

xaa'ifa ʕaleeh
   "(I'm) worried about
   him"

Haraara
   temperature, fever

ʕaali
   high

yasʕul
   he coughs

ʕam yasʕul
   he is coughing

wajaʕ (awjaaʕ)
   pain; ache

raas (ruus)
   head

wajaʕ raas
   headache

taqdari
   you (f) are able

tiiji
   you come

Haqiiqatan
   really, actually

muta'akkid (-iin)
   certain; sure

ʕiyaada
   clinic

bint (banaat)
   daughter, girl

taaxudh
   she takes

taaxudhu
   she takes him

raaHat
   she went

imbaariH
   yesterday

tazuur
   she visits

jadda
   grandmother

raajiʕ (-iin)
   returning

masa
   evening

basiiTa
   "that's okay,"
   "take it easy"

tahtammi
   you (f) are concerned,
   worried

la tahtammi
   don't worry

diiri baalik
   "be careful,"
   "take care"

mushkila (mashaakil)
   problem

yakuun
   it is, it may be

rashH
   cold (n.)

axadhu ʕadwa
   he caught it

ibn ʕamm
   paternal cousin (m)

taʕni
   you mean

mufakkir (-iin)
   thinking

nimoonya
   pneumonia

yaquul
   he says

Tabiib (aTibbaa')
   doctor, physician

abʕath
   I send

abʕath lik
   I send (to) you

SubuH
   morning

quuli
   tell (f)

quuli laha
   tell her

takuun
   she is

bakkiir
   early

109

SUPPLEMENTARY VOCABULARY

Terms for Parts of the Body

iid (iideen)
hand

iSbaʕ (aSaabiʕ)
finger

qalb (quluub)
heart

sinn (asnaan)
tooth

qadam (aqdaam)
foot

maʕida
stomach

ʕeen (ʕuyuun)
eye

rijil (arjul)
leg

baTn (buTuun)
stomach

fam (afwaah)
mouth

Sadr (Suduur)
chest

shaʕr
hair

Hanjara
throat

dhiraaʕ (adhruʕ)
arm

ʕaDHm (ʕiDHaam)
bone

udhun (adhaan)
ear

katif (aktaaf)
shoulder

Terms for Relatives

umm (ummahaat)
mother

ʕamm
paternal uncle

jadd
grandfather

ab / abu (aabaa')
father

ʕamma
paternal aunt

zawj
husband

ax / axu (ixwa, ixwaan)
brother

xaal
maternal uncle

zawja
wife

uxt (axawaat)
sister

xaala
maternal aunt

Miscellaneous Terms

Hasaasiyya
allergy

ʕaDHm maksuur
broken bone

sayyaarat isʕaaf
ambulance

Harq (Huruuq)
burn (n.)

mumarriDa (-aat)
nurse

saaʕad / yusaaʕid
to help

ishaal
diarrhea

booliis
police

I. WORKING WITH WORDS AND PHRASES

A. Matching English with Arabic
Match the English expressions with their Arabic equivalents.

1.	I'm speaking	a.	_____	mariid
2.	village	b.	_____	bintik
3.	sick	c.	_____	wajaʕ raas
4.	temperature	d.	_____	raajiʕa
5.	headache	e.	_____	ʕam aHki
6.	clinic	f.	_____	diiri baalik
7.	returning	g.	_____	imbaariH
8.	cousin	h.	_____	qarya
9.	your daughter	i.	_____	jadda
10.	yesterday	j.	_____	ibn ʕamm
11.	take care	k.	_____	Haraara
12.	grandmother	l.	_____	ʕiyaada

B. Completion of Arabic Dialogue
In the following dialogue, certain words have been left out of the conversation. Complete these nineteen sentences by filling in the missing words.

AMERICAN says:

1: aloo, _____ ʕam yatakallam?

3: _____ in shaa' allaah?

5: ʕafwan, ya fawziyya, shu yaʕni "ayyaan?" ma _____ .

7: _____ in shaa' allaah shi basiiT.

9: salaamtu. yaʕni ma raaH _____ tiiji l-yoom?

11: mish munkin bintik il-kabiira taaxudhu li _____ ?

13: basiiTa, la tahtammi, diiri _____ ʕala ibnik. ma fii mushkila.

15: taʕni _____ ʕindu nimoonya?

17. in shaa' allaah la. _____

19. Tayyib. quuli laha takuun huna bakkiir min faDlik.

ARAB says:

2: aloo, ana fawziyya. ʕam _____ min il-qarya.

4: ibni S-Saghiir _____ kathiir.

6: yaʕni _____ , mish mabsuuT.

8: wallaah xaa'ifa ʕaleeh. _____ ʕaaliya wa ʕam yasʕul wa ʕindu _____ raas.

10: Haqiiqatan ana mish _____ . laazim aaxudhu li-l-ʕiyaada.

12: binti l-kabiira raaHat _____ tazuur jaddatha fi qaryat karwaan, wa raajiʕa l-yoom il-masa.

14: xaa'ifa ʕindu _____ axadhu ʕadwa min ibn ʕammu.

16: mish muta'akkida. raH ashuuf shu _____ iT-Tabiib.

18: allaah yusallimik, mumkin abʕath lik binti bukra S-SubuH idha taHibbi.

111

II. WORKING WITH SENTENCES

A. Matching Spoken Arabic to English (listening)

Listen to Cassette 5 (side 2) or to your teacher, and match the spoken Arabic with the correct English sentence among the eight sentences below:

_____ My young son is very sick.

_____ Can't your older daughter take him to the clinic?

_____ Take care of your son.

_____ His temperature is high and he has a headache.

_____ What does "ʕayyaan" mean? I didn't understand.

_____ Tell her to be here at 9:00.

_____ You mean you think he has pneumonia?

_____ Actually, I'm not sure. I have to take him to the clinic.

B. Scrambled Arabic Dialogue

Reconstruct the dialogue below by numbering the nineteen sentences so they are in a meaningful sequence.

_____ mish muta'akkida. raH ashuuf shu yaquul iT-Tabiib.

_____ salaamtu. yaʕni ma raaH taqdari tiiji l-yoom?

_____ xeer in shaa' allaah?!

_____ xaa'ifa ʕindu rashH axaadhu ʕadwa min ibn ʕammu.

_____ Tayyib. quuli laha takuun huna bakkiir min faDlik.

_____ yaʕni mariiD, mish mabsuuT.

_____ mish mumkin bintik il-kabiira taaxudhu li-l-ʕiyaada?

_____ wallaah xaa'ifa ʕaleeh. Haraaratu ʕaaliya wa ʕam yasʕul wa ʕindu wajaʕ raas.

_____ aloo, ana fawziyya. ʕam aHki min il-qarya.

_____ Haqiiqatan ana mish muta'akkida. laazim aaxudhu li-l-ʕiyaada.

_____ ʕafwan, ya fawziyya, shu yaʕni "ʕayyaan?" ma fahimt.

_____ in shaa' allaah la. salaamtu.

_____ basiiTa, la tahtammi. diiri baalik ʕala ibnik. ma fii mushkila.

_____ taʕni mufakkira ʕindu nimoonya?

_____ aloo, miin ʕam yatakallam?

_____ salaamtu. in shaa' allaah shi basiiT.

_____ allaah yusallimik, mumkin abʕath lik binti bukra S-SubuH idha taHibbi.

_____ ibni S-Saghiir ʕayyaan kathiir.

_____ binti l-kabiira raaHat imbaariH tazuur jaddatha fi qaryat karwaan, wa raajiʕa l-yoom il-masa.

C. Matching English with Arabic
Match each English sentence with its Arabic counterpart.

id-dars
il-ʕaashir:
ʕala
t-talifoon

1. Hello, who's calling?

a. *quuli laha takuun huna bakkiir.*

2. I'm worried about him.

b. *raaHat imbaariH tazuur jaddatha.*

3. That means you can't come today?

c. *aloo, miin ʕam yatakallam?*

4. May I send you my daughter tomorrow morning?

d. *yaʕni maa raH tiiji l-yoom?*

5. I'm speaking from the village.

e. *wallaah xaa'ifa ʕaleeh.*

6. Tell her to be here early.

f. *ʕam aHki min il-qarya.*

7. She went yesterday to visit her grandmother.

g. *mumkin abʕath lik binti bukra S-SubuH?*

D. Matching Written Arabic
Match each of the Arabic sentences in the left-hand column with the appropriate response at the right.

1. *aloo, miin ʕam yatakallam?*

a. *yaʕni mariiD, mish mabsuuT.*

2. *ʕafwan yaa fawziyya, shu yaʕni "ʕayyaan"?*

b. *binti raaHat imbaariH.*

3. *xeer in shaa' allaah?*

c. *aloo, ana fawziyya.*

4. *salaamtu, in shaa' allaah shi basiiT.*

d. *mish muta'akkida, raH ashuuf shu yaquul iT-Tabiib.*

5. *taʕni mufakkira ʕindu nimoonya?*

e. *ibni S-Saghiir ʕayyaan kathiir.*

6. *mish mumkin bintik il-kabiira taaxudhu li-l-ʕiyaada?*

f. *wallaah xaa'ifa ʕaleeh.*

E. Translation into Arabic
Translate the eight sentences in Exercise **A** on the facing page into Arabic.

113

III. WORKING WITH THE LANGUAGE

A. Defective verbs

"Defective" verbs are verbs whose stems or citation forms end in a vowel. Some of those which have been used so far in this *FAST* text are listed below:

masha to go, walk	*aʕTa* to give	*Haka* to talk, speak
ʕana to mean	*ishtara* to buy	

These verbs have two stem variants in the past tense, a short one for the third person and a longer one for the first and second person. They are typically conjugated in the past tense as charted below:

masha he walked	*mash-at* she walked	*mash-u* they walked
mashee-t you walked	*mashee-ti* you walked	*mashee-tu* you walked

mashee-t I walked	*mashee-na* we walked

In the present tense, these same "defective" verbs take regular prefixes for the first, second, or third person, and they always end in a vowel, as illustrated in the present tense conjugation below:

yamshi he walks	*tamshi* she walks	*yamshu* they walk
tamshi you walk	*tamshi* you walk	*tamshu* you walk

amshi I walk	*namshi* we walk

A. Imperative Forms

The masculine and feminine imperative forms of these verbs are alike, both ending in **-i**, as follows:

Verb	Imperative
masha	*imshi*
ishtara	*ishtari*
aʕTa	*aʕTi*
Haka	*iHki*

B. Suffixed object pronouns

When an object pronoun suffix is attached to a verb form that ends in a vowel, that vowel is generally **lengthened and stressed**, as illustrated below:

aʕTíini give me	*ishtaráaha* he bought it (*f*)	*aʕTáah* he gave him

Drill 1: PAST TENSE CONJUGATION

First: Teacher goes over conjugation of *masha* in the past tense while students listen.

Second: Teacher recites *masha* in the past tense and students repeat.

Third: Teacher repeats first and second steps for *Haka, ishtara,* and *aʕTa.*

Fourth: Students conjugate the verbs in the following sentences:

1. *Haka maʕu.*
2. *ishtara l-akil.*
3. *aʕTaah l-fuluus.*

Drill 2: PRESENT TENSE CONJUGATION

As in Drill 1, go through the four steps, using the present tense of each verb.

1. *yaHki maʕu.*
2. *yashtari l-akil.*
3. *yaʕTiih l-fuluus.*

Drill 3: TRANSLATION INTO ARABIC

Provide the Arabic equivalent for each of the following ten sentences, taking care to use the necessary person, tense, and gender for each.

1. Go (walk) to the store and buy some bread.
2. I bought this meat yesterday but it's not fresh.
3. She spoke with me on the phone.
4. I speak a little Arabic.
5. Do you (*m*) mean that you are sick?
6. Give me those tomatoes, please.
7. He gave me this address.
8. I want to buy these things, please.
9. Would you (*m*) like to talk to him?
10. I want to give it to you.

B. The verb *ija*, "to come"

The verb *ija* "to come" is a very common and useful one, but is exceptional in its conjugation, so the best thing to do is memorize the forms and practice them as much as possible. The full paradigm is charted below:

Past tense

ija	*ijat*	*iju*
he came	she came	they came
jiit	*jiiti*	*jiitu*
you came	you came	you came

jiit	*jiina*
I came	we came

Present Tense:

yiiji	*tiiji*	*yiiju*
he comes	she comes	they come
tiiji	*tiiji*	*tiiju*
you come	you come	you come

aaji	*niiji*
I come	we come

For *ija*, these imperative forms are irregular:

taʕaal (m)!	*taʕaali (f)!*	*taʕaalu (pl)!*

Drill 4: CONJUGATION OF "ija" IN THE PAST TENSE

Practice conjugating *ija* in the past tense and then conjugate it in the three sentences below:

1. *ija imbaariH.*
2. *ija qabl saʕateen.*
3. *ija qabl xams daqaa'iq.*

Drill 5: CONJUGATION OF "ija" IN THE PRESENT TENSE

Practice conjugating *ija* in the present tense and then conjugate it in these three sentences:

1. *yiiji bakkiir.*
2. *raH yiiji bukra.*
3. *laazim yiiji halla.*

Drill 6: TRANSLATION OF "come" INTO ARABIC
Give the Arabic:

1. Can you (*m*) come tomorrow afternoon?
2. Can they come with us?
3. Will she come early?
4. I want her to come at 9:00.
5. We want to come with you.
6. They came yesterday.
7. Won't you (*f*) be able to come?
8. I'm sorry, I can't come.
9. Why can't you (*pl*) come?
10. She doesn't like to come here.

C. Use of ʕam
The particle ʕam is a progressive marker; that is, it emphasizes that the action of the verb is *ongoing*. It is widely used to mark ongoing, progressive activity in the Arabic speech of the Levant area: Lebanon, Syria, and Jordan.

It is not necessary for you to incorporate it into your speech at this level of proficiency, since it is a colloquial and somewhat redundant expression. However, you will hear it frequently in the everyday speech of Arabs from those areas.

D. Use of the present tense of "kaan"
In a regular Arabic equational sentence the forms of the verb "to be" are not used. In certain circumstances, however, they do occur. Usually, this happens when the equivalent in English is either "be" or "to be." The most common usages follow in the three sets of examples below:

1. After the helping words *laazim, mumkin* and *Hatta*:

   laazim takuuni huna bukra.
   You (*f*) have to be here tomorrow.

   mumkin takuun hunaak?
   Can you (*m*) be there?

   raaH bakkiir Hatta yakuun ʕala il-waqt.
   He went early in order to be on time.

2. In the future tense with *raH*:

   raH yakuun mawjuud.
   He'll be there.

   raH akuun maʕak.
   I'll be with you.

3. As the second or third element in a verb string:

   ma aqdar akuun hunaak.
   I can't be there.

   Haawil takuun ʕala-l-waqt.
   Try to be on time.

Drill 7: COMPLETION OF ARABIC USES OF "kaan"

Fill in each missing word with an appropriate form of the present tense of *kaan* in the five sentences below:

1. *mumkin _____ huna bakkiir, ya saʕiid?*
2. *ʕindi mawʕid is-saaʕa arbaʕa, wa laazim _____ hunaak ʕala l-waqt.*
3. *quul lahum _____ fi l-maTam is-saaʕa sabʕa.*
4. *Haawili _____ fi l-beet lamma narjaʕ.*
5. *naHna raH _____ fi s-suuq il-yoom.*

IV. WORKING WITH VARIANTS

A. Translation into Arabic

Translate the following eight sentences into Arabic:

1. I'm sorry. I don't understand.
2. Do you (*m*) have a problem?
3. Are you (*f*) sick?
4. I have a fever.
5. I don't know what to do.
6. I'm worried about her.
7. Did you talk to the police?
8. I have to see a doctor. I'm sick.

B. Comprehension of Spoken Arabic

Listen to the Arabic sentences on the cassette and determine which among the following English sentences corresponds in meaning to the taped Arabic.

1. _____ My young daughter is sick today.
   _____ My young son is sick today.
   _____ My eldest daughter is sick today.

2. _____ Fawziyya went to the clinic yesterday.
   _____ Fawziyya went to the clinic today.
   _____ Fawziyya will go to the clinic tomorrow.

3. _____ I must visit my grandfather in two days.
   _____ I must visit my grandmother in two days.
   _____ I must visit my aunt in two days.

4. _____ There is a doctor in the village clinic.
   _____ The village clinic doesn't have a doctor.
   _____ The village doctor doesn't have a clinic.

5. _____ Tell me what the doctor tells you.
   _____ I'll tell you what the doctor tells me.
   _____ The doctor will tell you what he wants to tell me.

6. _____ That means you can't come this morning?
   _____ That means you can't come tomorrow morning?
   _____ That means you can't come every morning?

C. Question formation in Arabic

Formulate questions in Arabic to which the following ten sentences could be appropriate responses:

1. *naʕam, ʕindi wajaʕ raas.*
2. *zawjati mish mawjuuda halla.*
3. *ʕindna binteen wa ibn.*
4. *ism ibni aHmad.*
5. *ana mish muta'akkid; laazim ashuuf iT-Tabiib.*
6. *zawji raajiʕ il-masa.*
7. *ʕam aHki min il-maktab.*
8. *uxti raH tiiji tazuurna bukra.*
9. *ʕindu wajaʕ fi baTnu.*
10. *ana saakina fi T-Taabiq il-xaamis.*

V. WORKING WITH THE SITUATION

There are any number of situations that might arise involving some sort of problem: illness, accident, misunderstanding, etc.

With your teacher, make a list of possible problems you may encounter and will have to deal with using a limited amount of spoken Arabic. Again, prepare and rehearse a set of "key lines" that you can comfortably use under such circumstances, for example:

I've lost my _____.

I need help. Can you help me?

What happened?

This is an emergency.

I'm sorry. I can't help you.

I don't understand.

What's the problem?

Practice the key lines with your instructor until you feel ready to role-play the scenarios for situations you have chosen.

الدرس الحادي عشر

مع الخادمة

١. العربـــية : شو بدك اياني اعمل هلا ؟

٢. الامريكية : اول شي بدي اياك تنظفي غرف النوم وبعدين الصالون .

٣. العربـــية : تريدي اغير الشراشف في غرف النوم ؟

٤. الامريكية : مش ضروري . غيرناها امبارح .

٥. العربـــية : طيب . متى بدك اياني اغسل الغسيل ؟

٦. الامريكية : خلي الغسيل لبعد الظهر ، فيه شغل كثير في المطبخ .

٧. العربـــية : اذا نشرنا الغسيل بعد الظهر ما رح ينشف اليوم .

٨. الامريكية : معليش ، تقدري تستعملي النشافة الكهربائية .

٩. العربـــية : طيّب رايحة ارتب غرف النوم .

١٠. الامريكية : لا تنسي تمسحي الغبار عن الأثاث .

١١. العربـــية : من كل بد . رح امسح الغبار بعد ما اكنس وامسح الارض .

LESSON ELEVEN: Around the House

id-dars il-Haadi ʕashar: Hawl il-beet

The dialogue in this lesson is structured as a typical scenario for a Foreign Service spouse who will probably need to interact with local employees regarding housework services and in the preparation of food. This is necessary because it is rare to find hired help in the Arab countries who speak English. For Arabic language learners who do not anticipate being in this specific situation, the terminology is still useful because it provides practice dealing with household issues and needs that are of general use with landlords, repairmen, delivery men, neighbors, and shopkeepers.

Because this two-part dialogue has twenty-four sentences and is quite long, it will take longer than most of those in the other lessons.

Sample Dialogue:

ARAB says:

AMERICAN says:

1: *shu biddik iyyaani aʕmal halla'?*
What would you like me to do now?

2: *awwal shi biddi yyaaki tunaDHDHifi ghuraf in-noom wa baʕdeen iS-Saaloon.*
First thing, I'd like you to clean the bedrooms and then the living room.

3: *turiidi ughayyir ish-sharaashif fi ghuraf in-noom?*
Do you want me to change the sheets in the bedrooms?

4: *mish Daruuri. ghayyarnaaha imbaariH.*
That's not necessary. We changed them yesterday.

5: *Tayyib. mata biddik iyyaani aghsil il-ghasiil?*
All right. When do you want me to do the laundry?

6: *xalli l-ghasiil li-baʕd iDH-DHuhur, fii shughul kathiir fi l-maTbax.*
Leave the laundry till this afternoon. There's a lot of work in the kitchen.

7: *idha nasharna l-ghasiil baʕd iDH-DHuhur ma raH yanshaf il-yoom.*
If we hang the laundry out this afternoon, it won't dry today.

8: *maʕalesh, taqdari tastaʕmili n-nashshaafa l-kahrabaa'iyya.*
That's all right. You can use the [electric] dryer.

9: *Tayyib, raayiHa urattib ghuraf in-noom.*
Okay. I'm going to straighten up the bedrooms.

10: *la tansi tamsaHi l-ghubaar ʕan il-athaath.*
Don't forget to dust the furniture.

11: *min kull budd. raH amsaH il-ghubaar baʕdma ukannis wa amsaH il-arD.*
Sure. I'll dust after I sweep and mop the floor.

121

في المطبخ

١٢. العربـــية : خلصت تنظيف البيت .

١٣. الامريكية : خلص ؟ الله يعطيك العافية . ارتاحي شوي قبل شغل المطبخ .

١٤. العربـــية : والله مش تعبانة . انا مستعدة .

١٥. الامريكية : اذاً تقدري تبدئي . الصحون والكاسات والطناجر والصواني مكدّسة بعد حفلة امبارح .

١٦. العربـــية : رح اجليها وبعدين رح انشفها واحطها في الخزانة .

١٧. الامريكية : لما تخلصي الجلي ممكن تساعديني في تحضير العشا ؟

١٨. العربـــية : طبعا يا مدام . شو رح نحضّر اليوم .

١٩. الامريكية : انا مفكرة نحضّر دجاج مع رز وسلطة .

٢٠. العربـــية : بدك اياني اروح اشتري دجاج من عند ابو خالد ؟

٢١. الامريكية : لا، مش ضروري . اشتريت دجاج امبارح، هو في البرّاد .

٢٢. العربـــية : يعني لازم نشوي الدجاج ونقطّعة منشان نخلطة مع الرز .

٣٢. الامريكية : ايوه، ومن فضلك، اعملي الرز على الطريقة العربية .

٢٤. العربـــية : اكيد . رح ابدأ بالطبخ لما اخلّص الجلي .

ARAB says:

12: xallaالسt tanDHiif il-beet.
I finished cleaning the house.

14: wallaah mish taʕbaana. ana mustaʕidda.
Really, I'm not tired. I'm ready.

16: raH ajliiha wa baʕdeen raH unashshifha wa aHuTTha fi l-xazaana.
I'll wash them, then dry them and put them in the cupboard.

18: Tabʕan ya madaam. shu raH nuHaDDir il-yoom?
Certainly, madam. What shall we prepare today?

20: biddik iyyaani aruuH ashtari dajaaj min ʕind abu xaalid?
Do you want me to go buy chicken from Abu Khalid?

22: yaʕni laazim nashwi d-dajaaj wa nuqattiʕu minshaan naxluTu maʕ ir-ruzz?
So we have to roast the chicken and cut it up to mix it with the rice?

24: akiid. raH abda' bi-T-Tabx lamma uxalliS il-jali.
Sure. I'll start cooking when I finish the dishes.

AMERICAN says:

13: xalaS? allaah yaʕTiiki l-ʕaafiya. irtaaHi shwayy qabl shughul il-maTbax.
Finished? "May God give you strength!" Rest a bit before working in the kitchen.

15: idhan taqdari tabda'i. is-suHuun wa l-kaasaat wa t-tanaajir wa s-sawaani mukaddasa baʕd Haflat imbaariH.
Then you can start. The dishes, glasses, pans, and serving plates are piled up from yesterday's party.

17: lamma tuxalliSi l-jali, mumkin tusaaʕidiini fi taHDiir il-ʕashaa'?
When you finish the dishes would you help me prepare dinner?

19: ana mufakkira nuHaDDir dajaaj maʕ ruzz wa salaTa.
I think we'll fix chicken with rice, and salad.

21: la, mish Daruuri. ishtareet dajaaj imbaariH, huwa fi l-barraad.
No, that's not necessary. I bought chicken yesterday. It's in the refrigerator.

23: aywa. wa min faDlik, iʕmali r-ruzz ʕala T-Tariiqa l-ʕarabiyya.
Yes. And please, make the rice the Arab way.

123

VOCABULARY

Haadi Sashar
eleventh

awwal shi
first thing, first of all

ghuraf
rooms

noom
sleep

ghuraf in-noom
bedrooms

ghurfat in-noom
bedroom

Saaloon
living room

ughayyir
I change

sharshaf (sharaashif)
sheet, linen

ghayyarna
we changed

ghayyarnaaha
we changed them

mata
when

ghasiil
laundry, wash

xalli
leave, let, keep

shughul
work

maTbax (maTaabix)
kitchen

nasharna
we hung out (laundry)

yanshaf
it dries (out)

tastaSmili
you (f) use

nashshaafa
dryer

kahrabaa'i
electric

urattib
I arrange, tidy up

tansi
you (f) forget

la tansi
don't forget

tamsaHi
you (f) wipe

ghubaar
dust

masaH il-ghubaar
to dust

San
from, away from;
about

athaath
furniture

amsaH il-ghubaar
I dust

ukannis
I sweep

arD
floor, earth

masaH il-arD
to mop

xallaSt
I finished

allaah yaS Tiiki l-Saafiya
"May God give
you strength."
(said to someone
engaged in or
finishing work)

irtaaHi
relax (f)

taSbaan (-iin)
tired

mustaSidd (-iin)
ready

tabda'i
you (f) begin

SaHn (SuHuun)
dish, plate

kaas (-aat)
cup, glass

Tanjara (Tanaajir)
pan, pot

Siiniyya (Sawaani)
tray

mukaddas
piled up, heaped up

ajli
I wash (dishes)

ajliiha
I wash them
(the dishes)

unashshif
I dry

unashshifha
I dry them

aHuTT
I put

aHuTTha
I put them

xazaana (-aat; xazaa'in)
cupboard, cabinet

tuxallisi
you (f) finish

jali
dishwashing

tusaaSidi
you (f) help

tusaaSidiini
you (f) help me

taHDiir
preparation

Sashaa'
dinner,
evening meal

nuHaDDir
we prepare

ruzz
rice

salaTa
salad

124

Sind
  at the place (of)
	nuqaTTiS
	  we cut
		Tariiqa
		  way, method
			**d-dars
			il-Haadi
			Sashar:
			Hawl il-beet**

Sind abu xaalid
  Abu Khalid's place
	nuqaTTiSu
	  we cut it
		Sala T-Tariiqa l-Sarabiyya
		  the Arab way	

ishtareet
  I bought
	minshaan
	  in order to
		Tabx
		  cooking	

barraad
  refrigerator
	naxluT
	  we mix
		uxalliS
		  I finish	

nashwi
  we roast
	iSmali
	  make (f. imperative)		

SUPPLEMENTARY VOCABULARY

Hammaam (-aat)
  bathroom
	furn (afraan)
	  stove, oven
		naaDHiif
		  clean

maghsala (maghaasil)
  sink
	miknasa
	  broom
		Saabuun
		  soap

baanyo
  tub
	mamsaHa
	  mop (n.)
		xaadima
		  hired woman, maid

unbuub (anaabiib)
  pipe
	Haa'iT (HiiTaan)
	  wall
		Tabax / yaTbux
		  to cook

Hanafiyya
  faucet
	wasix
	  dirty	

I. WORKING WITH WORDS AND PHRASES

A. Matching English with Arabic
Match each English expression in the left-hand column with its Arabic equivalent by writing the appropriate number next to the correct Arabic on the right:

1.	bedrooms	a.	_____	tansi
2.	sheets	b.	_____	tastaSmili
3.	you begin	c.	_____	barraad
4.	you use	d.	_____	allaah yaSTiiki l-Saafiya.
5.	you forget	e.	_____	taHDiir
6.	you dust	f.	_____	iT-Tariiqa l-Sarabiyya
7.	furniture	g.	_____	ghuraf in-noom
8.	"May God give you strength."	h.	_____	taSbaana
9.	kitchen	i.	_____	athaath
10.	rest a bit	j.	_____	sharaashif
11.	preparation	k.	_____	tamsaHi l-ghubaar
12.	I mop the floor	l.	_____	irtaaHi shwayy
13.	refrigerator	m.	_____	amsaH il-arD
14.	the Arab way	n.	_____	tabda'i
15.	tired	o.	_____	maTbax

B. Completion of Arabic Dialogue

In the following dialogue, certain words have been left out. Complete the conversation by filling in the missing words in the twenty-four sentences below:

ARAB says:

1: shu biddik _____ aʕmal
halla'?

3: turiidi _____
ish-sharaashif fi ghuraf in-noom?

5: Tayyib. mata biddik iyyaani
_____ il-ghasiil?

7: idha nasharna l-ghasiil baʕd iDH-
DHuhur ma raH _____ il-yoom.

9: Tayyib, raayiHa _____
ghuraf in-noom.

11: min kull _____. raH
amsaH il-ghubaar baʕdma
_____ wa amsaH il-arD.

AMERICAN says:

2: _____ shi biddi yyaaki
tunaDHDHifi _____
in-noom wa baʕdeen iS-Saaloon.

4: mish Daruuri. ghayyarnaaha
_____.

6: xalli l-ghasiil li-baʕd iDH-DHuhur,
fii _____ kathiir fi l-maTbax.

8: maʕaleesh, taqdari _____
n-nashshaafa l-kahrabaa'iyya.

10: la tansi tamsaHi
_____ ʕan il-athaath.

[fi l-maTbax]

12: xallaSt _____ il-beet.

14: wallaah mish _____.
ana mustaʕidda.

16: raH _____ wa baʕdeen
raH unashshifha wa aHuTtha fi
_____.

18: _____ ya madaam. shu
raH nuHaDDir il-yoom?

20: biddik iyyaani aruuH
_____ dajaaj min ʕind
abu xaalid?

22: yaʕni laazim _____
d-dajaaj wa nuqaTTiʕu minshaan
naxluTu maʕ ir-ruzz?

24: akiid. raH abda' bi-T-Tabx lamma
_____ il-jali.

13: xalaS? allaah yaʕTiiki l-_____.
irtaaHi shwayy qabl _____
il-maTbax.

15: idhan taqdari _____.
iS-SuHuun wa l-kaasaat wa T-
Tanaajir wa S-Sawaani mukaddasa
baʕd _____ imbaariH.

17: lamma tuxalliSi _____
mumkin tusaaʕidiini fi taHDiir
_____?

19: ana mufakkira nuHaDDir dajaaj
maʕ _____ wa salaTa.

21: la, mish Daruuri. ishtareet dajaaj
imbaariH, huwa fi
_____.

23: aywa. wa min faDlik,
_____ r-ruzz ʕala
T-Tariiqa l-ʕarabiyya.

II. WORKING WITH SENTENCES

A. Matching Spoken Arabic to English (listening)

Listen to Cassette 6 (side 2) or to your teacher, and then match what is said in Arabic with the appropriate English sentence among the nine below.

_____ I'm really not tired; I'm ready.

_____ Please make the rice the Arab way.

_____ Okay. I'm going to take care of the bedrooms.

_____ What would you like me to do now?

_____ Do you want me to change the sheets?

_____ Don't forget to dust.

_____ I finished cleaning the house.

_____ Could you help me prepare dinner when you're done with the dishes?

B. Scrambled Arabic Dialogue

Reconstruct the two-part Arabic dialogue below by numbering all twenty-four sentences so they are in a meaningful sequence.

_____ akiid. raH abda' bi-T-Tabx lamma uxalliS il-jali.

_____ wallaah mish taʕbaana. ana mustaʕidda.

_____ awwal shi biddi yyaaki tunaDHDHifi ghuraf in-noom wa baʕdeen iS-Saaloon.

_____ Tayyib, raayiHa urattib ghuraf in-noom.

_____ mish Daruuri. ghayyarnaaha imbaariH.

_____ xallaSt tanDHiif il-beet.

_____ xalli l-ghasiil li-baʕd iDH-DHuhur, fii shughul kathiir fi l-maTbax.

_____ ana mufakkira nuHaDDir dajaaj maʕ ruzz wa salaTa.

_____ maʕaleesh, taqdari tastaʕmili n-nashshaafa l-kahrabaa'iyya.

_____ turiidi ughayyir ish-sharaashif fi ghuraf in-noom?

_____ la tansi tamsaHi l-ghubaar ʕan il-athaath.

_____ la, mish Daruuri. ishtareet dajaaj imbaariH, huwa fi l-barraad.

_____ lamma tuxalliSi l-jali mumkin tusaaʕidiini fi taHDiir il-ʕashaa'?

_____ aywa. wa min faDlik, iʕmali r-ruzz ʕala T-Tariiqa l-ʕarabiyya.

---

fi l-maTbax

_____ Tayyib. mata biddik iyyaani aghsil il-ghasiil?

_____ xalaS? allaah yaʕTiiki l-ʕaafiya. irtaaHi shwayy qabl shughul il-maTbax.

_____ shu biddik iyyaani aʕmal halla'?

_____ idhan taqdari tabda'i. iS-SuHuun wa l-kaasaat wa T-Tanaajir mukaddasa baʕd Haflat imbaariH.

_____ Tabʕan ya madaam. shu raH nuHaDDir il-yoom?

_____ idha nasharna l-ghasiil baʕd iDH-DHuhur maa raH yanshaf il-yoom.

_____ biddik iyyaani aruuH ashtari dajaaj min ʕind abu xaalid?

_____ min kull budd. raH amsaH il-ghubaar baʕdma ukannis wa amsaH il-arD.

_____ raH ajliiha wa baʕdeen raH unashshifha wa aHuTTha fi l-xazaana.

_____ yaʕni laazim nashwi d-dajaaj wa nuqaTTiʕu minshaan naxluTu maʕ ir-ruzz?

127

C. Matching English with Arabic
Match each English sentence with its Arabic counterpart.

1. What do you want me to do?   *a.* fii shughul kathiir.

2. That's not necessary.   *b.* mata biddik iyyaani aghsil il-ghasiil?

3. You can use the dryer.   *c.* xalaSʔ allaah yaʕTiiki l-ʕaafiya.

4. There's a lot of work.   *d.* shu biddik iyyaaani aʕmal?

5. Finished? "May God give you   *e.* raH ajliiha wa unashshifha.
strength."

6. When do you want me to do the   *f.* haadha mish Daruuri.
laundry?

7. I'll wash them, then dry them.   *g.* taqdari tastaʕmili n-nashshaafa.

D. Matching Arabic Lines
Match the seven Arabic remarks on the left with the appropriate responses in the right-hand column.

1. xallaSt tanDHiif il-beet.   *a.* min kull budd.

2. shu biddik iyyaani aʕmal?   *b.* Tabʕan.

3. turiidi ughayyir ish-sharaashif?   *c.* xalaSʔ allaah yaʕtiiki l-ʕaafiya.

4. la tansi tamsaHi l-ghubaar.   *d.* mish Daruuri.

5. irtaaHi shwayy qabl shughul   *e.* akiid, raH abda' bi-T-Tabx lamma
il-maTbax.   uxalliS il-jali.

6. mumkin tusaaʕidiini?   *f.* biddi iyyaaki tunDHDHifi ghuraf
in-noom.

7. iʕmali ir-ruzz ʕala T-Tariiqa   *g.* wallaah mish taʕbaana.
l-ʕarabiyya.

E. Translation
Translate the sentences in Exercise **A** of this section (p. 127) into Arabic.

III. WORKING WITH THE LANGUAGE

A. Verb review

A number of new verbs occur in this lesson. Using the vocabulary list, take all the new verbs and derive the citation forms for each one (third person masculine singular, past tense, and present tense).

How many of these verbs are regular? How many are hollow? How many are defective?

B. Negative imperative

The negative imperative is formed by using the word *la* before the second person verb:

la tansi!	*la tantaDHiru!*
Don't forget (*f*)!	Don't wait (*pl*)!
la taruuH!	*la tarjaʕi!*
Don't go (*m*)!	Don't come back (*f*)!

Drill 1: IMPERATIVE ---> NEGATIVE IMPERATIVE

Change each of these ten imperative sentences to the appropriate negative imperative:

1. *ishtariiha!*	**6.** *iftaHu l-baab!*
2. *imshi!*	**7.** *rattibi l-maTbax!*
3. *aʕTiini l-ʕinwaan!*	**8.** *taʕaal!*
4. *jarrib haadha!*	**9.** *HuTT iT-Tanjara fi l-xazaana!*
5. *liff ʕa-l-yasaar!*	**10.** *jiibuu-li finjaan qahwa!*

C. Verb plus pronoun object (review)

The direct object of a verb, when it is a pronoun, is suffixed to the verb, as follows:

ghayyarnaa-ha	*raH aHuTT-ha fi-l-xazaana*
We changed them.	I'll put them in the cupboard.
raH ajlii-ha	*nuqaTTiʕ-uh*
I'll wash them.	We are cutting it up.

Note: Remember that adding a pronoun suffix lengthens the word and often affects the stress placement:

ghayyarnáa-ha	*shaafát-na*	*HaTTúu-h*
ajlíi-ha	*aʕTíi-ni*	*xallíi-ni*

Drill 2: TRANSFORMATION OF VERB OBJECTS
Change the object of the verb in the following sentences to the appropriate pronoun:

1. *raH unaDHDHif il-beet.*
2. *ishtareet xiyaar imbaariH.*
3. *taqdari tastaʕmili n-nashshaafa.*
4. *xallaSti kull shi?*
5. *biddi iyyaak taghsil is-sayaara.*
6. *ma ʕindi waqt Hatta ashuuf il-mudiir.*
7. *Tayyib, xudh qiTʕa Saghiira.*
8. *jaabat iS-SuHuun.*
9. *raaH yazuur jadduh imbaariH.*

IV. WORKING WITH VARIANTS

A. Translation
Put the following ten sentences into Arabic:

1. Could you tell me what I should do now?
2. Would you please help me clean the kitchen?
3. You're tired. "May God give you strength."
4. It's not necessary for you to cook.
5. Please rest a bit. You worked hard.
6. Could you please wash the windows?
7. Can you prepare lunch for us tomorrow?
8. Who is going to wash the dishes?
9. Can your son come to help me?
10. Don't do that now.

B. Comprehension of Spoken Arabic
Listen to the Arabic sentences on the cassette and determine which among the following English sentences corresponds in meaning to the taped Arabic.

1. _____ I'll dust the bedrooms after I clean the kitchen.
   _____ I'll dust the bedrooms after 1 clean the living room.
   _____ I'll clean the bedrooms after I dust the living room.

2. _____ There's no problem. You can use my home.
   _____ There's no problem. You can use my bedroom.
   _____ There's no problem. You can use my sheets.

3. _____ You must be tired. You can use my home.
   _____ You must be tired. You worked all night.
   _____ You must be hungry. You haven't eaten all day.

4. _____ After you clean the kitchen, I want you to prepare supper.
_____ After you clean the kitchen, I want you to prepare lunch.
_____ After you clean the kitchen, I want you to prepare breakfast.

5. _____ After you roast the chicken, cook the rice the Arab way.
_____ After you roast the meat, cook the rice the Arab way.
_____ After you roast the fish, cook the rice the Arab way.

6. _____ Could you help me dry the laundry?
_____ Could you help me dry the cups?
_____ Could you help me dry the dishes?

7. _____ When do you want me to do the laundry?
_____ When do you want me to dry the clothes?
_____ When do you want me to hang out the wash?

8. _____ Could you sweep the floor in the bedroom?
_____ Could you mop the floor in the bedroom?
_____ Could you clean the floor in the bedroom?

V. WORKING WITH THE SITUATION

Working with household help requires that you be able to specify certain tasks, talk about household chores, and respond to questions or comments. It also involves some knowledge of Arabic society and culture since their expectations of what their jobs entail may be different from yours. Before you role-play this situation with your teacher, check with him or her about attitudes and expectations that you will encounter in the Arab world as an employer of a host-country national. Then work up a list of "key lines" based on what you think you will need to get done in this situation.

In addition to role-playing this particular scenario, or instead of it, work up situations where this type of dialogue may be of use even though you are not employing a host-country national. Typically these could include: giving instructions to a repairman, a furniture mover, or a deliveryman; or explaining something to a landlord; or asking a neighbor for information about something.

الدرس الثاني عشر

الموظف المسؤول

١. الاميركي : مرحبا.

٢. العربـــي : مرحبتين.

٣. الاميركي : انا الموظف المناوب اليوم. اي خدمة؟

٤. العربـــي : نعم من فضلك. ابني طالب في جامعة ولاية مشغان، واليوم وصلتنا مكالمة تلفونية خبرتنا انه مريض كثير وهو في المستشفى وانا لازم اسافر للولايات المتحدة بكرة الصبح حتى اكون معه.

٥. الاميركي : عفواً، ممكن تقول لي المشكلة مرة ثانية؟ انا ما أفهم عربي كثير.

٦. العربـــي : ابني مريض في المستشفى، في مدينة ديترويت ولازم اروح لعنده.

٧. الاميركي : ابنك مريض في المستشفى؟ سلامته. يعني، انت بدك فيزا، مش هيك؟

٨. العربـــي : ايوه، من فضلك لان لازم اسافر بكره.

٩. الاميركي : مع الاسف، السفارة مسكرة اليوم. لازم ترجع بكره الصبح.

١٠. العربـــي : لكن طائرتي رح تترك الساعة عشرة الصبح وانا لازم اكون في المطار الساعة تسعة.

١١. الاميركي : متأسف، القنصل مش هنا. وانا ما اقدر اعطيك فيزا.

١٢. العربـــي : ارجوك يا اخ، ابني في خطر، لازم اروح لعنده بسرعة. هذي حالة طارئة مش ممكن اتأخر يوم ثاني.

١٣. الاميركي : معك تذكرة سفر بالطائرة؟

١٤. العربـــي : ايوه، تفضل شوف، عندي حجز في طائرة بكرة.

١٥. الاميركي : ممكن اشوف جواز سفرك؟

١٦. العربـــي : نعم تفضل، هذا هو.

١٧. الاميركي : دقيقة من فضلك، لازم اتلفن للقنصل انتظر هنا.

١٨. العربـــي : شكراً. الله يخليك.

LESSON TWELVE: The Duty Officer

id-dars ith-thaani ʕashar: il-muwaDHDHaf il-munaawib

This situation again is adapted from Foreign Service life, yet it represents a broader category of interaction since it concerns an emergency which requires dealing with someone in Arabic despite a very limited knowledge of the language. In such a situation, certain conversation strategies need to be used, such as asking for repetition and then re-phrasing what you think you have understood so that the Arabic speaker can confirm that you have indeed gotten the gist of his or her message.

Sample Dialogue:

AMERICAN says:	ARAB says:
1: *marHaba.* Hello.	**2:** *marHabteen.* Hello.
3: *ana l-muwaDHDHaf il-munaawib il-yoom. ayy xidma?* I'm the duty officer today. May I assist you?	**4:** *naʕam min faDlak. ibni Taalib fi jaamiʕat wilaayat "Michigan," wa l-yoom waSalatna mukaalama talifooniyya xabbaratna innu mariiD kathiir wa huwa fi l-mustashfa, wa ana laazim usaafir li-l-wilaayaat il-muttaHida bukra S-SubuH Hatta akuun maʕu.* Yes, please. My son is a student at Michigan State University, and today we got a phone call informing us that he's very sick and in the hospital, and I have to travel to the U.S. tomorrow morning to be with him!
5: *ʕafwan, mumkin taquul lii l-mushkila marra thaaniya? ana ma afham ʕarabi kathiir.* Excuse me, could you tell me the problem again? I don't understand much Arabic.	**6:** *ibni mariiD fi l-mustashfa fi madiinat "Detroit," wa laazim aruuH li-ʕindu.* My son is sick in the hospital in Detroit and I have to go to him.
7: *ibnak mariiD fi l-mustashfa? salaamtu. yaʕni inta biddak viiza, mish heek?* Your son is sick in the hospital? I hope he gets well. So, you want a visa, right?	**8:** *aywa, min faDlak, li'ann laazim usaafir bukra.* Yes, please, because I have to leave tomorrow.

133

AMERICAN says:

9: maʕ il-asaf, is-safaara musakkira l-yoom, laazim tarjaʕ bukra S-SubuH.
Unfortunately, the Embassy is closed today. You have to come back tomorrow.

11: muta'assif, il-qunsul mish huna. wa ana ma aqdar aʕTiik viiza.
I'm, sorry. The Consul isn't here, and I can't give you a visa.

13: maʕak tadhkarat safar bi-T-Taa'ira?
Do you have a plane ticket?

15: mumkin ashuuf jawaaz safarak?
May I see your passport?

17: Daqiiqa min faDlak, laazim utalfin li-l-qunSul. intaDHir huna.
One moment, please. I have to phone the Consul. Wait here.

ARAB says:

10: laakin Taa'irati raH tatruk is-saaʕa ʕashara S-SubuH wa ana laazim akuun fi l-maTaar is-saaʕa tisʕa!
But my plane leaves at 10:00 a.m. and I have to be at the airport at 9:00!

12: arjuuk ya ax, ibni fi xaTar, laazim aruuH li-ʕindu bi-surʕa. haadhi Haala Taari'a, mish mumkin ata'axxar yoom thaani!
I beg of you, sir (brother), my son is in danger. I have to go quickly! This is an emergency. I can't delay another day.

14: aywa, tafaDDal—shuuf! ʕindi Hajz fi Taa'irat bukra.
Yes. Here, see, I have a reservation for tomorrow.

16: naʕam, tafaDDal, haadha huwa.
Yes, here it is.

18: :shukran. allaah yuxalliik.
Thank you. May God preserve you.

VOCABULARY

thaani ʕashar
twelfth

munaawib (-iin)
on duty, detailed

Taalib (Tullaab)
student

jaamiʕa (-aat)
university

waSalat
it (f) arrived, reached

waSalatna
it reached us,
we received

mukaalama
conversation, talk

mukaalama talifooniyya
phone call

xabbarat
it (f) informed

inn
that

innu
that he

mustashfa (-ayaat)
hospital

usaafir
I travel

wilaaya (-aat)
state, province

taquul lii
you say to me

marra (-aat)
time, instance

li-ʕindu
to the place
where he is

viiza / fiiza (-aat, viyaz)
visa

mish heek?
not so?, right?

musakkir
closed

Taa'ira (-aat)
airplane

tatruk
it (f) leaves

maTaar (-aat)
airport

muta'assif (-iin)
sorry

qunSul (qanaaSil)
consul

ma aqdar
I can't

arjuuk
I beg you

xaTar
danger

bi-surʕa
quickly, fast

Haala (-aat)
state, condition

Haala Taari'a
emergency

ata'axxar
I delay, am late

tadhkara (tadhaakir)
ticket

Hajz
reservation

jawaaz safar
passport

utalfin
I telephone

allaah yuxalliik
"May God keep you"

**id-dars
ith-thaani
ʕashar:
il-muwaDHDHaf
il-munaawib**

135

I. WORKING WITH WORDS AND PHRASES

A. Matching English with Arabic

Match each of the fifteen English expressions with its Arabic equivalent. Then mark the appropriate number for the English next to its lettered Arabic counterpart:

1.	on duty	a. _____	maTaar
2.	student	b. _____	musakkira
3.	university	c. _____	jaamiʕa
4.	phone call	d. _____	Haala Taari'a
5.	hospital	e. _____	tadhkara
6.	I travel	f. _____	munaawib
7.	closed	g. _____	Hajz
8.	ticket	h. _____	mukaalama talifooniyya
9.	airport	i. _____	muta'assif
10.	sorry	j. _____	Taalib
11.	I beg you	k. _____	mustashfa
12.	danger	l. _____	jawaaz safar
13.	emergency	m. _____	xaTar
14.	reservation	n. _____	usaafir
15.	passport	o. _____	arjuuk

B. Completion of Arabic Dialogue

In the following Arabic dialogue, certain words have been left out. Complete each of the eighteen sentences by filling in the missing words.

id-dars
ith-thaani
ʕashar:
il-muwaDHDHaf
il-munaawib

AMERICAN says:

1: marHaba.

3: ana l-muwaDHDHaf
_____ il-yoom.
ayy xidma?

5: ʕafwan, mumkin _____ lii
l-mushkila marra thaaniya? ana ma
_____ ʕarabi kathiir.

7: ibnak mariiD fi l-mustashfa?
_____. yaʕni inta biddak
viiza, mish heek?

9: maʕ il-asaf, is-safaara
_____ l-yoom, laazim
tarjaʕ bukra S-SubuH.

11: _____, il-qunSul mish
huna. wa ana ma aqdar
_____ viiza.

13: maʕak _____ safar
bi-T-Taa'ira?

15: mumkin ashuuf _____
safarak?

17: daqiiqa min faDlak, laazim _____
li-l-qunSul. intaDHir huna.

ARAB says:

2: _____.

4: naʕam min _____. ibni
Taalib fi jaamiʕat wilaayat "Michigan," wa l-yoom waSalatna
_____ talifooniyya
xabbaratna innu mariiD kathiir wa
huwa fi _____ , wa
ana laazim usaafir li-l-wilaayaat
il-muttaHida bukra S-SubuH Hatta
akuun maʕu.

6: ibni _____ fi l-mustashfa fi
madiinat "Detroit," wa laazim aruuH
li-_____.

8: aywa, min faDlak, li'ann laazim
_____ bukra.

10: laakin Taa'irati raH _____
is-saaʕa ʕashara S-SubuH wa ana
laazim akuun fi l-maTaar is-saaʕa
tisʕa!

12: arjuuk ya ax, ibni fi xaTar, laazim
aruuH li-ʕindu bi-surʕa. haadhi
Haala _____, mish
mumkin ata'axxar yoom thaani!

14: aywa. tafaDDal, shuuf, ʕindi
_____ li-Taa'irat bukra.

16: naʕam _____, haadha
huwa.

18: shukran. _____ yuxalliik.

137

II. WORKING WITH SENTENCES

A. Matching Spoken Arabic with English (listening)

Listen to Cassette 6 (side 2) or to your teacher, and match what is said in Arabic with the appropriate English sentence among the eight below:

_____ I'm the duty officer today. Can I help you?

_____ Excuse me, could you tell me the problem again?

_____ My son is sick in the hospital. I have to go to him.

_____ Sorry, the Consul is not here, and I can't give you a visa.

_____ My son is in danger. I must get to him quickly.

_____ One minute, please. I have to call the Consul. Wait here.

_____ Do you have your passport?

_____ Sorry, the Embassy is closed today. You'll have to return tomorrow morning.

B. Scrambled Arabic Dialogue

Reconstruct the dialogue by numbering the eighteen Arabic sentences below so they are in a meaningful sequence.

_____ aywa, tafaDDal, shuuf, ʕindi Hajz li-Taaʕirat bukra.

_____ laakin Taaʼirati raH tatruk is-saaʕa ʕashara S-SubuH wa ana laazim akuun fi l-maTaar is-saaʕa tisʕa!

_____ naʕam min faDlak, ibni Taalib fi jaamiʕat wilaayat "Michigan," wa l-yoom waSalatna mukaalama talifooniyya xabbaratna innu mariiD kathiir wa huwa fi l-mustashfa, wa ana laazim usaafir li-l-wilaayaat il-muttaHida bukra S-SubuH Hatta akuun maʕu.

_____ naʕam tafaDDal, haadha huwa.

_____ arjuuk ya ax, ibni fi xaTar, laazim aruuH li-ʕindu bi-surʕa. haadhi Haala Taariʼa, mish mumkin ataʼaxxar yoom thaani!

_____ ibnak mariiD fi l-mustashfa? salaamtu. yaʕni inta biddak viiza, mish heek?

_____ marHabateen.

_____ maʕ il-asaf, is-safaara musakkira l-yoom, laazim tarjaʕ bukra S-SubuH.

_____ shukran. allaah yuxalliik.

_____ mutaʼassif, il-qunSul mish huna. wa ana ma aqdar aʕTiik viiza.

_____ ʕafwan, mumkin taquul lii l-mushkila marra thaaniya? ana ma afham ʕarabi kathiir.

_____ maʕak tadhkarat safar bi-T-Taaʼira?

_____ marHaba.

_____ mumkin ashuuf jawaaz safarak?

_____ aywa, min faDlak, liʼann laazim usaafir bukra.

_____ daqiiqa min faDlak, laazim utalfin li-l-qunSul. intaDHir huna.

_____ ibni mariiD fi l-mustashfa fi madiinat "Detroit," wa laazim aruuH li-ʕindu.

_____ ana l-muwaDHDHaf il-munaawib il-yoom. ayy xidma?

138

C. Matching English with Arabic

Match each of the eight English sentences with its correct Arabic counterpart in the right-hand column:

id-dars
ith-thaani
ʕashar:
il-muwaDHDHaf
il-munaawib

1. Wait a minute.

2. See, I have a reservation.

3. Sorry, the embassy is closed.

4. Your son is in the hospital?

5. I must travel tomorrow.

6. May I see your passport?

7. I'm the duty officer.

8. I'm sorry, the consul isn't here.

a. maʕ il-asaf is-safaara musakkira.

b. laazim usaafir bukra.

c. shuuf, ʕindi Hajz.

d. ana l-muwaDHDHaf il-munaawib.

e. daqiiqa min faDlak.

f. muta'assif. il-qunSul mish huna.

g. ibnak fi l-mustashfa?

h. mumkin ashuuf jawaaz safarak?

D. Matching Arabic Lines

Match the Arabic sentences on the left with the appropriate Arabic responses on the right.

1. ibnak mariiD fi l-mustashfa?

2. maʕ il-asaf is-safaara musakkira.

3. maʕak tadhkarat safar bi-T-Taa'ira?

4. intaDHir huna. laazim utalfin li-l-qunSul.

5. mumkin ashuuf jawaaz safarak?

6. muta'assif. il-qunsul mish huna.

7. marra thaaniya, ana maa afham ʕarabi kathiir.

a. aywa, shuuf-ʕindi Hajz.

b. aywa, min faDlak, laazim usaafir bukra.

c. shukran, allaah yuxalliik.

d. laakin Taa'irati raH tatruk is-saaʕa ʕashara.

e. arjuuk yaa ax, ibni fi xaTar.

f. ibni mariiD wa laazim aruuH ashuufu.

g. naʕam, tafaDDal, haadha huwa.

E. Translation into Arabic

Translate the eight English sentences in Exercise **A** of this lesson (facing page) into Arabic.

III. WORKING WITH THE LANGUAGE

A. Verb review

Make a list of all the new verbs that have occurred so far in this lesson and derive the citation forms for each one.

B. Future tense review

The future tense is made by placing the word *raH* before the present tense verb. The future of "to be" requires the use of the present tense of *kaan*.

Drill 1: COMPLETION OF FUTURE TENSE VERBS
Complete the following sentences with *raH* plus an appropriate verb.

1. _____ fi-l-maktab bukra.
2. taʕrif mata _____ ila r-riyaaD?
3. _____ maʕna li-l-Hafla?
4. huwa ma _____ il-yoom.
5. _____ il-maTaar bukra S-SubuH.

Drill 2: TRANSLATION INTO ARABIC
Translate the following ten sentences into Arabic.

1. I'm going to work at home today.
2. Are you (*f*) going to be there?
3. Will you (*pl*) come see us when you return?
4. I won't forget what you (*m*) told me.
5. They will finish in half an hour.
6. We will prepare the food quickly.
7. When will they begin?
8. He will know who you are.
9. Are you (*pl*) going to visit your son?
10. He will come soon.

C. Present tense verbs: Review

Drill 3: CONJUGATION OF VERBS IN ALL PERSONS
Conjugate the verbs in the following sentences in all persons:

1. laazim usaafir il-yoom.
2. mish mumkin ata'axxar.
3. ma aqdar aʕTiiha viiza.
4. laazim utalfin li-l-qunSul.
5. laazim akuun fi-l-maTaar is-saaʕa tisʕa.
6. mumkin ashuuf jawaaz is-safar?
7. ma afham ʕarabi kathiir.

IV. WORKING WITH VARIANTS

A. Translation into Arabic
Convert the following eight sentences into Arabic:
1. Who is in charge here?
2. She is very sick, and has to go to the hospital.
3. Please come back the day after tomorrow. The Embassy is closed today.
4. Please, we are in danger! Can you help us?
5. Did you buy a plane ticket to travel to the U.S.?
6. Please wait here. I have to see what the military attaché wants to do.
7. Why do you have to get your visa today? Can't you wait till tomorrow?
8. Can't you make a telephone call to the hospital in the U.S.?

B. Comprehension of Spoken Arabic
Listen to the Arabic sentences on the cassette and determine which among the seven triplets of English corresponds in meaning with the spoken Arabic.

1. _____ My daughter is sick in the hospital in the U.S.
   _____ My son is sick in the hospital in the U.S.
   _____ My cousin is sick in the hospital in the U.S.

2. _____ The consul is not here and I can't give you a visa.
   _____ The consul is not here, but I will give you a visa.
   _____ The consul is here, but he can't give you a visa.

3. _____ What time does your plane leave tomorrow?
   _____ What time do you want to leave tomorrow?
   _____ What time do you want to arrive in the U.S.?

4. _____ The Embassy is closed today. Come back tomorrow.
   _____ The Embassy is closed today. Come in the afternoon.
   _____ The Embassy is closed today. Come tomorrow afternoon.

5. _____ Where are your passport and airplane ticket?
   _____ Do you have your passport and airplane ticket?
   _____ Did you bring your passport and airplane ticket?

6. _____ This is an emergency. Please give me a visa.
   _____ This is an emergency. I need a visa.
   _____ This is an emergency. I want a visa today.

7. _____ Excuse me, could you tell me the problem again?
   I don't know Arabic.
   _____ Excuse me, could you tell me the problem again?
   I don't know English.
   _____ Excuse me, could you tell me the problem again?
   I don't speak Arabic.

V. WORKING WITH THE SITUATION

In this situation the American is on duty alone when approached by a local citizen with an urgent request. The Arab knows no English, so the duty officer has to use his or her limited knowledge of Arabic to deal with the situation and resolve it—at least temporarily.

The "key lines" here are of three types: those that get the Arab to slow down, repeat, or verify what was said ("I don't understand much Arabic"); those that state some basic information ("I'm sorry, the embassy is closed today."); and those that elicit some basic information ("May I see your passport?").

This kind of situation (dealing with requests) could occur under many different circumstances, and with your limited Arabic, you should have a standard set of "key lines" ready for use in almost any situation where someone needs you to do something.

Key lines that help you control the level, speed, and complexity of the conversation have a specific name. They are called "conversation managment devices" (CMD's), and you should have a repertoire of these ready to use when confronted with language that is above your head (e.g., "I only speak a little Arabic," "I'm sorry, I don't understand," "Would you repeat what you said?" etc.)

With your teacher, prepare a list of "key lines" for this type of situation, and a special list of CMD's for general use. Then role-play this situation with your teacher.

142

LESSON THIRTEEN: Weather and Leisure Time

id-dars ith-thaalith Sashar:
San iT-Taqs wa waqt il-faraagh

Sample Dialogue:

ARAB says:

1: ana musaafir ila l-wilaayaat il-muttaHida Hatta adrus fi jaamiSat "Georgetown" fi waashinTun, wa aHibb as'alak kam su'aal, idha mumkin.

I'm going to the U.S. to study at Georgetown University in Washington, and I'd like to ask you a few questions, if I may?

3: quul lii, kiif iT-Taqs fi l-wilaayaat il-muttaHida?

Tell me, how's the weather in the U.S.?

5: kiif iT-Taqs fi waashinTun il-SaaSima?

How's the weather in Washington, the capital?

7: qaddeesh tanzil darajat il-Haraara fi sh-shitaa'?

How low does the temperature drop in winter

9: mata mawsim il-maTar fi madiinat waashinTun?

When is the rainy season in the city of Washington?

11: halla Saar Sindi fikra waaDiHa San Taqs waashinTun. mumkin as'alak kiif yaSrif ish-shaSb il-ameerki waqt faraaghu?

Now I have a clear idea about Washington's weather. Could I ask you how American people spend their spare time?

AMERICAN says:

2: tafaDDal, bi-kull suruur.

Please, go right ahead.

4: il-wilaayaat il-muttaHida bilaad kabiira wa T-Taqs fiiha yaxtalif min makaan ila aaxar.

The United States is a big country and the weather there differs from one place to another.

6: fi faSl iS-Seef iT-Taqs Haarr wa raTib bi-Suura Saamma, taqriiban mithil bayruut. laakin fi sh-shitaa' iT-Taqs baarid jiddan mithil jibaal lubnaan.

In the summer season the weather is generally hot and humid, about like Beirut. But in winter the weather is very cold, like the mountains of Lebanon.

8: fi baSD il-awqaat il-Haraara tanzil taHt iS-Sifir mi'awiyya li-waqt Tawiil.

Sometimes the temperature drops below zero centigrade for a long time.

10: fi l-Haqiiqa il-maTar yanzil fi kull fuSuul is-sana, xaaSSatan fi faSl ir-rabiiS.

Actually, rain falls in every season of the year, especially in spring.

12: akthar in-naas fi l-wilaayaat il-muttaHida Saadatan mashghuuliin jiddan min yoom il-ithneen li-yoom il-jumSa wa yaHibbu yastariiHu baSd dhaalik. li haadha s-sabab yaSrifu aHyaanan is-sabt aw il-aHad xaarij buyuuthum fi r-riHlaat wa n-nuzhaat.

Most people in the U.S. are usually very busy from Monday to Friday and they like to relax after that. For this reason, sometimes they spend Saturday or Sunday outside their homes, on trips or excursions.

الدرس الثالث عشر

عن الطقس ووقت الفراغ

١. العربـــي : انا مسافر للولايات المتحدة حتى ادرس في جامعة جورج تاون في واشنطن ، واحب اسألك كم سؤال اذا ممكن .

٢. الاميركي : تفضل ، بكل سرور .

٣. العربـــي : قول لي ، كيف الطقس في الولايات المتحدة ؟

٤. الاميركي : الولايات المتحدة بلاد كبيرة والطقس فيها يختلف من مكان إلى آخر .

٥. العربـــي : كيف الطقس في واشنطن العاصمة ؟

٦. الاميركي : في فصل الصيف الطقس حار ورطب بصورة عامة ، تقريبا مثل بيروت، لكن في الشتاء الطقس بارد جدا مثل جبال لبنان .

٧. العربـــي : قديش تنزل درجة الحرارة في الشتاء ؟

٨. الاميركي : في بعض الأوقات الحرارة تنزل تحت الصفر مئوية لوقت طويل .

٩. العربـــي : متى موسم المطر في مدينة واشنطن ؟

١٠. الاميركي : في الحقيقة المطر ينزل في كل فصول السنة ، خاصة في فصل الربيع.

١١. العربـــي : هلا صار عندي فكرة واضحة عن طقس واشنطن . ممكن اسألك كيف يصرف الشعب الاميركي وقت فراغه ؟

١٢. الاميركي : اكثر الناس في الولايات المتحدة عادة مشغولين جدا من يوم الاثنين ليوم الجمعة . ويحبوا يستريحوا بعد ذلك . لهذا السبب يصرفوا احيانا السبت والاحد خارج بيوتهم في الرحلات والنزهات .

١٣. العربـــي : شو هي الاماكن اللي يفضلوا يروحوا الها؟

١٤. الاميركي : بعضهم يروحوا الى الشاطئ والبعض الى الجبل وبعض اللي يبقوا في المدينة يتفرجوا على الالعاب الرياضية وافلام السينما ويأكلوا في المطاعم ويزوروا المتاحف .

ARAB says:

AMERICAN says:

**id-dars
ith-thaalith
ʕashar:
ʕan iT-Taqs
wa waqt
il-faraagh**

13: shu hiya il-amaakin illi yufaDDilu
yaruuHu ilha?
What places do they like to go to?

14: baʕDhum yaruuHu ila sh-shaaTi' wa
l-baʕD ila l-jibaal wa baʕD illi yabqu
fi l-madiina yatafarraju ʕala l-alʕaab
ir-riyaaDiyya wa aflaam is-siinama
wa yaakulu fi l-maTaaʕim wa
yazuuru il-mataaHif.
Some go to the shore and some to
the mountains. Others who stay in
the city watch sports or movies,
eat in restaurants, and visit museums.

15: shu hiya l-alʕaab ir-riyaaDiyya
il-mufaDDala fi ameerka?
What are the favorite sports in
America?

16: ashhar il-alʕaab hiya il-fuTbool
il-ameerki wa l-beesbool wa t-tanis
wa kurat is-salla.
The most popular sports are American football, baseball, tennis, and
basketball.

17: shukran jaziilan ʕala haadhi
l-maʕluumaat il-mufiida.
Thanks a lot for the helpful
information.

18: ʕafwan. muwaffaq, in shaa' allaah.
You're welcome. I wish you luck.

١٥.   العربـــي : شو هي الألعاب الرياضية المفضلة في أميركا ؟

١٦.   الاميركي : أشهر الألعاب هي الفطبول الاميركي والبيسبول والتنس وكرة السلة .

١٧.   العربـــي : شكراً جزيلاً على هذي المعلومات المفيدة .

١٨.   الاميركي : عفواً . موفق إن شاء الله.

VOCABULARY

thaalith ʕashar
thirteenth

Taqs
weather

waqt (awqaat)
time

faraagh
empty space, void

waqt faraagh
spare time, leisure

musaafir (-iin)
going, traveling

adrus
I study

su'aal (as'ila)
question

suruur
pleasure, happiness

bi-kull suruur
with pleasure

quul (imperative)
tell, say

bilaad (buldaan)
country

yaxtalif
it (*m*) differs

makaan (amaakin)
place

aaxar (-iin)
other, another

ʕaaSima (ʕawaaSim)
capital

faSl (fuSuul)
season

Seef
summer

Haarr
hot

raTib
humid

bi-Suura ʕaamma
in general, generally

taqriiban
approximately

mithil
like, as

shitaa'
winter

jiddan
very

jabal (jibaal)
mountain

tanzil
it (*f*) falls, drops

daraja (-aat)
degree

Haraara
heat

darajat il-Haraara
temperature

baʕD
some, some of

fi baʕD il-awqaat
sometimes

taHt
under

Sifir
zero

mi'awiyya
centigrade

Tawiil (Tiwaal)
long; tall

mawsim (mawaasim)
season

maTar
rain

madiina (mudun)
city

Haqiiqa
fact, truth

fi l-Haqiiqa
in fact, actually

xaaSSatan
especially

rabiiʕ
spring

Saar ʕindi
I got, I acquired

fikra
idea

waadiH
clear

yaSrif
he spends

shaʕb (shuʕuub)
people
(nationals of a
country or region)

akthar
more; most

naas
people (in general)

ʕaadatan
usually

mashghuul (-iin)
busy

il-ithneen
Monday

il-jumʕa
Friday

yastariiHu
they rest

dhaalik
that

baʕd dhaalik
after that

sabab (asbaab)
reason

aHyaanan
sometimes

is-sabt
Saturday

il-aHad
Sunday

xaarij
outside

riHla (-aat) trip	*film (aflaam)* film, movie	*beesbool* baseball	***id-dars*** ***ith-thaalith*** ***ʕashar:*** ***ʕan iT-Taqs*** ***wa waqt*** ***il-faraagh***
nuzha (-aat) outing, excursion	*siinama* movie house	*tanis* tennis	
yufaDDilu they prefer	*yazuuru* they visit	*kura (-aat)* ball	
shaaTi' shore, beach	*matHaf (mataaHif)* museum	*salla (-aat, silaal)* basket	
yabqu they stay, remain	*yaakulu* they eat	*shukran jaziilan* thanks a lot	
yatafarraju (ʕala) they watch	*mufaDDal* favorite	*maʕluumaat* information	
luʕba (alʕaab) game	*ashhar* popular; most famous	*mufiid* useful, beneficial	
riyaaDiyya athletic (adj.)	*futbool* football, soccer	*muwaffaq* good luck	
alʕaab riyaaDiyya sports			

SUPPLEMENTARY VOCABULARY

il-xariif autumn	*Hilu (Hilwiin)* nice, pretty	*jaww* air, atmosphere
muʕtadil moderate	*shams* sun	*ith-thalaatha* Tuesday
daafi warm	*DHill* shade	*il-arbaʕa* Wednesday
thalj snow; ice	*gheem (ghuyuum)* clouds	*il-xamiis* Thursday
ʕaaSifa (ʕawaaSif) storm		

I. WORKING WITH WORDS AND PHRASES

A. Matching English with Arabic

Match each of the fifteen English expressions with its Arabic equivalent by writing the appropriate numbers to the left of the Arabic:

1.	with pleasure	a. _____	darajat il-Haraara
2.	weather	b. _____	jibaal
3.	free time	c. _____	maՏluumaat
4.	temperature	d. _____	yaxtalif
5.	winter	e. _____	bi-kull suruur
6.	games	f. _____	yastariiHu
7.	information	g. _____	waqt faraagh
8.	mountains	h. _____	mawsim ish-shitaa'
9.	good luck	i. _____	alՏaab
10.	museums	j. _____	il-jumՏa
11.	differs	k. _____	mataaHif
12.	rainy season	l. _____	mi'awiyya
13.	centigrade	m. _____	shitaa'
14.	they rest	n. _____	Taqs
15.	Friday	o. _____	muwaffaq

B. Completion of Arabic Dialogue

In the following dialogue, certain Arabic words have been left out. Complete the conversation by filling in the missing words in each of the eighteen sentences:

id-dars
ith-thaalith
ʕashar:
ʕan iT-Taqs
wa waqt
il-faraagh

ARAB says:

AMERICAN says:

1: ana _____ ila il-wilaayaat il-muttaHida Hatta adrus fi jaamiʕat 'Georgetown' fi waashinTun, wa _____ as'alak kam su'aal idha mumkin.

2: tafaDDal, bi-kull _____.

3: quul lii; kiif _____ fi l-wilaayaat il-muttaHida?

4: il-wilaayaat il-muttaHida _____ kabiira wa T-Taqs fiiha yaxtalif min _____ ila aaxar.

5: kiif iT-Taqs fi waashinTun _____?

6: fi _____ iS-Seef iT-Taqs Haarr wa _____ bi-Suura ʕaamma, taqriiban mithil bayruut. laakin fi sh-shitaa' iT-Taqs _____ jiddan mithil jibaal lubnaan.

7: qaddeesh tanzil _____ il-Haraara fi sh-shitaa'?

8: fi baʕD il-awqaat il-Haraara tanzil taHt _____ mi'awiyya li-waqt Tawiil.

9: mata _____ il-maTar fi madiinat waashinTun?

10: fi l-Haqiiqa _____ yanzil fi kull fuSuul _____, xaaSSatan fi faSl ir-rabiiʕ.

11: halla Saar ʕindi _____ waadiHa ʕan Taqs waashinTun. mumkin as'alak kiif yaSrif _____ il-ameerki waqt faraaghu?

12: akthar _____ fi l-wilaayaat il-muttaHida ʕaadatan mashghuuliin jiddan min yoom _____ li-yoom il-jumʕa wa yaHibbu yastariiHu baʕd dhaalik. li haadha _____, yaSrifu aHyaanan is-sabt aw il-aHad xaarij buyuuthum fi r-riHlaat wa n-nuzhaat.

13: shu hiya _____ illi yufaDDilu yaruuHu ilha?

14: baʕDhum yaruuHu ila _____ wa l-baʕD ila l-jabal wa baʕD illi yabqu fi l-madiina yatafarraju ʕala _____ ir-riyaaDiyya wa _____ is-siinama wa yaakulu fi l-maTaaʕim wa yazuuru il-mataaHif.

15: shu hiya l-alʕaab ir-riyaaDiyya _____ fi ameerka?

16: ashhar il-alʕaab hiya il-futbool il-ameerki wa l-beesbool wa t-tanis wa _____ is-salla.

17: sukran jaziilan ʕala haadhi _____ il-mufiida.

18: ʕafwan. _____ in shaa' allaah.

149

II. WORKING WITH SENTENCES

A. Matching Spoken Arabic with Written English (listening)

Listen to Cassette 7 (side 1) or to your teacher, and match what is said in Arabic with these eight English sentences.

_____ Now I have a clear idea about the weather in Washington.

_____ What are the places they prefer to go to?

_____ The United States is a big country and the weather there differs from place to place.

_____ In summer the weather is hot and humid.

_____ Some of them go to the beach, and some go to the mountains.

_____ When is the rainy season in Washington?

_____ But sometimes they spend Saturday or Sunday outside their homes.

_____ Some of those who stay in the city eat in restaurants and visit museums.

B. Scrambled Arabic Dialogue

Reconstruct the dialogue by numbering the following lines so the eighteen statements and questions are in meaningful sequence.

_____ fi faSl iS-Seef iT-Taqs Haarr wa raTib bi-Suura Saamma, taqriiban mithil bayruut. laakin fi sh-shitaa' iT-Taqs baarid jiddan mithil jibaal lubnaan.

_____ Safwan. muwaffaq, in shaa' allaah.

_____ il-wilaayaat il-muttaHida bilaad kabiira wa T-Taqs fiiha yaxtalif min makaan ila aaxar.

_____ ana musaafir ila il-wilaayaat il-muttaHida Hatta adrus fi jaamiSat 'Georgetown' fi waashinTun, wa aHibb as'alak kam su'aal, idha mumkin.

_____ shu hiya il-amaakin illi yufaDDilu yaruuHu ilha?

_____ qaddeesh tanzil darajat il-Haraara fi sh-shitaa'?

_____ mata mawsim il-maTar fi madiinat waashinTun?

_____ shukran jaziilan Sala haadhi l-maSluumaat il-mufiida.

_____ tafaDDal, bi-kull suruur.

_____ fi l-Haqiiqa il-maTar yanzil fi kull fuSuul is-sana, xaaSSatan fi faSl ir-rabiiS.

_____ shu hiya, l-alSaab ir-riyaaDiyya il-mufaDDala fi ameerka?

_____ fi baSD il-awqaat il-Haraara tanzil taHt iS-Sifir mi'awiyya li-waqt Tawiil.

_____ quul lii, kiif iT-Taqs fi l-wilaayaat il-muttaHida?

_____ akthar in-naas fi l-wilaayaat il-muttaHida Saadatan mashghuuliin jiddan min yoom il-ithneen li-yoom il-jumSa wa yaHibbu yastariiHu baSd dhaalik. li haadha s-sabab, yaSrifu aHyaanan is-sabt aw il-aHad xaarij buyuuthum fi r-riHlaat wa n-nuzhaat.

_____ kiif iT-Taqs fi waashinTun il-SaaSima?

_____ baSDhum yaruuHu ila sh-shaaTi' wa l-baSD ila l-jabal wa baSD illi yabqu fi l-madiina yatafarraju Sala l-alSaab ir-riyaaDiyya wa aflaam is-siinama wa yaakulu fi l-maTaaSim wa yazuuru il-mataaHif.

_____ halla Saar Sindi fikra waadiHa San Taqs waashinTun. mumkin as'alak kiif yaSrif ish-shaSb il-ameerki waqt faraaghu?

_____ ashhar il-alSaab hiya il-futbool il-ameerki wa l-beesbool wa t-tanis wa kurat is-salla.

C. Matching English with Arabic

Match each of the eight English sentences with its Arabic counterpart.

id-dars
ith-thaalith
ʕashar:
ʕan iT-Taqs
wa waqt
il-faraagh

1. Sometimes the temperature goes below zero.

a. ana musaafir ila l-wilaayaat il-muttaHida.

2. What are the favorite games in America?

b. fi sh-shitaa' iT-Taqs baarid jiddan.

3. In the winter the weather is very cold.

c. akthar in-naas ʕaadatan mashghuuliin jiddan.

4. Most people are usually very busy.

d. shu hiya il-alʕaab il-mufaDDala fi ameerka?

5. Tell me how the weather is in the U.S.

e. kiif ish-shaʕb yaʕrif waqt faraaghu?

6. Actually, rain falls in all seasons.

f. quul lii kiif iT-Taqs fi l-wilaayaat il-muttaHida?

7. I'm traveling to the U.S.

g. baʕD il-awqaat darajat il- Haraara tanzil taHt iS-Sifr.

8. How do American people spend their time?

h. fi l-Haqiiqa l-maTar yanzil fi kull fuSuul is-sana.

D. Matching Arabic Lines

Match each of the eight Arabic sentences on the left with the appropriate response in the right-hand column.

1. aHibb as'alak kam su'aal.

a. ʕafwan. muwaffaq in shaa' allaah.

2. mumkin as'alak kiif yaʕrif ish-shaʕb il-ameerki waqt faraaghu?

b. fi baʕD il-awqaat tanzil taHt iS-Sifr.

3. mata mawsim il-maTar fi waashinTun?

c. ashhar il-alʕaab hiya l-futbool.

4. shukran jaziilan ʕala l-maʕluumaat.

d. yaʕrifu s-sabt aw il-aHad xaarij buyuuthum.

5. qaddeesh tanzil darajat il-Haraara?

e. fi l-Haqiiqa il-maTar yanzil fi kull fuSuul is-sana.

6. kiif iT-Taqs fi waashinTun?

f. tafaDDal, bi-kull suruur.

7. shu hiya ashar il-alʕaab ir-riyaaDiyya l-mufaDDala fi ameerka?

g. taqriiban mithil beeruut.

8. shu hiya l-amaakin illi yufaDDilu yaruuHu ilha?

h. ila sh-shaaTi' wa ila il-jabal.

151

E. Translation into Arabic
Translate each of the eight sentences in Exercise **A** (p. 150) in this lesson into Arabic.

III.   WORKING WITH THE LANGUAGE

A. Comparative adjective forms
Arabic makes comparatives of most adjectives by changing the vowel pattern of the word to a _ _ a _. Study the five examples below:

kabiir ---> akbar	big ---> bigger
sahl---> ashal	easy ---> easier
ʕaali ---> aʕlaa	high ---> higher
kathiir ---> akthar	much ---> more
qaliil ---> aqall	little, few ---> less, fewer

Sometimes (as in English) Arabic uses the word *akthar* "more" plus the adjective:

mashghuul	mariiD	taʕbaan
busy	sick	tired
mashghuul akthar	mariiD akthar	taʕbaan akthar
busier	sicker	more tired

The word *akthar* is used mainly for adjectives that start with *ma-* or *mu-*, and adjectives that end in *-aan*.

When comparing two things, "than" is expressed by the word *min*:

hiya akbar min uxtha.	yadrus akthar minni.
She is older than her sister.	He studies more than I.

Drill 1: TRANSFORMATION TO THE COMPARATIVE FORM
Change each of the following ten adjectives to the comparative form, and then use each in a sentence.

1. baʕiid	6. Hasan
2. qariib	7. Hilu
3. sahl	8. ghaali
4. Tayyib	9. kathiir
5. qaliil	10. jawʕaan

B. Superlative adjective forms
The superlative form of the adjective is similar to the comparative form. It is used in either of the following ways:

1. Superlatives with the definite article:

il-akbar	il-akthar
the biggest, the oldest	the most
il-aSghar	il-aqall
the smallest, the youngest	the least

2. Superlatives as the first term of a construct phrase:

*id-dars
ith-thaalith
ʕashar:
ʕan iT-Taqs
wa waqt
il-faraagh*

> akbar madiina
> > the biggest city
>
> ashhar film
> > the most famous movie
>
> aHsan waaHid
> > the best one

Drill 2: TRANSLATION INTO ARABIC

Convert each of the five sentences below into Arabic:

1. This was the easiest lesson.
2. I know that he is the oldest.
3. Where is the nearest restaurant?
4. This is the most expensive one.
5. Do you think this is the best?

C. Active participles

Active participles are derived from verbs and are often used as verb substitutes in Arabic. They can be recognized by their vowel "patterns": either _ aa _ i _ or prefix *mu-*. The following is a list of active participles that have occurred in this text so far:

> saakin (-iin)
> > living
>
> xaa'if (-iin)
> > afraid
>
> raa'iH / raayiH (-iin)
> > going
>
> musaafir (-iin)
> > traveling
>
> HaaDir (-iin)
> > ready
>
> mufakkir (-iin)
> > thinking
>
> raajiʕ (-iin)
> > returning
>
> mustaʕidd (-iin)
> > ready

Active participles behave like adjectives. That is, they are inflected for number (singular or plural) and gender (masculine or feminine), the way adjectives are. When used as verb substitutes in spoken Arabic, the plural is normally *-iin*.

> hiya saakina fi l-madiina.
> > She lives (is living) in the city.
>
> naHna raayiHiin halla.
> > We are going now.
>
> ana musaafir bukra.
> > I (*am*) am leaving (travelling) tomorrow.

Drill 3: TRANSFORMATION OF GENDER AND NUMBER

Change the five sentences below to the feminine (singular) and then to the plural. The example is typical of this sort of inflection:

> ween inta saakin? -->
> ween inti saakina? -->
> ween intu saakiniin?

1. ween inta raayiH?
2. huwa raajiʕ baʕd nuSS saaʕa.
3. ana xaa'if ʕaleeh.
4. inta mufakkir tazuur il-matHaf?
5. huwa musaafir li-miSr.

153

IV. WORKING WITH VARIANTS

A. Translation into Arabic

Translate the following eight sentences into Arabic:

1. When is the hot season in the Middle East?
2. Most people in the Middle East are not very busy on Friday.
3. Do the people in the Middle East like to go to the beach?
4. Now I have a clear idea about how people spend their time in Oman.
5. The weather in Riyadh is approximately like the weather in Phoenix.
6. In the Middle East, the rain falls between the end of fall and the beginning of spring.
7. Where do the people of the Middle East like to go in their free time?
8. I'm going to the Middle East to work in Kuwait, and I would like to ask you some questions, if that's okay.

B. Comprehension of Spoken Arabic

Listen to the Arabic sentences on Cassette 7 (side 1) and determine which in the following ten English triplets corresponds in meaning to the taped Arabic sentences.

1. _____ Most people in the United States are very busy.
   _____ Most people in the United States work on Friday.
   _____ Most people in the United States eat in restaurants.

2. _____ In summer the weather is generally hot and humid.
   _____ In summer the weather is generally humid and hot.
   _____ In winter the weather is generally cold and humid.

3. _____ Now I have a clear idea about the weather in Washington.
   _____ Now I have a clear idea about the people in Washington.
   _____ Now I have a clear idea about sports in Washington.

4. _____ The most popular sports are football, baseball, and basketball.
   _____ The most popular sports are football, baseball, and tennis.
   _____ The most popular sports are football, basketball, and baseball.

5. _____ Some of them go to the beach and some go the mountains.
   _____ Some of them go to the mountains and some go to restaurants.
   _____ Some of them go to the beach and some go to restaurants.

6. _____ Most people are very busy from Monday to Friday.
   _____ Most people are very busy from Tuesday to Saturday.
   _____ Most people are very busy from Sunday to Friday.

7. _____ What is the temperature in the summer?
   _____ What is the temperature in the spring?
   _____ What is the temperature in the fall?

154

8. _____ The weather in the United States differs from place to place.

_____ The weather in the United States differs from state to state.

_____ The weather in the United States differs from city to city.

9. _____ When is the cold season in Saudi Arabia?

_____ When is the hot season in Saudi Arabia?

_____ When is the rainy season in Saudi Arabia?

10. _____ I am going to the U.S. to study at Georgetown University.

_____ I am going to the U.S. to visit Georgetown University.

_____ I am traveling to the U.S. to study in Washington, the capital.

id-dars
ith-thaalith
ʕashar:
ʕan iT-Taqs
wa waqt
il-faraagh

V. WORKING WITH THE SITUATION

It is possible that you may be called upon to answer questions about the United States or about Americans in general while you are in the Arab world. Moreover, you may have the opportunity to reverse roles and elicit social and cultural information about life in the Arab world. While it is not the goal of this course to enable you to discuss these things at length, you will want to be able to give some basic information about what the U.S. is like, or to inquire about life in an Arab country, engaging in small talk and narrative to a limited extent.

Before you begin role-playing with your teacher, ask him or her what topics of conversation are likely to come up with Arabs, especially in standard social situations. You may also want to learn how to inquire politely about similar information yourself, especially if you are unsure about which topics are culturally appropriate.

155

الدرس الرابع عشر

مشاكل مع الشرطة

١.   الامـيركي : عفوا يا أخ، شفت ولد صغير ماشي لوحده ؟

٢.   العربي ١ : شو اوصافه ؟

٣.   الامـيركي : هو اشقر، وعمره ست سنين و لابس بنطلون اخضر و قميص اصفر .

٤.   العربي ١ : لا والله ما شفته . ليش ما تخبر الشرطة ؟

٥.   الامـيركي : وين مركز الشرطة ؟

٦.   العربي ١ : في هذيك البناية الصغيرة اللي عليها العلم .

٧.   العربي ٢ : شو تعمل هنا ؟

٨.   الامـيركي : ابني ضايع و احتاج مساعدتكم .

٩.   العربى ٢ : وليش فاتح كاميرتك ؟ ممنوع التصوير في هذي المنطقة .

١٠. الامـيركي : انا ما صورت هنا . اخذت صورة عند الآثار وبعدين ضاع ابني .

١١. العربي ٢ : هذي مش حجة . انت مخالف القانون ولازم تبقى تحت الحجز .
     ادخل في هذيك الغرفة .

١٢. الامـيركي : انا دبلوماسي وعندي حصانة دبلوماسية ، ما تقدر تحجزني .

١٣. العربي ٢ : طيب ، انتظر حتى يوصل الضابط .

١٤. الامـيركي : ارجوك ياأخ ، انا ما صورت اي شيء هنا، انا بدي مساعدة
     حتى الاقي ابني هو صغير وما يتكلم عربي ويحتاج مساعدة ارجوك .

LESSON FOURTEEN: Problems with the Police

id-dars ir-raabiʕ ʕashar:
mashaakil maʕ ish-shurTa

Sample Dialogue:

AMERICAN says:

1: ʕafwan ya ax, shuft walad Saghiir maashi li-waHdu?
Pardon me, sir. Have you seen a little boy walking by himself?

3: huwa ashqar, ʕumru sitt saniin wa laabis banTaloon axDar wa qamiiS aSfar.
He's blond, six years old, wearing green trousers and a yellow shirt.

5: ween markaz ish-shurTa?
Where's the police station?

ARAB says:

2: shu awSaafu?
What does he look like?

4: la wallaah ma shuftu. leesh ma tuxabbir ish-shurTa?
No, really, I haven't seen him. Why don't you inform the police?

6: fi hadhiik il-binaaya iS-Saghiira illi ʕaleeha l-ʕalam.
In that little building with the flag on it.

[The American enters the police station, but finds no one there. Then an angry policeman enters the station where the American is waiting.]

7: shu taʕmal huna?
What are you doing here?

8: ibni Daayiʕ wa aHtaaj musaaʕadatkum.
My son is lost and I need your help.

9: wa leesh faatiH kamratak? mamnuuʕ it-taSwiir fi haadhi l-manTiqa.
Why is your camera open? It is forbidden to take pictures in this area.

10: ana ma Sawwart huna. axadht Suura ʕind il-aathaar wa baʕdeen Daaʕ ibni.
I didn't take any pictures here. I took a picture at the ruins and then my son got lost.

11: haadhi mish Hujja. inta muxaalif il-qaanuun wa laazim tabqa taHt il-Hajz. udxul fi hadhiik il-ghurfa.
That's no excuse. You've broken the law and will have to be detained. Go into that room.

12: ana dibluumaasi wa ʕindi HaSaana dibluumaasiyya, ma taqaar taHjizni.
I'm a diplomat and I have diplomatic immunity. You can't detain me.

13: Tayyib, intaDHir Hatta yuuSal iD-DaabiT.
Okay, wait until the officer comes.

١٥. العربي ٣ : شو المشكلة ؟

١٦. الامريكي : يا حضرة الضابط، انا موظف دبلوماسي في السفارة الامريكية . انا وعائلتي في رحلة سياحية لهذي المدينة اولادي كانوا يلعبوا في الدرج الروماني بعدين ضاع ابني الصغير وبدي مساعدتكم .

١٧. العربـــي ٣ : قديش صار له ضايع ؟

١٨. الاميركي : حوالي عشرين دقيقة .

١٩. العربـــى ٣ : لا تهتم، رح ابعث شرطي يفتش عليه . اكيد هو في واحدة من الغرف تحت الدرج . صارت هذي الحادثة مرات كثيرة من قبل .

٢٠. الامريكى : الف شكر على مساعدتكم . الله يخلي لك اولادك .

id-dars
ir-raabiʕ ʕashar:
mashaakil
maʕ ish-shurTa

AMERICAN says:

*14: arjuuk ya ax, ana ma Sawwart ayy
shi huna. ana biddi musaaʕada Hatta
ulaaqi ibni. huwa Saghiir wa ma
yatakallam ʕarabi wa yaHtaaj
musaaʕada, arjuuk.*

Please, sir, I didn't photograph
anything here. I want help to find
my son. He's small and doesn't
speak Arabic and needs help. I
beg you.

[A police official enters.]

ARAB says:

15: shu il-mushkila?
What's the problem?

*16: ya HaDrat iD-DaabiT, ana
muwaDHDHaf dibluumaasi min
is-safaara l-ameerkiyya. ana wa
ʕaa'ilati fi riHla siyaaHiyya li-haadhi
l-manTiqa. awlaadi kaanu yalʕabu fi
l-mudarraj ir-ruumaani, baʕdeen
Daaʕ ibni S-Saghiir, wa biddi
musaaʕadatkum.*

Officer, I'm a diplomat from the
American Embassy. My family and
I are on a sightseeing trip in this
area. My children were playing in
the Roman amphitheater and my
little son got lost. I need your help.

17: qaddeesh Saar lu Daayiʕ?
How long has he been lost?

18: Hawaali ʕiishriin daqiiqa.
About twenty minutes.

*19: la tahtamm, raH abʕath shurTi
yufattish ʕaleeh. akiid huwa fi
waaHida min il-ghuraf taHt
il-mudarraj. Saarat haadhi l-Haaditha
marraat kathiira min qabl.*

Don't worry, I'll send a policeman
to look for him. He's sure to be in
one of the rooms under the
amphitheater. This [event] has
happened many times before.

*20: alf shukr ʕala musaaʕadatkum.
allaah yuxallii-lak awlaadak.*
Thanks a million for your help.
May God keep your children safe.

159

VOCABULARY

raabiʕ ʕashar
  fourteenth

shurTa
  police

maashi (-iin)
  walking

li-waHdu
  by himself

waSf (awSaaf)
  description,
  characteristic

ashqar (shuqur)
  blond

ʕumr (aʕmaar)
  age

sana (saniin, sanawaat)
  year

laabis (-iin)
  wearing

tuxabbir
  you inform

markaz (maraakiz)
  center, headquarters

markaz ish-shurTa
  police station

hadhiik
  that (f)

binaaya (-aat)
  building

ʕalam (aʕlaam)
  flag

Daayiʕ
  lost

faatiH
  open

kamara (-aat)
  camera

mamnuuʕ
  forbidden, not allowed

taSwiir
  taking pictures,
  photographing

manTiqa (manaaTiq)
  region, area

Sawwart
  I took photographs

Suura (Suwar)
  picture

aathaar
  ruins

Daaʕ
  he got lost

Hujja (Hujaj)
  excuse, pretext

muxaalif (-iin)
  violator, violating

qaanuun (qawaaniin)
  law

muxaalif il-qaanuun
  breaking the law

tabqa
  you (m) stay

Hajz
  detention; reservation

udxul
  enter, go in
  (imperative)

dibluumaasi (n. & adj.)
  diplomat, diplomatic

HaSaana
  immunity

taHjiz
  you (m) detain; reserve

DaabiT (DubbaaT t)
  officer
  (police or military)

ulaaqi
  I find, I meet

ʕaa'ila (-aat)
  family

siyaaHi
  sightseeing, tourist
  (adj.)

walad (awlaad)
  child; boy

kaanu yalʕabu
  they were playing

mudarraj (-aat)
  amphitheater;
  auditorium

ruumaani
  Roman

Saar lu
  he has been

tahtamm
  you (m) worry

la tahtamm
  Don't worry.

shurTi (shurTa)
  policeman

yufattish (ʕala)
  he looks for

Haaditha (Hawaadith)
  event, incident

min qabl
  previously, before

alf shukr
  Thanks a million
  ("A thousand thanks").

allaah yuxalliilak
awlaadak.
  "May God keep your
  children safe."

I. WORKING WITH WORDS AND PHRASES

id-dars
ir-raabiʕ ʕashar:
mashaakil
maʕ ish-shurTa

A. Matching
Match each English expression with its Arabic equivalent.

1.	by himself	a.	_____	ʕalam
2.	immunity	b.	_____	yalʕabu
3.	they play	c.	_____	shurTi
4.	law	d.	_____	li-waHdu
5.	I need	e.	_____	markaz ish-shurTa
6.	flag	f.	_____	tuxabbir
7.	amphitheater	g.	_____	la tahtamm
8.	you detain	h.	_____	aHtaaj
9.	trip	i.	_____	qaanuun
10.	ruins	j.	_____	taHjiz
11.	policeman	k.	_____	mudarraj
12.	police station	l.	_____	aathaar
13.	don't worry	m.	_____	riHla
14.	you inform	n.	_____	HaSaana
15.	area	o.	_____	manTiqa

B. Completion

In the following version of the dialogue, certain words have been left out. Complete the sentences by filling in the missing words.

AMERICAN says:

1: ʕafwan ya ax, shuft _____ Saghiir maashi li-waHdu?

3: huwa _____, ʕumru sitt saniin wa _____ banTaloon axDar wa qamiiS aSfar.

5: ween _____ ish-shurTa?

8: ibni Daayiʕ wa _____ musaaʕadatkum.

10: ana ma _____ huna. axadht Suura ʕind _____ wa baʕdeen Daaʕ ibni.

12: ana dibluumaasi wa ʕindi _____ dibluumaasiyya; ma taqdar taHjizni.

14: _____ ya ax, ana ma Sawwart ayy shi huna, ana biddi musaaʕada Hatta _____ ibni. huwa Saghiir wa ma _____ ʕarabi wa yaHtaaj musaaʕada. arjuuk.

16: yaa HaDrat _____, ana muwaDHDHaf dibluumaasi min is-safaara l-ameerkiyya. ana wa ʕaa'ilati fi _____ siyaaHiyya li-haadhi l-manTiqa. _____ kaanu yalʕabu fi _____ ir-ruumaani baʕdeen Daaʕ ibni S-Saghiir wa biddi musaaʕadatkum.

18: Hawaali _____ daqiiqa.

20: alf _____ ʕala musaaʕadatkum. allaah _____ awlaadak.

ARAB says:

2: shu _____?

4: la wallaah ma shuftu. leesh ma _____ ish-shurTa?

6: fi hadhiik il-_____ iS-Saghiira illi ʕaleeha l-ʕalam.

7: shu _____ huna?

9: wa leesh faatiH kamratak? _____ it-taSwiir fi haadhi l-_____.

11: haadhi mish _____. inta muxaalif il-_____ wa laazim tabqa taHt _____. udxul fi hadhiik il-ghurfa.

13: Tayyib, _____ Hatta yuuSal iD-DaabiT.

15: shu _____?

17: qaddeesh _____ lu Daayiʕ?

19: la tahtamm, raH abʕath _____ yufattish ʕaleeh. akiid huwa fi waaHida min _____ taHt il-mudarraj. Saarat haadhi l-_____ marraat kathiira min qabl.

II. WORKING WITH SENTENCES

id-dars
ir-raabiʕ ʕashar:
mashaakil
maʕ ish-shurTa

A. Matching Spoken Arabic with Written English (listening)

Listen to Cassette 7 (side 2) or to your teacher, and match what is said in Arabic with the correct English among the following eight sentences.

_____ Where is the police station?

_____ What is the problem?

_____ How long has he been lost?

_____ What does he look like?

_____ Thank you for your help.

_____ Did you see a young boy?

_____ What are you doing here?

_____ I need your help.

B. Scrambled Arabic Dialogue

Reconstruct the dialogue by numbering the following lines from one to twenty so they are in a meaningful sequence.

_____ ibni Daayiʕ wa aHtaaj musaaʕadatkum.

_____ huwa ashqar, ʕumru sitt saniin wa laabis banTaloon axDar wa qamiiS aSfar.

_____ shu awSaafu?

_____ ween markaz ish-shurTa?

_____ shu taʕmal huna?

_____ ʕafwan ya ax, shuft walad Saghiir maashi li-waHdu?

_____ wa leesh faatiH kamratak? mamnuuʕ it-taSwiir fi haadhi l-manTiqa.

_____ la wallaah ma shuftu. leesh ma tuxabbir ish-shurTa?

_____ ana ma Sawwart huna. axadht Suura ʕind il-aathaar wa baʕdeen Daaʕ ibni.

_____ ya HaDrat iD-DaabiT, ana muwaDHDHaf dibluumaasi min is-safaara l-ameerkiyya. ana wa ʕaa'ilati fi riHla siyaaHiyya li-haadhi l-manTiqa. awlaadi kaanu yalʕabu fi l-mudarraj ir-ruumaani. baʕdeen Daaʕ ibni S-Saghiir wa biddi musaaʕadatkum.

_____ haadhi mish Hujja. inta muxaalif il-qaanuun wa laazim tabqa taHt il-Hajz. udxul fi hadhiik il-ghurfa.

_____ fi hadhiik il-binaaya iS-Saghiira illi ʕaleeha l-ʕalam.

_____ la tahtamm, raH abʕath shurTi yufattish ʕaleeh. akiid huwa fi waaHida min il-ghuraf taHt il-mudarraj. Saarat haadhi l-Haaditha marraat kathiira min qabl.

_____ ana dibluumaasi wa ʕindi HaSaana dibluumaasiyya, ma taqdar taHjizni.

_____ qaddeesh Saar lu Daayiʕ?

_____ arjuuk ya ax, ana ma Sawwart ayy shi huna. ana biddi musaaʕada Hatta ulaaqi ibni. huwa Saghiir wa maa yatakallam ʕarabi wa yaHtaaj musaaʕada. arjuuk.

_____ shu il-mushkila?

_____ Tayyib, intaDHir Hatta yuuSal iD-DaabiT.

_____ Hawaali ʕishriin daqiiqa.

_____ alf shukr ʕala musaaʕadatkum. allaah yuxallii-lak awlaadak.

C. Matching English with Arabic
Match each of the eight English sentences with its Arabic counterpart.

1. What does he look like?

2. Around twenty minutes.

3. How long has he been lost?

4. I haven't seen him.

5. Where's the police station?

6. Thank you for your help.

7. I have diplomatic immunity.

8. Wait till the officer arrives.

a. *intaDHir Hatta yuuSal iD-DaabiT.*

b. *alf shukr Sala musaaSadatkum.*

c. *ma shuftu.*

d. *Sindi HaSaana dibluumaasiyya.*

e. *ween markaz ish-shurTa?*

f. *shu awSaafu?*

g. *qaddeesh Saar lu Daayi S?*

h. *Hawaali Sishriin daqiiqa.*

D. Matching Arabic Lines
Match the Arabic lines on the left with one of the eight responses on the right.

1. *shu awSaafu?*

2. *shu taSmal huna?*

3. *wa leesh faatiH kamratak?*

4. *ween markaz ish-shurTa?*

5. *shu il-mushkila?*

6. *inta muxaalif il-qaanuun wa laazim tabqa taHt il-Hajz.*

7. *la tahtamm, raH abSath shurTi yufattish Saleeh.*

8. *qaddeesh Saar lu Daayi S?*

a. *fi hadhiik il-binaaya S-Saghiira.*

b. *ana dibluumaasi, ma taqdar taHjizni.*

c. *Hawaali Sishriin daqiiqa.*

d. *huwa ashqar, Sumru sitt saniin.*

e. *axadht Suura Sind il-aathaar.*

f. *ibni DaayiS wa aHtaaj musaaSadatkum.*

g. *DaaS ibni S-Saghiir wa biddi musaaSadatkum.*

h. *alf shukr Sala musaaSadatkum.*

E. Translation into Arabic
Put the sentences in Exercise **A** of this lesson (p. 163) into Arabic.

III. WORKING WITH THE LANGUAGE

id-dars
ir-raabiʕ ʕashar:
mashaakil
maʕ ish-shurTa

A. *Saar li-* "have been, has been"

Spoken Arabic has an idiomatic way of expressing "have been" or "has been." It consists of the verb *Saar*, "to happen, to become" plus the preposition *li-* or *la-* "to, for" with pronoun suffixes. The full paradigm for *Saar li* is charted below:

Saar lu(h)	*Saar laha*	*Saar lahum*
he has been	she has been	they have been
Saar lak	*Saar lik*	*Saar lakum*
you (*m*) have been	you (*f*) have been	you (*pl*) have been

Saar lii   *Saar lana*
I have been   we have been

Examples:

qaddeesh Saar lu Daayiʕ?
How long has he been lost?

Saar lii sabʕ asaabiiʕ fi hadha l-balad.
I've been in this country seven weeks.

kam Saar lak huna?
How long have you (*m*) been here?

qaddeesh Saar lik tadrusi ʕarabi?
How long have you (f) been studying Arabic?

Note: *Saar* is only used to refer to action during a definite period of time, and always has such a period of time as its reference. It is used to describe explicitly *how long* an action has gone on:

Saar lii Taaliba sittat ashhur.
I have been a student for six months.

Saar lana fi dimashq ʕashrat ayyaam.
We've been in Damascus ten days.

But it is not used to state that an action occurred during an indefinite, previous period:

kunt Taaliba.
I have been (was / at some point in the past) a student.

kunti fi dimashq?
Have you (*f*) been (at some point in the past) to Damascus?

naʕm, kunt hunaak.
Yes, I've been there.

Drill 1: CONJUGATION OF "Saar li-"

Conjugate *Saar li-* in the following sentences. Make any other necessary changes.

1. Saar lii adrus xams asaabiiʕ.
2. Saar lii arbaʕat ayyaam fi-l-madiina.
3. Saar lii muwaDHDHaf sanateen.
4. Saar lii yoomeen huna.
5. Saar lii saaʕateen ufattish ʕaleeh.

Drill 2: CONVERSATION PRACTICE IN ARABIC

a. Using *Saar li-* each student asks the teacher a different question. For example:

-*kam Saar lak muʕallim?*
-*kam Saar lak tashtaghil huna?*
-*kam saar lak mutazawwij?*

b. Then the teacher asks similar questions of each student, and summarizes the information at the end of the exercise, while the students listen to the summary.

B. Past Progressive Tense

To describe any action that occurred either over a period of time in the past or habitually in the past ("was *describ*-ing," "were *describ*-ing;" "used to *describe*"), the verb *kaan* is used plus the present tense of the appropriate descriptive verb. Study the four examples below:

kaanu yalʕabu fi-l-aathaar.
They were playing in the ruins.

kunna nantaDHir nuSS saaʕa.
We were waiting for half an hour.

kunt uSawwir huna.
I was taking pictures here.

kaanat tuuSal kull yoom is-saaʕa tisʕa.
She used to arrive every day at 9:00.

Drill 3: CONJUGATION OF "kunt"

Conjugate the verbs in the following sentences:

1. kunt ufattish ʕala il-binaaya.
2. kunt adxul il-beet kull yoom.
3. kunt atakallam maʕhum.
4. ma kunt ashrab biira.

Drill 4: TRANSLATION INTO ARABIC
Put the following eight sentences into Arabic.

id-dars
ir-raabiʕ ʕashar:
mashaakil
maʕ ish-shurTa

1. He was putting something in the car.
2. They were eating dinner.
3. We used to buy vegetables there.
4. They were cleaning the house.
5. She was finishing the lesson.
6. What were you (*m*) doing there?
7. I was writing a letter.
8. He was inflating the tire.

Drill 5: OBJECT PRONOUN REVIEW
Using the sentences in Drill **4**, change the noun objects of the verbs to pronoun objects. For example, instead of "She was finishing the lesson," use "She was finishing it."

IV. WORKING WITH VARIANTS

A. Translation into Arabic
Put the following ten sentences into Arabic:

1. Did you see a blond girl on this street?
2. What are you doing in my office?
3. Please wait until the duty officer comes in.
4. How long has he been in that room?
5. Please, sir, try to help me.
6. I didn't take pictures in this room.
7. All diplomats have diplomatic immunity.
8. Picture-taking is prohibited in this area.
9. Don't worry, he will call you in a few minutes.
10. Thanks a million for your help.

B. Comprehension of Spoken Arabic

Listen the the Arabic sentences on the cassette and determine which among the triplets of the following eight English sentences corresponds in meaning with the taped Arabic sentences.

1. _____ What are you doing in my home?
   _____ What are you doing in my office?
   _____ What are you doing in my car?

2. _____ What were they doing in that area?
   _____ What was he doing in that area?
   _____ What were you doing in that area?

3. _____ Please, I've lost my children and I need your help.
   _____ Please, I lost my youngest child and I need your help.
   _____ Please, I lost my daughter and I need your help.

4. _____ That's not an excuse, you are not supposed to be here.
   _____ That's not an excuse, you were supposed to be here.
   _____ That's not an excuse, you were supposed to be there.

5. _____ He is blond, about six years old, and he's wearing blue jeans.
   _____ He is blond, about six years old, and he is wearing a blue shirt.
   _____ He is blond, about six years old, and he is wearing blue pants.

6. _____ Did you see a little boy walking by himself?
   _____ Did you see a little girl walking by herself?
   _____ Did you see a blond boy walking by himself?

7. _____ He is young and can't speak Arabic. I must find him.
   _____ She is young and can't speak Arabic. I must find her.
   _____ He is young and can't understand Arabic. I must find him.

8. _____ My children and I are on a sightseeing trip.
   _____ My family and I are on a sightseeing trip.
   _____ My friends and I are on a sightseeing trip.

V. WORKING WITH THE SITUATION

*id-dars
ir-raabiʕ ʕashar:
mashaakil
maʕ ish-shurTa*

In this lesson two overlapping situations arise: being in need of help and being confronted with a hostile authority. In both cases, you would again be in need of some stock phrases or "key lines" ("I have diplomatic immunity," "I need help"), should such situations actually occur. If you are not a Foreign Service Officer, then you will need a different set of lines explaining who you are ("I am a tourist, a foreign student, an archaeologist," "Please let me contact the American consul," etc.). You should also ask your teacher about expected behavior under these circumstances (e.g., is it better to be appeasing or firm? Should behavior differ for men and for women? If so, how so?)

You can then role-play these situations (separately or together) with your teacher.

NAMES OF THE MONTHS OF THE YEAR

THE GREGORIAN CALENDAR:

English-speaking world SOLAR MONTHS		*The Arab East* (EQUIVALENT NAMES)	*Egypt & North Africa* (EQUIVALENT NAMES)
1. January	31 days	kaanuun ith-thaani	yanaayir
2. February	28 or 29 days	shubaaT	fibraayir
3. March	31 days	aadhaar	maaris
4. April	30 days	niisaan	abriil
5. May	31 days	ayyaar	maayu
6. June	30 days	Haziiraan	yuunyu
7. July	31 days	tammuuz	yuulyu
8. August	31 days	aab	aghusTus
9. September	30 days	ayluul	sibtambir
10. October	31 days	tishriin il-awwal	uktoobar
11. November	30 days	tishriin ith-thaani	nufambir
12. December	31 days	kaanuun il-awwal	disambir

THE ISLAMIC CALENDAR:

LUNAR MONTHS

1. *muHarram*
2. *Safar*
3. *rabiiʕ il-awwal*
4. *rabiiʕ ith-thaani*
5. *jumaada il-uula*
6. *jumaada ith-thaaniya*
7. *rajab*
8. *shaʕbaan*
9. *ramaDaan*
10. *shawwaal*
11. *dhu l-qiʕda*
12. *dhu l-Hijja*

ARABIC NAMES OF GOVERNMENT MINISTRIES

Ministry of Agriculture
wazaarat iz-ziraaʕa

Ministry of Culture
wazaarat ith-thaqaafa

Ministry of Defense
wazaarat id-difaaʕ

Ministry of Education
wazaarat it-tarbiya

Ministry of Finance
wazaarat il-maaliyya

Ministry of Foreign Affairs
wazaarat il-xaarijiyya

Ministry of Health
wazaarat iS-SiHHa

Ministry of Housing
wazaarat it-taʕmiir wa l-iskaan

Ministry of Industry
wazaarat iS-Sinaaʕa

Ministry of the Interior
wazaarat id-daaxiliyya

Ministry of Justice
wazaarat il-ʕadl

Ministry of Labor
wazaarat il-ʕamal

Ministry of Oil
wazaarat in-nafT

Ministry of Public Works
wazaarat il-ashghaal il-ʕaamma

Ministry of Religious Affairs
wazaarat il-awqaaf

Ministry of Tourism
wazaarat is-siyaaHa

Ministry of Trade
wazaarat it-tijaara

ARAB COUNTRIES AND THEIR CAPITAL CITIES

ALGERIA
il-jazaaʕir
  ALGIERS
    il-jazaaʕir
BAHRAIN
il-baHreen
  MANAMA
    il-manaama
DJIBOUTI
jibuuti
  DJIBOUTI
    jibuuti
EGYPT
miSr
  CAIRO
    il-qaahira
IRAQ
il-ʕiraaq
  BAGHDAD
    baghdaad
JORDAN
il-urdun
  AMMAN
    ʕammaan
KUWAIT
il-kuweet
  KUWAIT CITY
    madiinat il-kuweet
LEBANON
lubnaan
  BEIRUT
    beeruut
LIBYA
liibya
  TRIPOLI
    Taraablus
MAURITANIA
muuritaanya
  NOUAKCHOTT
    nuwaakshuuT

MOROCCO
il-maghrib
  RABAT
    ir-ribaaT
OMAN
ʕumaan
  MUSCAT
    masqaT
QATAR
qaTar
  DOHA
    id-dooHa
SAUDI ARABIA
is-saʕuudiyya
  RIYADH
    ir-riyaaD
SOMALIA
iS-Suumaal
  MOGADISCIO
    maqadiishu
SUDAN
is-suudaan
  KHARTOUM
    il-xarTuum
SYRIA
suuriya
  DAMASCUS
    dimashq
TUNISIA
tuunis
  TUNIS
    tuunis
UNITED ARAB EMIRATES
il-imaaraat il-ʕarabiyya il-muttaHida
  ABU DHABI
    abu DHabi
YEMEN
il-yaman
  SANA
    Sanʕaa'

COURTESY EXPRESSIONS & IDIOMS OF THE ARAB EAST

COURTESY EXPRESSIONS	TRADITIONAL RESPONSES
1: Goodbye *maʕ is-salaama*	**R:** *allaah yusallimak / -ik / -kum*
2: Good morning *SabaaH il-xeer*	**R:** *SabaaH in-nuur*
3: Hello *marHaba*	**R:** *marHabteen*
4: How are you? *kiif il-Haal (kiif Haalak / -ik)*	
5: Fine (thanks be to God) *il-Hamdu li-llaah (bi-xeer)*	
6: I hope he gets well. *salaamtu*	**R:** *allaah yusallimak / -ik*
7: It's a pleasure to meet you. *tasharrafna*	**R:** *ish-sharaf la-na*
8: May God give you strength! *allaah yaʕtiik / -ki l-ʕaafiya*	**R:** *allaah yaʕaafiik / -ki*
9: May your food be everlasting! *sufra daayma*	**R:** *SaHteen*
10: I'm sorry. *muta'assif / muta'assifa*	**R:** *il-ʕafu*
11: Thank you. *shukran*	
12: You're welcome. *ʕafwan*	
13: To your health / *bon appétit!* *SaHteen*	**R:** *SaHteen ʕala qalbak / -ik*
14: Welcome. *ahlan wa sahlan*	**R:** *ahlan biik / -ki*

actually
  fi l-Haqiiqa, Haqiiqatan

again
  marra thaaniya

all right, okay
  Tayyib

Anything else?
  ayy shi thaani?

anyway; anyhow
  ʕala kull Haal

At your service.
  Haadir, tikram, ʕala raasi

be careful; take care
  diir baalak / diiri baalik

busy
  mashghuul / mashghuula

by all means
  min kull budd

Don't worry.
  la tahtamm / la tahtammi

emergency
  Haala Taari'a

especially
  xaaSSatan

finished, done
  xalaS

first thing, first of all
  awwal shi

generally
  bi-Suura ʕaamma

God willing; hopefully
  in shaa' allaah

Good luck.
  muwaffaq

How wonderful!
  ma shaa' allaah!

I'm in a hurry.
  ana mustaʕjil / mustaʕjila.

I'm mistaken.
  ana ghalTaan / ghalTaana.

I beg you.
  arjuuk / arjuuki.

I hope nothing's wrong.
  xeer in shaa' allaah

if possible
  idha mumkin

if you please
  law samHt / samaHti

Keep the change.
  xalli l-baaqi

May God keep you.
  allaah yuxalliik / -ki.

May God keep your children safe.
  *allaah yuxallii-lak awlaadak /
  yuxallii-lik awlaadik.*

May I help you?
  ayy xidma? shu tu'mur / tu'muri?

maybe
  yumkin, mumkin

My goodness!
  ya salaam!

naturally, of course
  Tabʕan

never mind; it's okay
  maʕaleesh

no problem
  ma fii mushkila

not at all; never
  abadan

not certain, not sure
mish muta'akkid / muta'akkida

not necessary
mish Daruuri

not really
la wallaah

one minute
daqiiqa waaHida

One moment, please.
laHdha min faDlak / -ik

pardon me, excuse me
la mu'aaxadha

pardon; with your permission
ʕan idhnak / -ik

please; go ahead; come in
tafaDDal / tafaDDali / tafaDDalu

quickly, fast
bi-surʕa

ready
mustaʕidd / mustaʕidda

really, indeed
fiʕlan

really, actually
Haqiiqatan

regretfully, unfortunately
maʕ il-asaf

Rest a bit.
irtaaH / irtaaHi shwayy.

slowly
shway-shway

surely; for sure
akiid

Thanks a million.
alf shukr

Thanks for your help.
shukran ʕala musaaʕadatak / -ik.

That's all right; take it easy.
basiiTa.

That's all right; no problem.
ma fii maaniʕ.

That's nice of you.
haadha min luTfak / -ik

That's what I was afraid of.
haadha illi kunt xaayif / xaayfa minnu.

the Arab way
ʕala T-Tariiqa l-ʕarabiyya

to your liking
ʕala keefak / -ik

Wait a minute.
intaDHir / intaDhiri daqiiqa

Welcome.
ahlan wa sahlan

What's the problem?
shu l-mushkila?

why not?
leesh la?

with pleasure
bi-kull suruur

would that, I wish, if only
ya reet

FORMAL SPOKEN ARABIC FAST COURSE GLOSSARIES

These two glossaries use the following abbreviations within parentheses for English terms:

(adj.) adjective   **(demons.)** demonstrative   **(f.)** feminine   **(m.)** masculine
(n.) noun   **(pl.)** plural   **(pron.)** pronoun   **(s.o.)** someone   **(sth.)** something

Plurals of Arabic nouns and adjectives are in parentheses after the singular. Past and present tenses of Arabic verbs are cited together, separated by a slash mark (/). The regular Arabic citation form for adjectives and flexible nouns is masculine singular; and where colors are cited, the masculine form is given first, then the feminine.

English-*Arabic* GLOSSARY

a

to be able
    qadir / yaqdar
above
    fawq
ache (n.)
    wajaʕ (awjaaʕ)
actually
    fi l-Haqiiqa, Haqiiqatan
address
    ʕinwaan (ʕanaawiin)
afraid, fearful
    xaa'if (-iin)
after
    baʕd
after that, then
    baʕdeen
afternoon
    baʕd iDH-DHuhur
again
    marra thaaniya
age
    ʕumr (aʕmaar)
ahead
    quddaam
air, atmosphere
    jaww
air pressure
    daghT il-hawa
airplane
    Taa'ira (-aat)

airport
    maTaar (-aat)
all
    kull
all right
    Tayyib
allergy
    Hasaasiyya
almonds
    looz
almost
    taqriiban
also
    kamaan
ambassador
    safiir (sufaraa')
ambulance
    sayyaarat isʕaaf
America
    ameerka
American
    ameerki
amphitheater
    mudarraj (-aat)
and
    wa
angry
    zaʕlaan (-iin)
another
    aaxar (-iin)

177

anyhow, anyway
Sala kull Haal
apartment
shiqqa (shiqaq)
appetizers
muqabbilaat
apples
tuffaaH
appointment
mawSid (mawaaSid)
approximately
Hawaali, taqriiban
apricots
mishmish
Arab
Sarabi (Sarab)
Arabic
Sarabi
arm
dhiraaS (adhruS)
army
jeesh
around
Hawl

to arrange
rattab / yurattib
to arrive
waSal / yuuSal
as long as
ma daam
as much as
qadarma
to ask
sa'al / yas'al
assistance, help
musaaSada
"at your service"
tikram, Sala raasi, Sala Seeni
attache
mulHaq (-iin)
auditorium
mudarraj (-aat)
aunt (maternal; paternal)
xaala (-aat); Samma (-aat)
autumn
il-xariif

b

ball
kura (-aat)
banana
smooz
baseball
beesbool
basket
salla (-aat, silaal)
bathroom
Hammaam (-aat)
to be
kaan / yakuun
beach
shaaTi' (shawaaTi')
beans (green)
fasuulya
because
li'ann
to become
Saar / yaSiir
bedroom
ghurfat noom

beef
laHm baqar
beer
biira
before (+ n.)
qabl
before (+ verb)
qablma
to beg (s.o.) for a favor
raja / yarju
to begin
bada' / yabda'
below, under
taHt
belt
zunnaar (zanaaniir)
beneficial, useful
mufiid
beside
janb
big
kabiir (kibaar)

black
aswad, sawdaa'
black (of coffee)
saada
blond
shqar (shuqur)
blouse
bluuza (bluwaz)
blue
azraq, zarqaa'
bone
ʕaDHm (ʕiDHaam)
to bother; to fatigue (s.o.)
taʕʕab / yutaʕʕib
box
Sanduuq (Sanaadiiq)
boy; child
walad (awlaad)
bread
xubz
breakfast
fuTuur
to bring
jaab / yajiib
to bring near
qarrab / yuqarrib
broiled, grilled
mashwi
broken; out of order
maksuur; xarbaan

broken bone
ʕaDHm maksuur
broom
miknasa
brother
ax / axu (ixwa)
brown
bunni, bunniyya
building
ʕamaara (-aat), binaaya (-aat)
bulgur wheat
burghul
burn (n.)
Harq (Huruuq)
bus
baaS (-aat)
busy
mashghuul (-iin)
but, however
laakin
butter
zibda
button
zirr (azraar)
to buy
ishtara / yashtari
by all means
min kull budd

c

cabbage
malfuuf
camera
kamara (-aat)
can (n.)
ʕilba (ʕilab)
can, (be able)
qadir / yaqdar
capital
ʕaaSima (ʕawaaSim)
car
sayyaara (-aat)
"Be careful!"
diir baalak
carrots
jazar

cauliflower
zahra (qarnabiit)
center
markaz (maraakiz)
centigrade
mi'awiyya
certain, sure (adj.)
muta'akkid (-iin)
chair
kursi (karaasi)
to change (sth.)
ghayyar / yughayyir
characteristic (n.)
waSf (awSaaf)
cheap, inexpensive
raxiiS

179

to check
    kashaf / yakshif
cheese
    jibna
chest
    Sadr (Suduur)
chick peas
    Hummus
chicken
    dajaaj, farruuj (faraariij)
child
    walad (awlaad)
city
    madiina (mudun)
clean (*adj.*)
    naDHiif
to clean
    naDHDHaf / yunaDHDHif
cleaners (dry-cleaners)
    maSbagha
cleaning
    tanDHiif
clear
    waaDiH
clinic
    ʕiyaada
close (to); near
    qariib (min)
to close, to shut
    sakkar / yusakkir
closed
    musakkir
clothes
    malaabis
clouds
    gheem (ghuyuum)
coat
    kabbuut (kabaabiit)
coffee
    qahwa
cold (*adj.*)
    baarid
cold (*n.*), flu
    rashH
cold, chilly (of persons)
    bardaan (-iin)

colonel
    ʕaqiid
color
    loon (alwaan)
to come
    ija / yiiji
to come to have; to acquire
    Saar ʕind-
to be concerned, interested in
    ihtamm / yahtamm (bi-)
condition
    Haal (aHwaal), Haala (-aat)
conflicting
    muxaalif (-iin)
consul
    qunSul (qanaaSil)
container
    ʕilba (ʕilab)
conversation
    mukaalama
to cook
    Tabax / yaTbux
cooking
    Tabx
corner
    zaawiya (zawaayaa)
to cough
    saʕal / yasʕul
country
    balad, bilaad (buldaan)
cousin (maternal; paternal)
    ibn xaal, bint xaal; ibn ʕamm,
    bint ʕamm
crazy
    majnuun (majaaniin)
cucumbers
    xiyaar
cup, glass
    kaas (-aat)
cup
    finjaan (fanaajiin)
cupboard
    xazaana (xazaa'in)
to cut (up)
    qaTTaʕ / yuqaTTiʕ

dairy products
  albaan
danger
  xaTar
dates
  tamr
daughter
  bint (banaat)
day
  yoom (ayyaam)
day after tomorrow
  baʕd bukra
defense
  difaaʕ
degree, step, rank
  daraja (-aat)
delicious
  Tayyib, ladhiidh
to deliver (*sth.* to *s.o.*)
  sallam / yusallim
description
  waSf (awSaaf)
detention
  Hajz
diarrhea
  ishaal
to differ
  ixtalaf / yaxtalif
dinar
  diinaar (danaaniir)
dinner
  ʕasha / ʕashaa'
diplomat, diplomatic
  dibluumaasi (-iyyin)
dirty
  wasix

dish, plate
  SaHn (SuHuun)
dish (of food)
  akla (-aat)
dishwashing
  jali
distance
  masaafa (-aat)
to do
  ʕamal / yaʕmil
doctor
  Tabiib (aTibbaa')
dollar
  doolaar (-aat)
door
  baab (abwaab)
dress
  fustaan (fasaatiin)
to drink
  sharib / yashrab
drinks
  mashruub
to drop, to descend
  nazal / yanzil
drunk
  sakraan (-iin)
to dry out
  nashaf / yanshaf
to dry (*sth.*)
  nashshaf / yunashshif
dryer (clothes dryer)
  nashshaafa
dust
  ghubaar
to dust
  masaH il-ghubaar

e

ear
  udhun (adhaan)
early
  bakkiir
earth
  arD
East
  sharq
easy
  sahl

to eat
  akal / yaakul
eggplant
  baadhinjaan
eggplant purée
  baaba ghannuuj
eggs
  bayD
eight
  thamaaniya

eighteen
thamanta ʕsh(ar)

eighth
thaamin

eighty
thamaaniin

electric
kahrabaa'i

eleven
iHda ʕsh(ar)

eleventh
Haadi ʕashar

embassy
safaara (-aat)

emergency
Haala Taari'a

employee
muwaDHDHaf (-iin)

empty space
faraagh

enough
kifaaya, kaafi

to enter
daxal / yadxul

especially
xaaSSatan

evening
masa

event
Haaditha (Hawaadith)

every
kull

exactly
tamaaman

excellent
mumtaaz

excuse (*n.*)
Hujja (Hujaj)

excuse me
la mu'aaxadha

expensive
ghaali

eye
ʕeen (ʕuyuun)

f

facing
muqaabil

fact
Haqiiqa (Haqaa'iq)

to fall
nazal / yanzil

family
ʕaa'ila (-aat)

far (from)
ba ʕiid (min)

fare
ujra

fast
bi-sur ʕa

father
ab / abu (aabaa')

faucet
Hanafiyya

fava beans
fuul

favorite
mufaDDal

fever, temperature
Haraara

few
qaliil, shwayy

fifteen
xamsta ʕsh(ar)

fifth
xaamis

fifty
xamsiin

figs
tiin

to fill
ʕabba / yu ʕabbi

film
film (aflaam)

final, last
aaxir (-iin)

to find
laaqa / yulaaqi

fine, good
kwayyis (-iin)

finger
iSba ʕ (aSaabi ʕ)

to finish
xallaS / yuxalliS

first
awwal

first of all
awwalan

first thing
awwal shii

fish
samak

five
xamsa

to fix
SallaH / yuSalliH

flag
ʕalam (aʕlaam)

flat (of a tire)
munaffis

floor (of a bldg.)
Taabiq (Tawaabiq)

floor (ground level)
arD

flour
TaHiin

flower
zahra (zuhuur)

food
akil

foot
qadam (aqdaam)

football
futbool

for sure
akiid

"for your (m) sake"
kirmaalak

forbidden
mamnuuʕ

to forget
nasi / yansa

fork
shawka (shuwak)

forty
arbaʕiin

four
arbaʕa

fourteen
arbaʕtaʕsh(ar)

fourteenth
raabiʕ ʕashar

fourth
raabiʕ

fresh
Taaza

Friday
(yoom) il-jumʕa

from
min

fruit
faakiha (fawaakih)

full (no longer hungry)
shabʕaan (-iin)

furniture
athaath

g

game
luʕba (alʕaab)

garage
karaaj (-aat)

garden
Hadiiqa (Hadaa'iq)

garlic
thuum

garment
thoob (thiyaab)

gas station
maHaTTat banziin

gasoline
banziin

to get lost
Daaʕ / yaDiiʕ

girl
bint (banaat)

to give
aʕTa / yuʕTi

glass
kaas (-aat)

to go
raaH / yaruuH; masha / yamshi

to go down, descend
nazal / yanzil

"God willing"
in shaa' allaah

going
raayiH (-iin)

going, traveling
musaafir (-iin)

good
kwayyis (-iin)

"good luck"
muwaffaq (-iin)

"good morning"
SabaaH il-xeer
"good morning" (as a response)
SabaaH in-nuur
"good-bye"
maʕ is-salaama
"good-bye" (as a response)
allaah yusallimak
grandfather
jadd (juduud, ajdaad)

grandmother
jadda (-aat)
grapes
ʕinab
grass
Hashiish
green
axDar, xaDraa'

h

hair
shaʕr
half
nuSS
hand
iid (iideen)
to hang clothing
nashar / yanshur
happiness
suruur
happy
farHaan (-iin), mabsuuT (-iin)
he
huwa
head
raas (ruus)
headache
wajaʕ raas
headquarters
markaz (maraakiz)
heart
qalb (quluub)
heat
Haraara
"hello"
marHaba
help (n.)
musaaʕada
to help
saaʕad / yusaaʕid
here
huna

high
ʕaali
home, house
beet (buyuut)
to be honored
tasharraf / yatasharraf
hospital
mustashfa (-ayaat)
hot
Haarr
hot (of persons)
shawbaan (-iin)
hotel
funduq (fanaadiq)
hour
saaʕa (-aat)
house
beet (buyuut)
how
kiif
how many
kam (+ noun)
how much
qaddeesh, bikam
humid
raTib
hundred
miyya, miit
hungry
jawʕaan (-iin)
husband
zawj (azwaaj)

i

I (pronoun)
ana
ice
thalj

idea
fikra (fikar)
if
idha

"if you please"
  law samaHt
immunity
  HaSaana
in a hurry
  mustaʕjil (-iin)
in front (of)
  quddaam
in general
  bi-Suura ʕaamma
in order to
  minshaan, Hatta
in the past
  min qabl
in, at
  bi, fi
incident
  Haaditha (Hawaadith)

to inflate
  nafax / yanfux
to inform
  xabbar / yuxabbir
information
  maʕluumaat
to inspect
  kashaf / yakshif
instance, time
  marra (-aat)
ironing
  kawi
it is necessary
  laazim
it means
  yaʕni
it pleases (s.o.)
  yuʕjib

j

jacket
  jakeet (-aat)

juice
  ʕasiir

k

kibbee (ground lamb)
  kubba
kilogram
  kiilo
kind, sort
  nawʕ (anwaaʕ)

kitchen
  matTbax (maTaabix)
knife
  sikkiin (sakaakiin)
to know
  ʕaraf / yaʕrif

l

lamb (meat)
  laHm ghanam
language
  lugha (-aat)
last, final
  aaxir (awaaxir)
to be late
  ta'axxar / yata'axxar
laundry
  ghasiil
law
  qaanuun (qawaaniin)
lazy
  kaslaan (-iin)
lean meat
  laHma habra

to learn
  taʕallam / yataʕallam
to leave
  tarak / yatruk
left (as direction)
  yasaar
leg
  rijil (arjul)
lemons
  leemuun
lentils
  ʕadas
lesson
  dars (duruus)
to let, allow
  xalla / yuxalli

letter
risaala (rasaa'il)

lettuce
xass

like, similar to
mithil

to like
Habb / yaHibb

linen, sheets
sharshaf (sharaashif)

liter
litir

little, few
qaliil

a little
qaliilan; shwayy

living, residing
saakin (-iin)

living room
Saaloon

long; tall
Tawiil (Tiwaal)

to look for
fattash / yufattish (ʕala)

to look; to see
shaaf / yashuuf

lost
Daayiʕ

to love
Habb / yaHibb

lunch
ghada

---

m_____

made
maʕmuul

mail
bariid

to make, to do
ʕamal / yaʕmil

making (n.)
ʕamil

mangoes
manga

many
Kathiir (Kithaar)

map
xaariTa (xaraa'iT)

market place
suuq (aswaaq)

may, maybe
mumkin, yumkin

to mean, intend
ʕana / yaʕni

meat
laHm

medicine
dawa / dawaa' (adwiya)

to meet, encounter
qaabal / yuqaabil

melon
baTTiix

menu
liista

meter
ʕaddaad, mitir

method, way, manner
Tariiqa (Turuq)

military (adj.); a soldier (n.)
ʕaskari (-iyyiin)

military attaché
mulHaq ʕaskari

milk
Haliib

mineral water
mayy maʕdaniyya

ministry
wazaara, wizaara (- aat)

mint (herb)
naʕnaʕ

minute
daqiiqa (daqaa'iq)

miscellaneous (items)
munawwaʕaat

mistaken
ghalTaan

to mix
xalaT / yaxluT

moderate (adj.)
muʕtadil

moment
laHDHa (-aat)

Monday
(yoom) il-ithneen

money
fuluus

month
shahr (shuhuur)

mop; dustrag; eraser
  mimsaHa (mamaasiH)
to mop (as a floor); wipe off, erase
  masaH / yamsaH (il-arD)
more
  akthar
morning
  SubuH, SabaaH
most
  akthar; il-akthar
mother
  umm (ummahaat)
mountain
  jabal (jibaal)
mouth
  fam (afwaah)

movie
  film (aflaam)
movie house, theater
  siinama
Mr.
  sayyid, ustaadh
Mrs.
  sayyida, madaam
much
  kathiir / kithaar
museum
  matHaf (mátaaHif)
must
  laazim
"my goodness!"
  ya salaam!

n_____

name
  ism (asmaa')
napkin
  fuuTa (fuwaT)
naturally
  Tabʕan
near (to)
  qariib (min)
necessary
  laazim, Daruuri
to need (sth.), have need of (sth.)
  iHtaaj / yaHtaaj
never
  abadan
"never mind"
  maʕaleesh
new
  jadiid (judud)
nice; sweet
  Hilu (Hilwiin)
nine
  tisʕa
nineteen
  tisaʕtaʕash(ar)
ninth
  taasiʕ

ninety
  tisʕiin
no
  la
North
  shamaal, shimaal
not
  ma (negates verbal expressions)
not
  mish (negates adjectives, phrases, nouns)
not at all
  abadan
not really
  la wallaah
not so? right?
  mish heek?
not yet
  lissa
now
  halla, halla'
nurse
  mumarriDa (-aat)

o_____

objection
  maaniʕ

of course
  Tabʕan

187

to offer
qaddam / yuqaddim
office
maktab (makaatib)
officer (police or military)
DaabiT (DubbaaT)
official (n.)
mas'uul (-iin)
oil
zeet
okay
Tayyib, tamaam
okra
baamya
old, ancient
qadiim
olive oil
zeet zeeytuun
olives
zeetuun
on
ʕala
on duty
munaawib (-iin)
one
waaHid
onions
baSal
only
bass

open (adj.)
faatiH, maftuuH
to open
fataH / yaftaH
opinion
ra'y (aaraa')
opposite, facing
muqaabil
or
aw
orange (as color)
burtuqaali, burtuqaaliyya
oranges
burtuqaal
to order
amar / ya'mur
other
aaxar (-iin), thaani
other than
gheer
out of order, broken
xarbaan
outing, excursion
nuzha (-aat)
outside
xaarij
oven
furn (afraan)

p————————————————————————

pain
wajaʕ (awjaaʕ)
pan, pot
Tanjara (Tanaajir)
pants
banTaloon (-aat)
"pardon," "pardon me"
ʕan idhnak; la mu'aaxadha
parsley
baqduunis
party, festivity
Hafla (-aat)
to pass (by)
marr / yamurr (ʕala)
passport
jawaaz safar (jwaazaat safar)
to pay
dafaʕ / yadfaʕ

peaches
durraaq
peanuts
fustuq
pears
injaaS
peas
bazeella
people (of a country)
shaʕb (shuʕuub)
people (in general)
naas
peppers
filfil
perhaps
mumkin
pharmacy
Saydaliyya

phone call
mukaalama talifooniyya

photographing (n.)
taSwiir

pickled vegetables
muxallal

picture
Suura (Suwar)

piece, morsel
qiTʕa (qiTaʕ)

piece of paper
waraqa (awraaq)

piled up
mukaddas

pine nuts
Snoobar

pineapple
ananaas

pipe
unbuub (anaabiib)

pistachios
fustuq Halabi

place
makaan (amaakin)

plate
SaHn (SuHuun)

to play
laʕib / yalʕab

please (proceed m & f)
tafaDDal, tafaDDali

please (as a request)
min faDlak, -ik

to please (s.o.)
aʕjab / yuʕjib

pleasure
suruur

with pleasure
bi kull suruur

pneumonia
nimoonya

police
booliis, shurTa

police station
markaz ish-shurTa

policeman
shurTi (shurTa)

pomegranates
rummaan

pork
laHm xanziir

post office
maktab il-bariid

pot
Tanjara (Tanaajir)

potatoes
baTaaTa

pound (currency)
liira (-aat)

to prefer
faDDal / yufaDDil

to prepare
HaDDar / yuHaDDir

preparation
taHDiir

present (adj.)
mawjuud (-iin)

to present, offer
qaddam / yuqaddim

pretext, excuse
Hujja (Hujaj)

pretty, sweet
Hilu (Hilwiin)

price
thaman (athmaan)

problem
mushkila (mashaakil)

professor
ustaadh (asaatidha)

purse
juzdaan (jazaadiin)

to put
HaTT / yaHuTT

---

q

quarter
rubʕ

question
su'aal (as'ila)

quickly
bi-surʕa

r

radishes
  fijil

rain
  maTar

raisins
  zabiib

to reach, arrive at
  waSal / yuuSal

ready
  Haadir, mustaʕidd (-iin)

ready, at your service
  Haadir

really
  fiʕlan, Haqiiqatan

reason
  sabab (asbaab)

reasonable
  maʕquul

recipe
  waSfa (-aat)

red
  aHmar, Hamraa'

refrigerator
  barraad; thallaaja

regarding
  bi-xuSuuS

region, area
  manTiqa (manaaTiq)

regretfully, unfortunately
  maʕ il-asaf

to relax
  irtaaH / yartaaH

to remain
  baqi / yabqa

to repair
  SallaH / yuSalliH

reservation
  Hajz

to reserve
  Hajaz / yaHjis

to rest
  irtaaH / yartaaH

restaurant
  maTʕam (maTaaʕim)

return, to
  rajaʕ / yarjaʕ

returning
  raajiʕ (-iin)

rice
  ruzz

right (direction)
  yamiin

right?
  mish heek?

riyal
  riyaal (-aat)

roasted
  muHammar

to roast
  shawa / yashwi

Roman
  ruumaani

room
  ghurfa (ghuraf)

ruins
  aathaar

s

salad
  salaTa

salt
  milH

sandwich
  sandwiitsh

Saturday
  (yoom) is-sabt

Saudi
  saʕuudi (-iyyin)

to say
  qaal / yaquul

to search for
  fattash / yufattish (ʕala)

season
  faSl (fuSuul), mawsim (mawaasim)

second
  thaani

secretary
  sikriteer (-iin)

to see
  shaaf / yashuuf

to send
  baʕath / yabʕath

sergeant
 ʕariif
servant
 xaadim (xuddaam)
sesame seed
 simsim
seven
 sabʕa
seventeen
 sabaʕtaʕsh(ar)
seventh
 saabiʕ
seventy
 sabʕiin
shade
 DHill
she
 hiya
sheet
 sharshaf (sharaashif)
shirt
 qamiiS (qumSaan)
shoes
 kundura (kanaadir)
shop (n.)
 dukkaan (dakaakiin)
shore
 shaaTi' (shawaaTi')
shortening
 samna
shortly, in a little while
 baʕd swayy
shoulder
 katif (aktaaf)
to show
 dall / yadill
show me (sth.)
 dillni ʕala
sick
 ʕayyaan (-iin), mariiD (marDa)
sightseeing, tourist (adj.)
 siyaaHi
sign
 ishaara (-aat)
simple
 basiiT
sink (n.)
 maghsala (maghaasil)
sir
 ustaadh

sister
 uxt (axawaat)
to sit
 jalas / yajlis
six
 sitta
sixteen
 sittaʕsh(ar)
sixth
 saadis
sixty
 sittiin
skirt
 tannuura (tanaaniir)
sleep
 noom
sleepy
 naʕsaan (-iin)
slowly; a little bit
 sway-shway
small
 Saghiir (Sighaar)
snow
 thalj
soap
 Saabuun
soccer
 futbool
socks
 kalsaat
some
 baʕD
sometimes
 baʕD il-awqaat, aHyaanan
son
 ibn (abnaa')
sorry
 muta'assif (-iin)
sort, kind
 nawʕ (anwaaʕ)
soups
 hoorba
South
 januub
to speak
 takallam / yatakallam; Haka / yaHki
to spend
 Saraf / yaSrif

spices
bahaaraat
spinach
sabaanix
spoon
milʕaqa (malaaʕiq)
sports
alʕaab riyaaDiyya
spring (season)
rabiiʕ
squash
kuusa
state, province
wilaaya (-aat)
state, condition
Haala (-aat), Haal (attwaal)
station
maHaTTa (-aat)
to stay
baqi / yabqa
still, yet
lissa
stomach
baTn (buTuun)
store
dukkaan (dakaakiin)
storm
ʕaaSifa (ʕawaaSif)
story, floor (of a building)
Taabiq (Tawaabiq)
stove
furn (afraan)

straight ahead
dughri
street
shaariʕ (shawaariʕ)
student
Taalib (Tullaab)
to study
daras / yadrus
stuffed
maHshi
sugar
sukkar
suit
badla (-aat)
summer
Seef
sun
shams
Sunday
(yoom) il-aHad
sure, certain
muta'akkid (-iin)
surely; for certain
akiid
sweater
kanza (-aat)
to sweep
kannas / yukannis
sweets
Hilwayaat

t

table
Taawila (-aat)
to take
axadh / yaaxudh
"take care!"
diir baalak!
to take photographs
Sawwar / yuSawwir
to talk
takallam / yatakallam
talk (*n.*), conversation
mukaalama
tall; long
Tawiil (Tiwaal)
tangerines
mandaliina

tank (*e.g.* of a car)
xazzaan (-aat)
taxi
taksi
tea
shaay
teacher
mudarris (-iin)
telephone
talifoon (-aat)
to telephone
talfan / yutalfin
temperature (degree of heat)
darajat il-Haraara
temperature (fever)
Haraara

ten
ʕashara

tennis
tanis

tenth
ʕaashir

to test, to try out
jarrab / yujarrib

"thanks"
shukran

"Thanks (praise) be to God"
il-Hamdu li-llaah

that (*conjunction*)
inn

that (*demons. pron., m & f*)
dhaalik, hadhiik

then, after that
baʕdeen

there, over there
hunaak

there are
hunaak; fii(h)

there is
hunaak; fii(h)

therefore
idhan

these
hadhool

they
hum

thing
shi (ashyaa')

to think, to believe
iftakar / yaftakir

thinking (*adj.*)
mufakkir (-iin)

third
thaalith

thirsty
ʕaTshaan (-iin)

thirteen
thalaathtaʕsh(ar)

thirteenth
thaalith ʕashar

thirty
thalaathiin

this (*m & f*)
haadha, haadhi

thousand
alf (aalaaf)

three
thalaatha

throat
Hanjara

Thursday
(yoom) il-xamiis

ticket
tadhkara (tadhaakir)

to tidy up, arrange
rattab / yurattib

time, instance
marra (-aat)

time (in general)
waqt (awqaat)

tire (*n.*)
ʕajal (iʕjaal)

to tire (*s.o.*) out, to fatigue
taʕʕab / yutaʕʕib

tired
taʕbaan (-iin)

to, toward
ila, li-

"to your (*m*) liking"
ʕala keefak

today
il-yoom

tomatoes
banaduura

tomorrow
bukra

tonight
il-leela

too, also
kamaan

too much
kathiir

tooth
sinn (asnaan)

travel (n.)
safar

to travel
saafar / yusaafir

tray
Siiniyya (Sawaani)

tree
shajara (ashjaar)

trip
riHla (-aat)

truth, fact
Haqiiqa (Haqaa'iq)

to try out, to test
jarrab / yujarrib
to try, to attempt
Haawal / yuHaawil
tub
baanyo
Tuesday
(yoom) ith-thalaatha
to turn, change direction
laff / yaliff

turnips
lift
twelve
ithnaʕsh(ar)
twelfth
thaani ʕashar
twenty
ʕishriin
two
ithneen

u

umbrella
shamsiyya
uncle (maternal; paternal)
xaal (axwaal); ʕamm (aʕmaam)
uncomplicated, easy
basiiT
under, below
taHt
to understand
fahim / yafham
unfortunately
maʕ il-asaf

university
jaamiʕa (-aat)
United States
il-wilaayaat il-muttaHida
to use
istaʕmal / yastaʕmil
useful
mufiid
usually
ʕaadatan

v

veal
laHm ʕijil
vegetable
xuDra (xuDaar)
very
jiddan, kathiir
village
qarya (qura)

vinegar
xall
violator, violating
muxaalif (-iin)
visa
viiza (-aat, viyaz)
to visit
zaar / yazuur

w

to wait
intaDHar / yantaDHir
waiter
garsoon
to walk
masha / yamshi
walking
maashi (-iyyin)
wall
Haa'iT (HiiTaan)
walnuts
jooz
to want

araad / yuriid, bidd-
warm
daafi
washing
ghasiil
to wash (of dishes)
jala / yajli
to wash
ghasal / yaghsil
washed
maghsuul
watch (on wrist)
saaʕa (-aat)

194

to watch
tafarraj / yatafarraj (gala)

water
mayy

to water
saqa / yasqi

way
Tariiqa

we
naHna

wearing
laabis (-iin)

weather
Taqs

Wednesday
(yoom) il-arbaʕa

week
usbuuʕ (asaabiiʕ)

"welcome"
ahlan wa sahlan

West
gharb

what
shu, eesh

when (conjunction)
lamma

when (query word)
mata

where
feen, ween

whether
idha

which (relative pron.)
illi

white
abyaD, bayDaa'

who (query word)
miin

who, whom (relative pron.)
illi

why
leesh

wife
zawja (-aat)

window
shubbaak (shabaabiik)

wine
nabiidh

winter
shitaa'

to wipe
masaH / yamsaH

with
maʕ, bi-

"with pleasure"
bi-kull suruur

work
shughul

to work
ishtaghal / yashtaghil

to be worried
ihtamm / yahtamm

to write
katab / yaktub

wrong (mistaken)
ghalTaan

wrong number
in-numra ghalaT

---

y

year
sana (saniin, sanawaat)

yellow
aSfar, Safraa'

yes
naʕam, aywa

yesterday
imbaariH, ams

yoghurt
laban

you (f)
inti

you (m)
inta

you (pl)
intu

"you're welcome"
ʕafwan (response to shukran)

---

z

zero
Sifir

195

Arabic-English GLOSSARY

In order to accommodate the transcription system and the separate sounds used in the Arabic alphabet, the order of **initial consonant entries** used in this *Arabic-English* glossary is arranged as follows:

a	e	i	m	r	t T	v	z
b	f	j	n	s S	th	w	ʕ
d D	g(gh)	k	o	sh	u	x	
dh DH	h H	l	q			y	

a_____

aathaar
  ruins
aaxar (-iin)
  other
aaxir
  last, final, end
ab / abu (aabaa')
  father
abadan
  not at all, never
abyaD
  white
aHad
  (any)one
il-aHad
  Sunday
ahlan wa sahlan
  "welcome"
ahlan biik
  response to *"ahlan wa sahlan"*
aHmar
  red
aHyaanan
  sometimes
akal / yaakul
  to eat
akiid
  for sure; surely
akil
  food
akla (-aat)
  dish (of food)
akthar
  more; most

albaan
  dairy products
alf
  thousand
allaah
  God
allaah yusallimak
  "goodbye" (response to maʕa s-sallama)
allaah yuxalliik
  "May God keep you"
alʕaab riyaaDiyya
  sports
amar / ya'mur
  to order, ask for
ameerka
  America
ameerki / -iyya
  American
amr
  "at your service"
ana
  I
ananaas
  pineapple
araad / yuriid
  to want
arbaʕa
  four
arbaʕiin
  forty
arbaʕtaʕsh(ar)
  fourteen

197

il-arbiʕaa'
  Wednesday
arD
  floor, earth
aSfar
  yellow
ashhar
  most or more famous
ashqar (shuqur)
  blond
aswad
  black
athaath
  furniture
aw
  or
awwal
  first
awwal shi
  first thing

awwalan
  first, firstly
ax / axu (ixwa)
  brother
axadh / yaaxudh
  to take
axDar
  green
aywa
  yes (informal)
ayy xidma?
  "May I help you?" ("any service")
azraq
  blue
aʕjab / yuʕjib
  to please (s.o.)
aʕTa / yuʕTi
  to give

---

b_____

baab (abwaab)
  door
baaba ghannuuj
  eggplant purée
baadhinjaan
  eggplant
baamya
  okra
baanyo
  tub
baaqi
  rest, remainder
baarid
  cold (*adj.*)
baaS (-aat)
  bus
bada' / yabda'
  to begin
badla (-aat)
  suit
bahaaraat
  spices
bakkiir
  early
balad (bilaad, buldaan)
  country
banaduura
  tomatoes

banTaloon (-aat)
  pants
banziin
  gasoline
baqduunis
  parsley
baqi / yabqa
  to stay, remain
bardaan (-iin)
  cold, chilly (of persons)
bariid
  mail
barraad
  refrigerator
baSal
  onions
basiiT
  simple
basiiTa
  that's all right, take it easy
bass
  only, just
baTaaTa
  potatoes
baTn (buTuun)
  stomach
baTTiix
  melon

bayD
eggs

baʕath / yabʕath
to send

baʕd
after

baʕd bukra
day after tomorrow

baʕd idh-dhuhur
afternoon

baʕdeen
then, afterwards

baʕD
some (of)

baʕD il-awqaat
sometimes

baʕiid (min)
far (from)

bazeella
peas

beesbool
baseball

beet (buyuut)
house, home

bi-
in, at, with

bi-kam
how much

bi-kull suruur
with (every) pleasure

bi-surʕa
quickly, fast

bi-Suura ʕaamma
in general, generally

bi-xuSuuS
regarding, concerning

bidd- (+ pron. suffix)
to want

biira
beer

bilaad (buldaan)
country

binaaya (-aat)
building

bint (banaat)
daughter, girl

bluuza (bluwas)
blouse

booliiS
police

bukra
tomorrow

bunni
brown

burghul
bulgur wheat

burtuqaal
oranges

burtuqaali
orange (color)

---

d

daafi
warm

dafaʕ / yadfaʕ
to pay; to push

dajaaj
chicken

dall / yadill (ʕala)
to show s.o. (sth.)

daqiiqa (daqaa'iq)
minute

daraja (-aat)
degree

darajat il-Haraara
temperature

daras / yadrus·
to study

dars (duruus)
lesson

dawaa' (adwiya)

medicine

daxal / yadxul
to enter

dibluumaasi (n. & adj.)
diplomat, diplomatic

difaaʕ
defense

diinaar (danaaniir)
dinar

diir baalak
"be careful," "take care"

doolaar (-aat)
dollar

dughri
straight ahead

dukkaan (dakaakiin)
store, shop

durraaq
peaches

199

D

Daaʕ / yaDiiʕ
to get lost

DaabiT (DubbaaT)
officer (police or military)

Daayiʕ
lost

DaghT il-hawa
air pressure

Daruuri
essential, necessary

dh

dhaalik
that

dhiraaʕ (adhruʕ)
arm

DH

DHill
shade, shadow

e

eesh
what

f

faakiha (fawaakih)
fruit

faatiH
open

faatuura (fawaatiir)
bill, check

faDDal / yufaDDil
to prefer

fahim / yafham
to understand

falaafil
falafil

fam (afwaah)
mouth

farHaan (-iin)
happy, joyful

faraagh
empty space; spare time

faraariij
chicken(s)

faSl (fuSuul)
season

faSuulya
beans (green)

fataH / yaftaH
to open

fattash / yufattish (ʕala)
to look for, search for

feen
where

fi
in, at

fi l-Haqiiqa
actually

fii (or fiih)
there is, there are

ma fii (or ma fiih)
there isn't (any); there aren't (any)

fijil
radishes

fikra (fikar)
idea

filfil
peppers

film (aflaam)
film, movie

fils (fuluus)
fils (currency)

finjaan (fanaajiin)
cup

fuluus
money

funduq (fanaadiq)
hotel

furn (afraan)
stove, oven

fustaan (fasaatiin)
dress
fustuq
nuts (peanuts)
fustuq Halabi
pistachios
futbool
football, soccer

fuTuur
breakfast
fuul
fava beans
fuuTa (fuwaT)
napkin
fiʕlan
really, actually

g

garsoon
waiter
ghaali
expensive
ghadaa'
lunch
ghalaT (aghlaaT)
error, mistake
ghalTaan
mistaken, wrong
gharb
West
ghasal / yaghsil
to wash

ghasiil
laundry, wash (*n.*)
ghayyar / yughayyir
to change
gheem (ghuyuum)
clouds
gheer
other, other than
ghubaar
dust
ghurfa (ghuraf)
room

h

haadha
this (*m*)
haadhi
this (*f*)
hadhiik
that (*f*)
halla, halla'
now
hiya
she

hum
they
huna
here
hunaak
there
huwa
he

H

Haadi ʕashar
eleventh
HaaDir
"at your service" ("ready")
Haaditha (Hawaadith)
event, incident
Haal (aHwaal)
condition
Haala (-aat)
state, condition
Haala Taari'a
emergency

Haarr
hot
Haawal / yuHaawil
to try, attempt
Haa'iT (HiiTaan)
wall
Habb / yaHibb
to like, to love
HaDDar / yuHaDDir
to prepare
Hadiiqa (Hadaa'iq)
garden

201

HaDritak
polite form of "you"
HaDritik
polite "you" (f)
HaDritkum
polite "you" (pl)
Hafla (-aat)
party
Hajaz / yaHjiz
to reserve; detain
Hajz
reservation; detention
Haka / yaHki
to speak, to talk
Haliib
milk
Hamd
praise
il-Hamdu li-llaah
"Praise be to God"
Hammaam (-aat)
bathroom
Hanafiyya(-aat)
faucet
Hanjara
throat
Haqiiqa (Haqaa'iq)
fact, truth
Haqiiqatan
really, actually

Haraara
heat, fever, temperature
Harq (Huruuq)
burn (n.)
HaSaana
immunity
Hasaasiyya
allergy
Hashiish
grass
HaTT / yaHuTT
to put
Hatta
in order to
Hawaali
approximately
Hawl
around
Hilu (Hilwiin)
nice, pretty
Hilwayaat
sweets
Hisaab (-aat)
bill, invoice
Hujja (Hujaj)
excuse, pretext
HummuS
chick pea purée

i_____

iHdaʕsh(ar)
eleven
iHtaaj / yaHtaaj
to need
ibn (abnaa')
son
ibn ʕamm
paternal cousin
idha
if, whether
idhan
therefore, so
iftakar / yaftakir
to think, believe
ihtamm / yahtamm (bi-)
to be concerned, worried (about)
iid (iideen)
hand

ija / yiiji
to come
ila
to, towards
illi
which, who
imbaariH
yesterday
in shaa' allaah
"God willing", hopefully
injaaS
pears
inn
that (conj.)
int (a)
you (m)
intaDHar / yantaDHir
to wait, await

inti
  you (f)

intu
  you (pl)

irtaaH / yartaaH
  to rest

ishaal
  diarrhea

ism (asmaa')
  name; noun

istaraaH / yastariiH
  to rest, relax

istaʕmal / yastaʕmil
  to use

iSbaʕ (aSaabiʕ)
  finger

ishaara (-aat)
  sign

ishtaghal / yashtaghil
  to work

ishtara / yashtari
  to buy

ithnaʕsh(ar)
  twelve

ithneen
  two

il-ithneen
  Monday

ixtalaf / yaxtalif
  to differ

j

jaab / yajiib
  to bring

jaamiʕa (-aat)
  university

jabal (jibaal)
  mountain

jadd (juduud, ajdaad)
  grandfather

jadda (-aat)
  grandmother

jadiid (judud)
  new

jakeet (-aat)
  jacket

jala / yajli
  to wash dishes

jalas / yajlis
  to sit

jali
  dishwashing

januub
  South

jarrab / yujarrib
  to try out, test

jawaaz safar (jawaazaat safar)
  passport

jaww (ajwaa')
  air, atmosphere

jawʕaan (-iin)
  hungry

jazar
  carrots

jeesh
  army

jibna
  cheese

jiddan
  very

jooz
  walnuts

il-jumʕa
  Friday

juzdaan (jazaadiin)
  purse

k

kaafi
  enough (adj.)

kaan / yakuun
  to be

kaas (-aat)
  glass, cup

kabbuut (kabaabiit)
  coat

kabiir (kibaar)
  big, great, old

kahrabaa'i
  electric

kalsaat
  socks

kamaan
  also, too

kamara (-aat)
camera
kannas / yukannis
to sweep
kanza (-aat)
sweater
karaaj (-aat)
garage
kaslaan (-iin)
lazy
kashaf / yakshif
to check, inspect
katab / yaktub
to write
katif (aktaaf)
shoulder
kathiir (kithaar)
many, much, too much
kawi
ironing
kifaaya
enough (n.)

kiif
how
kiilo
kilogram
kirmaalik
"for your (f) sake"
kubba
kibbee
kull
all; every
kundara (kanaadir)
shoes
kura (-aat)
ball
kursi (karaasi)
chair
kuusa
squash
kwayyis (-iin)
good, fine

---

la
no
la muʃaaxadha
"pardon me"
la wallaah
not really
laabis (-iin)
wearing
laakin
but, however
laaqa / yulaaqi
to find
laazim
it is necessary; must, have to
laban
yoghurt
ladhiidh
delicious
laHDHa (-aat)
moment
laHm
meat
laHm baqar
beef
laHm ghanam
lamb

laHm xanziir
pork
laHm ʃijil
veal
laHma habra
lean meat
laff / yaliff
to turn
lamma
when
law samaHt / law samaHti
"if you please;"
"with your permission"
laʃib / yalʃab
to play
il-leela
tonight
leemuun
lemons
leemuunaada
lemonade
leesh
why
leesh la?
why not?

lift
turnips
liira (-aat)
pound (currency)
liista
menu
li'ann
because
lissa
still; not yet
litir
liter

li-waHdu
by himself
loon (alwaan)
color
looz
almonds
lubnaani (-iin)
Lebanese
luSba (alSaab)
game

---

m_____

ma (+ verb)
not (negates *verbs*)
ma fii
there isn't (any); there aren't (any)
ma aTyab!
how good!
ma daam
as long as
maaniS
objection
maashi (-iin)
walking
mabsuuT (-iin)
well, happy
madaam
Madam
madiina (mudun)
city
maghsala(maghaasil)
sink
maghsuul
washed
maHaTTa (-aat)
station
maHaTTat banziin
gas station
maHshi
stuffed
majnuun (majaaniin)
crazy
makaan (amaakin)
place
maktab (makaatib)
office
maktab il-bariid
post office

malaabis
clothes
malfuuf
cabbage
maksuur
broken
mamnuuS
forbidden
mamsaHa
mop
mandaliina
tangerines
manga
mangos
manTiqa (manaaTiq)
region, area
marHaba
"hello"
mariiD (marDa)
sick
markaz (maraakiz)
center, headquarters
marr / yamurr (Sala)
to pass (by)
marra (-aat)
time, instance
marra thaaniya
another time, again
masa / masaa'
evening
masaafa (-aat)
distance
masaH / yamsaH
to wipe
mas'uul (-iin)
official (n.)

205

maSbagha
dry cleaners

masha / yamshi
to walk, go

mashghuul (-iin)
busy

mashruub (-aat)
drinks, refreshments

mashwi
broiled

matHaf (mataaHif)
museum

mata
when

maTaar (-aat)
airport

maTar
rain

maTbax
kitchen

maTSam (maTaaSim)
restaurant

mawjuud (-iin)
present, here

mawsim (mawaasim)
season

mawSid (mawaaSid)
appointment

mayy
water

mayy maSdaniyya
mineral water

maS
with

maS il-asaf
regretfully, unfortunately

maS is-salaama
"goodbye"

maSaleesh
"never mind," "it's okay"

maSluumaat
information

maSmuul
made

maSquul
reasonable

mi'awiyya
centigrade

miin
who

miiteen
two hundred

miknasa (makaanis)
broom

milSaqa (malaaSiq)
spoon

milH
salt

min
from

min faDlak / -ik / -kum
"please"

min kull budd
"by all means"

min qabl
previously

minshaan
for, in order to

mish
not (negates nouns, adjectives,
phrases)

mish heek?
not so, right?

mish baTTaal
not bad

mishmish
apricots

mitir
meter

mithil
like, as, similar to

miyya (or miit)
hundred

mooz
bananas

muHammar
roasted

mudarraj (-aat)
auditorium; amphitheater

mufaDDal
favorite

mufakkir (-iin)
thinking

mufiid
useful, beneficial

mukaalama
conversation, talk

mukaalama talifooniyya
phone call

mukaddas
  piled up, heaped up
mulHaq (-iin)
  attaché
mumarriDa (-aat)
  nurse
mumkin
  may, maybe, can, could, perhaps
mumtaaz
  excellent
munaawib (-iin)
  on duty
munaffis
  flat, deflated
munawwaʕaat
  miscellaneous items
muqaabil
  facing, opposite
muqabbilaat
  appetizers
musaafir (-iin)
  going, traveling
musaaʕada
  help, assistance

musakkir
  closed
mustaʕidd (-iin)
  ready
mustaʕjil (-iin)
  rushed, in a hurry
mustashfa (mustashfayaat)
  hospital
mushkila (mashaakil)
  problem
muta'akkid (-iin)
  certain, sure
muta'assif (-iin)
  sorry
muwaDHDHaf (-iin)
  employee
muwaffaq (-iin)
  "good luck"
muxaalif (-iin)
  violating; conflicting
muxallal
  pickled vegetables
muʕtadil
  moderate

n

naas
  people (in general)
nabiidh
  wine
naDHDHaf / yunaDHDHif
  to clean
naDHiif
  clean
nafax / yanfux
  to inflate
naHna
  we
nasi / yansa
  to forget
nashaf / yanshaf
  to dry (out)
nashar / yanshur
  to hang (*sth.*) out
nashshaafa
  dryer (n.)
nashshaf / yunashshif
  to dry (sth.)

nawʕ (anwaaʕ)
  kind, sort
nazal / yanzil
  to fall, drop, descend
naʕam
  yes
naʕnaʕ
  mint (herb)
naʕsaan (-iin)
  sleepy
nimoonya
  pneumonia
noom
  sleep
numra (numar)
  number
in-numra ghalaT
  "wrong number"
nuSS
  half
nuzha (-aat)
  outing, excursion

q

qaabal / yuqaabil
  to meet

qaal / yaquul
  to say

qaanuun (qawaaniin)
  law

qabl
  before; ago

qadam (aqdaam)
  foot

qadarma
  as much as

qaddam / yuqaddim
  to offer, present

qaddeesh
  how much

qadiim
  old, ancient

qadir / yaqdar
  to be able

qahwa
  coffee

qalb (quluub)
  heart

qaliil
  little, few

qamiiS (qumSaan)
  shirt

qariib (min)
  near, close (to)

qarrab / yuqarrib
  to bring near

qarya (qura)
  village

qaTTaʕ / yuqaTTiʕ
  to cut up (sth.)

qiTʕa (qiTaʕ)
  piece, morsel

quddaam
  ahead, in front of

qunSul(qanaaSil)
  consul

r

raabiʕ
  fourth

raabiʕ ʕashar
  fourteenth

raaH / yaruuH
  to go

raajiʕ (-iin)
  returning

raas (ruus)
  head

raayiH (-iin)
  going

rabiiʕ
  spring

raH (+ present tense verb)
  = future tense

raja / yarju
  to beg, entreat (s.o.)

rajaʕ / yarjaʕ
  to return

ra'y (aaraa')
  opinion

rashH
  cold, flu

rattab / yurattib
  to arrange, tidy up

raTib
  humid

raxiiS
  cheap, inexpensive

riHla (-aat)
  trip

rijil (arjul)
  leg

risaala (rasaa'il)
  letter

riyaaDi
  sport (adj.)

riyaal (-aat)
  riyal

rubʕ
  quarter

rummaan
  pomegranates

s

saabiʕ
seventh

saada
black (coffee)

saadis
sixth

saafar / yusaafir
to travel

saakin (-iin)
living, dwelling

saaʕa (-aat)
hour, watch, clock

saaʕad / yusaaʕid
to help

sa'al / yas'al
to ask

sabaanix
spinach

sabab (asbaab)
reason

is-sabt
Saturday

sabaʕtaʕsh(ar)
seventeen

sabʕa
seven

sabʕiin
seventy

safaara (-aat)
embassy

safar
trip, traveling

safiir (sufaraa')
ambassador

sahl
easy

sakraan (-iin)
drunk

salaamtu
"I hope he gets well"
("his well-being")

salaTa
salad

salla (-aat, silaal)
basket

sallam / yusallim
to deliver (sth.) to (s.o.)

samak
fish

samna
shortening

sana (saniin, sanawaat)
year

sandwiitsh
sandwich

saqa / yasqi
to water, irrigate

sayyaara (-aat)
car

sayyaarat isʕaaf
ambulance

sayyid
Mr.

saʕal / yasʕul
to cough

saʕuudi (-iin)
Saudi

siinama
movie house

sikkiin (sakaakiin)
knife

sikriteer (-iin)
secretary

simsim
sesame seed

sinn (asnaan)
tooth

sitta
six

sittaʕsh(ar)
sixteen

sittiin
sixty

siyaaHi
tourist (n. & adj.)

sukkar
sugar

su'aal (as'ila)
question

suruur
pleasure, happiness

suuq (aswaaq)
marketplace

209

S

Saabuun
  soap
Saaloon
  living room
Saar / yaSiir
  to become
SabaaH il-xeer
  "good morning"
SabaaH in-nuur
  "good morning" (as a response)
Sadr (Suduur)
  chest, breast
Saghiir (Sighaar)
  small; young
SaHn (suHuun)
  plate, dish
SaHteen
  "to your health"
SallaH / yuSalliH
  to repair, fix
Sanduuq (Sanaadiiq)
  box, case

Saraf / yaSrif
  to spend
Sawwar / yuSawwir
  to take photographs
Saydaliyya (-aat)
  pharmacy
Seef
  summer
Sifir
  zero
Siiniyya (Sawaani)
  tray, pan
Snoobar
  pine nuts
SubuH
  morning
iS-SubuH
  this morning
Suura (Suwar)
  picture

sh

shaaf / yashuuf
  to see, look
shaariʕ (shawaariʕ)
  street
shaaTi'
  shore, beach
shaay
  tea
shabʕaan (-iin)
  full (no longer hungry)
shahr (ashhur; shuhuur)
  month
shajara (ashjaar)
  tree
shamaal
  North
shams
  sun
shamsiyya (-aat)
  umbrella
sharaf
  honor
ish-sharaf la-na
  "the honor is ours"

sharib / yashrab
  to drink
sharq
  East
sharshaf (sharaashif)
  sheet, linen
shawa / yashwi
  to roast
shawbaan (-iin)
  hot
shawka (shuwak)
  fork
shaʕb (shuʕuub)
  people
shaʕr
  hair
shi (ashyaa')
  (some) thing
shiqqa (shiqaq)
  apartment
shitaa'
  winter
shoorba
  soup

210

shubbaak (shabaabiik)
window
shughul
work
shukran
"thanks"
shurTa
police (in general)

shurTi (shurTa)
policeman
shu
what
shwayy
a little
shway-shway
slowly

t

taasiʕ
ninth
ta'axxar / yata'axxar
to delay, be late
tadhkara (tadhaakir)
ticket
tafaDDal / tafaDDali / tafaDDalu
please
tafarraj / yatafarraj (ʕala)
to watch
taHDiir
preparation
taHt
under
takallam / yatakallam
to speak
taksi
taxi
talfan / yutalfin
to telephone
talifoon
telephone
tamaam
O.K., fine
tamaaman
exactly
tamr
dates
tanis
tennis

tannuura (tanaaniir)
skirt
taqriiban
approximately, about, almost
tarak / yatruk
to leave
tasharraf / yatasharraf
to be honored
taSwiir
taking pictures, photographing
taʕallam / yataʕallam
to learn
taʕbaan (-iin)
tired
taʕʕab / yutaʕʕib
to fatigue (s.o.), wear out (s.o.)
tiin
figs
tikram
"at your service"
tisʕa
nine
tisʕiin
ninety
tisaʕ taʕsh(ar)
nineteen
tuffaaH
apples

T

Taa'ira (-aat)
airplane
Taabiq (Tawaabiq)
floor, story (of a bldg.)
Taalib (Tullaab)
student
Taawila (-aat)
table

Taaza
fresh
Tabax / yaTbux
to cook
Tabiib (aTibbaa')
doctor
Tabx
cooking

211

Tabʕan
  naturally, of course
TaHiin
  flour
Tanjara (Tanaajir)
  pan, pot
Taqs
  weather

Tariiqa (Turuq)
  way, method
Tawiil (Tiwaal)
  long, tall
Tayyib
  all right, okay; delicious

th_____

thaalith
  third
thaalith ʕashar
  thirteenth
thaamin
  eighth
thaani
  second, other
thaani ʕashar
  twelfth
thalaatha
  three
thalaathiin
  thirty
thalaathtaʕsh(ar)
  thirteen

ith-thalathaa'
  Tuesday
thalj
  ice; snow
thamaaniin
  eighty
thamaaniya
  eight
thamantaʕsh(ar)
  eighteen
thaman
  price
thoob (thiyaab)
  garment; robe
thuum
  garlic

u_____

udhun (adhaan)
  ear
ujra
  fare
umm (ummahaat)
  mother
unbuub (anaabiib)
  pipe

usbuuʕ (asaabiiʕ)
  week
ustaadh (asaatidha)
  professor; sir
uxt (axawaat)
  sister

v_____

viiza (-aat, viyaz)
  visa

w_____

wa
  and
waaHid
  one
waaDiH
  clear
wajaʕ (awjaaʕ)
  pain, ache

wajaʕ raas
  headache
walad (awlaad)
  child, boy
wallaah
  really! (a mild oath)
waqiyya
  a weight, 37g.–350g. depending
  on the country

212

waqt (awqaat)
  time
waraqa (awraaq)
  (piece of) paper
wasix
  dirty
waSal / yuuSal
  to reach, arrive
waSf (awSaaf)
  feature, characteristic

waSfa (-aat) recipe
wazaara (-aat)
  ministry
ween
  where
wilaaya (-aat)
  state, province
il-wilaayaat il-muttaHida
  The United States

x

xaadim (xuddaam)
  servant, hired man
xaal (axwaal)
  maternal uncle
xaala (-aat)
  maternal aunt
xaamis
  fifth
xaa'if (-iin)
  afraid, fearful
(ana) xaa'if ʕaleeh
  (I'm) worried about him
xaarij
  outside
xaariTa (xaraa'iT)
  map
xaaSSatan
  especially
xabbar / yuxabbir
  to inform
xalaT / yaxluT
  to mix
xall
  vinegar
xalla / yuxalli
  to let, allow; keep
xallaS / yuxalliS
  to finish

xamsa
  five
xamsiin
  fifty
xamstaʕsh(ar)
  fifteen
il-xamiis
  Thursday
xarbaan (-iin)
  out of order, broken
xariif
  autumn
xass
  lettuce
xaTar
  danger
xazaana (xazaa'in)
  cupboard
xazzaan (-aat)
  tank (*e.g.*, of a car)
xiyaar
  cucumbers
xubz
  bread
xuDra (xuDaar)
  vegetable

y

ya
  O, Oh
ya Haraam!
  "What a pity!," "too bad!"
ya salaam!
  "My goodness!"
ya reet
  "if only," "I wish"

ya tura
  "I wonder"
yamiin
  right (direction)
yasaar
  left (direction)
yaʕni
  well; sort of; that is to say

yoom (ayyaam)
  day
il-yoom
  today

z

zaar / yazuur
  to visit
zaawiya (zawaayaa)
  corner
zabiib
  raisins
zahra (zuhuur)
  flower
zahra (or qarnabiiT)
  cauliflower
zawj (azwaaj)
  husband
zawja (-aat)
  wife

zaʕlaan (-iin)
  angry
zeet
  oil
zeet zeeytuun
  olive oil
zeetuun
  olives
zibda
  butter
zirr (azraar)
  button
zunnaar (zanaaniir)
  belt

ʕ

ʕaadatan
  usually
ʕaali
  high
ʕaa'ila (-aat)
  family
ʕaaSifa (ʕawaaSif)
  storm
ʕaaSima (ʕawaaSim)
  capital
ʕaashir
  tenth
ʕabba / yuʕabbi
  to fill up (or out)
ʕadas
  lentils
ʕaddaad
  meter
ʕaDHm (ʕiDHaam)
  bone
ʕaDHm maksuur
  broken bone
ʕafwan
  "you're welcome"
ʕajal (iʕjaal, -aat)
  tire
ʕala
  on, upon

ʕala ʕeeni
  "at your service"
ʕala keefik
  "to your (f) liking"
ʕala kull Haal
  anyway, anyhow
ʕala raasi
  "at your service"
ʕalam (aʕlaam)
  flag
ʕamaara (-aat)
  building
ʕamal / yaʕmil
  to make, do
ʕamil
  making (n.)
ʕamm (aʕmaam)
  paternal uncle
ʕamma (-aat)
  paternal aunt
ʕan
  from; about, concerning
ʕan idhnak
  "pardon," "with your permission"
ʕana / yaʕni
  to mean
ʕaqiid
  colonel

yumkin
  maybe

214

ʕarabi
  Arabic
ʕarabi (ʕarab)
  Arab
ʕaraf / yaʕrif
  to know
ʕariif
  sergeant
ʕaSiir
  juice
ʕasha, ʕashaa'
  dinner
ʕashara
  ten
ʕaTshaan (-iin)
  thirsty
ʕayyaan (-iin)
  sick, ill

ʕeen (ʕuyuun)
  eye
ʕilba (ʕilab)
  can, box, container
ʕinab
  grapes
ʕind
  at the place (of)
ʕind (+ pron. suffix)
  to have
ʕinwaan (ʕanaawiin)
  address; title
ʕishriin
  twenty
ʕiyaada
  clinic
ʕumr (aʕmaar)
  age